Social Structure in Divided Germany

JAROSLAV KREJCI

ST. MARTIN'S PRESS NEW YORK

1-26-79

TO MY MOTHER

CONTENTS

LIST OF TABLES

ACKNOWLEDGEMENTS

The writing of this book has been made possible by the sponsorship of the Social Science Research Council in London and by the facilities of the University of Lancaster. The author is happy to express his acknowledgements for their support. He also feels indebted to all those who by their own research and publications, whether in West Germany, East Germany or elsewhere, have contributed to his knowledge of the subject. In particular he wishes to thank the Bundesminister für Innerdeutsche Beziehungen in Bonn and the Friedrich Ebert Stiftung in Bonn-Bad Godesberg for supplying relevant literature.

The author appreciates the permission granted by the following publishers, institutions or authors to quote from their publications:
Bundesminister für Innerdeutsche Beziehungen (Bericht zur Lage der Nation 1971, 1972, 1974; Zahlenspiegel, 1973 and 1974);
Deutsches Institut für Wirtschaftsforschung (DDR-Wirtschaft 1971 and 1974)
Deutschland Archiv (1974, 1975);
Dreste Vorlag (Marcus, Die Macht der Mächtigen);
Duncker and Humblot (Brinkmann, Berufsausbildung und Arbeitseinkommen);
Princeton University Press (Almond and Verba, The Civic Culture);
Professor P. Ludz (Die Entwicklung der DDR in Das 198. Jahrzehnt);
R. Piper & Co. Verlag (Zapf, Wandlungen der Deutschen Elite);
Verlag für Demoskopie (Jahrbuch der öffentlichen Meinung 1968– 1973);
Weidenfeld and Nicolson (Dahrendorf, Society and Democracy in Germany);
Westdeutscher Verlag (Ludz, Studien und Materialien zur Soziologie der DDR, and Ludz, The Changing Party Elite in East Germany).

The author would also like to express his gratitude to his friend Dr. Vitezslav Velimsky for assistance in collecting material and to Professor Charles W. Wheatley of Bucknell University for his helpful comments. Further, the author wishes to extend his thanks to Mrs Mavis Mason and Mrs. Ann Payne for typing, calculating, compiling the index etc. and to Messrs P. P. Burnett and J. P. Payne for their help in the preparation of the manuscript. Last but not least, the author has to thank his wife for her patience and understanding.

The responsibility for the contents of the book lies of course solely with the author.

1 INTRODUCTION

1a. Aims and methods

The aim of this study is expressed in its sub-title. It is intended as a contribution to the comparative analysis of social systems. This formulation gives rise to several questions. What is a social system? Is there any system at all in human relationships and organisations? What is the scope and method of dealing with such a topic? To what degree should such a study be factual or conceptual?

The term social system is used here as a comprehensive label for what is usually considered as two separate compounds: Marx's socio-economic formation or mode of production, and the type of government (political régime) and political culture as expounded by political scientists.

Undoubtedly the topic is of a complex nature, any aspect of which could be tackled by different methods; several middle-range theories can be tested or constructed on the basis of partial observations. But an 'understanding' of the whole tissue of positions, relationships, roles and tendencies requires an analysis embracing all relevant aspects of social life, and not merely those which, according to particular theories, provide the backbone of the whole structure.

My aim is to find out in concrete, tangible terms the distinction between two types of society which in contemporary usage are characterised, according to one's ideological background, as capitalist versus socialist; pluralistic versus totalitarian; democratic versus communist; bourgeois versus people's democratic, etc. These labels stand as abbreviations for, or symbols of, much more complex patterns, the detailed structuring of which may be differently understood by those who use them.

When I say that the analysis has to be undertaken in concrete terms, I have primarily in mind aspects and features which are relevant for common men and which are considered important by them; therefore, my concern with the theoretical concepts which lie behind institutions and relationships constituting the dichotomy above is to make them empirically observable and, as far as possible, quantifiable.

The quest for data, however, should not lead us to forget the importance of non-measurable aspects and issues. Both quantitative and qualitative information has to be combined. In order to keep a certain

7

balance between them, neither speculation nor statistical sophistication should be pushed too far. As all statistical data have to be taken with some reservation, different statistical investigations have to be mutually checked rather than elaborated for a display of sociometric methods; these can hardly make good any factual blunders.

Similarly, it would be inadequate to treat the basic dichotomy ('socialism versus capitalism', 'democracy versus totalitarianism', or whatever label may be used) in philosophical terms. In such a way contact with reality can easily be lost. Not only orthodox supporters of traditional social philosophies, but also many modernisers or 'revisionists' of such philosophies have found little courage to confront their views with adequate empirical tests.

Another supposition basic to this study is that all issues relevant for intersystemic analysis constitute an indivisible whole in the sense that any individual's position depends on some kind of comprehensive evaluation of these issues. Although particular aspects can be in the forefront of the individual's concern (some of them may be more in his consciousness than others), they are always an interconnected entity. Theoretical abstractions dividing man into an economic, political or cultural being may be useful for elaboration of particular relationships but can never help to understand individual and social behaviour in its entirety. For such an understanding partial description and middle-range theories may be misleading. Only the fact that we cannot tackle the problems all at once makes specialisation necessary. Moreover, advantages resulting from division of labour make it useful.

So we have to accept specialisation but not to develop it so far as to present disconnected details, but rather to pull the strings together and synthesise the results. Following the established lines of specialisation, comparative analysis of social systems as defined above can be subdivided into three main areas.

The first area can be described as socio-economic; it is centred around the problems of income and wealth and their distribution among social groups and individuals, or households. This area contains most of the material relevant to Marx's theory of value which in connection with the concept of ownership and exploitation provides the theoretical basis of the most popular dichotomy of our days, that of socialism versus capitalism.

The second area falls into the field of general sociology. It is centred around the problems of stratification and social mobility, concepts which were elaborated independently of Marx's dichotomy and which in a sense helped to overcome its monothematic bias. The concept of social stratification became more suited to the multi-faceted reality. Even some Marxists were able to make it a starting point for empirical structural analysis in societies where means of production became state-owned. The concept of social mobility too has also helped to provide some tangible framework for Marx's concept of alienation.

The third area of the inter-systemic analysis can be put under the heading of political science or, rather, political sociology. It is centred on the question of ruling and following, on the relationship between the rulers and their subjects and on their respective attitudes and forms of organisation. Although the hierarchy of power may constitute one additional variable in the stratification scheme, its proper understanding extends beyond the context of stratification. Since power is being exercised against other men, their respective position *vis-à-vis* those in power must also be taken into consideration. Therefore the focus of this section will be not only on those who are in power and how they got in, but also on the scope of their power and what those subject to their power can do to check or possibly evade it. Whatever definition of freedom one may adhere to, the function of individual self-assertion cannot be dismissed as irrelevant or as a matter of 'false consciousness'.

The more technical questions of the systemic dichotomy such as relationships of planning and market forces have already been amply discussed in specialist literature. Therefore they are only occasionally tackled in this study wherever they appear relevant.

In drawing conclusions from these three areas, a concrete and tangible basis for a comprehensive inter-systemic analysis can be obtained. Understandably, all this work cannot be undertaken in a void. Even those who are loath to wade in empirical detail and prefer to juggle with concepts and their nuances do from time to time descend from their lofty exercise to pick up a few examples from real life, Those who are involved in the daily struggle between political factions might especially like to know the practical results of their policy.

Up till now the main studies of inter-systemic differences have taken the USA and the USSR as their examples. Conclusions based on the comparison of these two countries, however, take into account not only differences in social systems but a wider field of social issues: different culture, different levels of technological and economic development, and last but not least, different political tradition. Some features of such a comparison may point to the concept of societies at different levels of otherwise similar development. Some features may be considered as permanently different; they may be metaphorically described as elements of *genius loci*. A quest for a satisfactory answer to these questions would expand the study far beyond the scope of the conventional academic disciplines.

In order to limit the inquiry to what might be considered a systemic analysis proper, one has to consider countries which differ least in culture, technology and historical background. One has to envisage countries in which any structural differences may be related to purposeful action by those within the society, action intended to organise society in a particular way and possibly educate or re-educate its members towards particular attitudes and value judgements. Only in the case of such countries can the respective merits of different social systems, such as capitalism on one side and socialism on the other, be properly evaluated.

There can be little doubt that for an inter-systemic comparison in the aforementioned sense, divided Germany provides the most suitable ground. There are still two other countries in a similar position, namely Korea and, until recently, Vietnam; but there are two particular reasons which make their study less relevant for our purpose. Firstly, information from these Asian countries is scarce, statistics seem to be less reliable (there is little opportunity for mutual checks) and last but not least there is, for me, the barrier of language and distance (both in the geographical and socio-cultural sense). Secondly, both Korea and Vietnam embarked on the 'capitalism/socialism' dichotomy from what Marxists and many non-Marxists alike consider as the 'pre-capitalist' stage of development. Consequently, 'socialism' there appears to be an alternative to 'capitalism' rather than its following stage.[1]

There are only two countries where the Marxist-Leninist brand of socialism can be considered as the successor to a genuine capitalist formation: East Germany and Czechoslovakia. Only in these two countries can there be talk of socialism according to Marx's expectations, i.e. according to his sequence of socio-economic formations. (It will be shown in the concluding section how tenable this supposition is.) But only the 'German Democratic Republic' has, from the point of view of its history, culture and technological development, an adequately comparable counterpart in the other camp, namely the Federal Republic of Germany.

Of course, even divided Germany does not provide all the necessary information. Data on some crucial issues are scarce, particularly from the East. Neither comprehensive statistics nor sample research in that part of Germany can match comparable data from the West. There are only a few items (such as for example the training level of working population or service industry for households) on which the GDR supplies more data than the FRG. Otherwise it is the detailed territorial breakdown of less relevant data which makes the statistical yearbooks of the GDR as thick as those of the FRG. It has also to be mentioned that the GDR is more restrictive in quantitative information than other Communist-dominated countries in Central Europe, such as Czechoslovakia, Poland and Hungary.

In spite of all these deficiences it is possible, especially with personal experience in dealing with statistics in the East, to derive from the available data more than simply their face value. On the other hand personal experience is hardly a substitute for the lack of genuine sociological research. Although the GDR has acknowledged sociology as a legitimate discipline since the early sixties, more has been said and written about its tasks and orientations than about its results. Again there is a considerable difference between East Germany on the one hand, and Poland, Hungary and Czechoslovakia on the other.

Fortunately for students of the GDR, the West German research institutes have made a tremendous effort to collect and republish whatever information can be obtained from the East. There is a lot of comparative analyses and statistical juxtapositions which more often than not reveal a genuine quest for objective information and understanding.

So, on the whole, as the testing ground of the systemic dichotomy, divided Germany is not only the most suitable but also the most accessible ground.

As I have said already, the aim of this study is a three-fold analysis: economic, sociological and political. This necessarily implies use of different methods and concepts. Neither conceptual rigidity nor epistemological elegance can be considered a virtue in this under-taking. Different concepts and methods are to be used in order to elucidate the state of the body social, just as in the medical profession different tests are combined in order to find and understand the real state of the human body.

For obvious reasons I have not been in the position to organise new research which might provide comparable results in the two countries in question. I have had to rely on available statistics and the results of investigations undertaken for purposes other than those followed in this study. This meant certain disadvantages but, on the other hand, some advantages. One shortcoming for instance was that I could not collect sufficient commensurate data for a correlation analysis of social status components; hence the question whether there is in individual parts of divided Germany a swing towards congruence or decomposition of social status could be answered only tentatively. On the other hand, it proved an advantage to be able to combine different data and observations. Wherever I found consistency between information from different sources, I could be more sure of the reliability of such data; where this was not the case I felt I had to be more cautious.

Sometimes I have had to return to a particular issue in different sections. Income distribution for example, is as important an element of social stratification as of socio-economic structure. Similarly distribution of wealth characterises both the economic and power structure. It seemed to me sensible to tackle these problems within both respective contexts. Also some aspects of the distribution of power, to which a special section has been devoted, could be dealt with in the section on stratification. Yet the lack of quantitative data which may be juxtaposed with other variables of social status makes it more expedient to discuss the whole complex of power separately. Only access to power by socio-economic groups is dealt with in the section on stratification.

As the first objective of the study is to find hard facts, theoretical concepts have had to be treated accordingly. If, for instance, Marx's concepts of exploitation and alienation are to have any real meaning, they have to be related to the real fate of men. The rate of exploitation, defined as the ratio of surplus value (gross profits) to variable capital (compensation of labour) cannot be meaningfully understood other than in quantitative terms. Marx himself continuously pointed at such a procedure.

It might be more difficult to translate alienation into tangible terms. Yet if it is to be understood by the supposed beneficiaries of Marx's philosophy — the workers, it must become, in a way, a tangible concept. Whatever Mészáros and other philosophers may consider as the true interpretation of Marx's transformation of Hegelian speculation and however they may rage against 'the artificial simplicity of commonplace mongering neo-empiricism',* just such an empiricism is the only way through which precepts of Marxist theory can be proven; only through empirical test can they become internalised by the working class, a class which Marxists themselves proclaim as the bearer and promoter of human progress.

In contrast to those who prefer theorising, but only pick up facts when they fit their theories, I have to re-emphasise that any theory has

*István Mészáros, *Marx's Theory of Alienation*, London, 1970, p. 13.

to comply with facts and real processes, not vice versa. On the other hand, with respect to the comprehensive nature of the topic, theoretical observations have to fit into a comprehensive framework. Therefore no attempt is undertaken to discuss or to construct a middle-range theory within the individual sections of investigation. Nevertheless applicability of some theoretical concepts (such as rate of surplus value, congruence and decomposition of social status, authoritarian and totalitarian constellation of power, convergence and divergence of socio-economic systems) and the validity of some theoretical statements (hypotheses) connected with them are tested. Only in the concluding chapter is there an attempt to unify individual results of the analyses in the three sections. The aim of this exercise is to find those variables which in the author's view can be considered as parameters of the 'social system' and consequently tested in any other inter-systemic analysis.

It might be objected that the author should have done this at the beginning and applied his framework to the whole study and so have tried to make it more unified conceptually and methodically. My answer to such a reproach is that I did not want to start with any *a priori* position. I preferred to follow different lines of conventional analysis and made necessary adaptations when the need arose.

Although I had some preliminary ideas concerning the general framework, I changed them often as the work progressed and I arrived at my final conclusions only when the work was finished. I still consider these conclusions as merely tentative suggestions which should be tested against other empirical material. If these conclusions are rejected by other researchers in the field, or if I change them in the further course of my own work, the individual sections of this study may nevertheless stand as factual comparisons of the three types of societal relationships: those of incomes and wealth, of stratification and mobility, and of power and freedom, in a nation which has been divided not only into two separate states but also into two different social systems.

1b. Historical and territorial considerations

Although there may be little doubt that divided Germany provides the best feasible ground for inter-systemic comparison, the question may arise whether the *best* in relative terms is *good* enough in absolute terms. Students of social history may point to some essential features which in the past made the countries east of the Elbe different from those to the west of this river. The second period of bondage, the patronising role of the small gentry, and the slower development of industry are the main points which eventually made the social climate in the German north-east less 'Western' than in other parts of Germany.

The GDR, however, does not merely contain the north-eastern territories beyond the Elbe but also a substantial part of the city of Berlin and the whole of Saxony and Thuringia. These two Länder became highly industrialised during the second half of the nineteenth century and workers there, as in Berlin, developed a high degree of class consciousness. In these Länder was one of the main territorial bases of the Social Democratic Party and Communists, in their bid for power in the early twenties, found more support there than elsewhere in Germany.

German historians have occasionally touched on the idea of the two-fold tradition of Germany: that of a rather cosmopolitan first empire (Holy Roman Empire of the Germanic nation) and that of a nationalist second empire, both based on different geographical areas; the first on the Rhine and Main in the West and the second in Brandenburg and Prussia in the East. I have even heard an opinion that the contemporary division of Germany is a culmination of this development.[2]

Many Western sociologists however would find such reasoning too speculative to be taken seriously. Although I am not so sceptical of the longevity of some socio-cultural features in the structure of society I nevertheless feel it expedient to disregard, at least within this particular inquiry, any such ideas the verification of which requires a far more extended analysis than is provided by methods used in this study.

For the particular purpose of this study it seems to be enough to accept that both the second (Hohenzollern) and third (Nazi) empires with the intermittent period of the Weimar Republic, altogether stretching over seventy-five years, exerted a strong unifying influence on what was then Germany. During that time the fruits of the industrial revolution spread more evenly between East and West, law, type of government and social institutions of individual 'Länder' were brought closer together, and a unified educational system provided a social layer from which rationalisation of any of the successive régimes originated.

To be faithful to one of the methodical principles of this study, this contention has to be illustrated by some data. Quantification of course cannot cover the whole ground. It can provide only a partial glimpse of what can be considered as the technico-economic level (level of

Table 1.1 Technico-Economic Levels in the FRG and GDR
           (Modernisation Ratios)

	1950		1970	
	FRG	GDR	FRG	GDR
Percentage of urban population (in communes of over 2000 inhabitants)	68.6[1]	65.4[1]	88.2[2]	73.8
Percentage of population in great cities of over 100,000 inhabitants	26.9	18.9	32.6[2]	22.0
Percentage of labour force in primary production	24.6	27.9	8.8	12.8
Percentage of labour force in secondary production	42.7	43.9	48.7	49.1
Percentage of labour force providing services	32.7	28.2	42.5	38.1
Rail length per 100 sq. kilometres	12.5	13.7	13.6	13.8
Per capita consumption of primary energy (tons of coal equivalent)	2.5	2.7	5.3	5.7
Per capita living space (square metres)	14.9	14.7	23.0[3]	18.6[3]
Doctors per 100,000 population	129	72	163	160
Infant mortality rate (per 1000)	56	72	23	18

1. 1946   2. 1973   3. 1968

Source: *Statistical Yearbooks* of the FRG and GDR respectively, *UN Demographic Yearbooks* and *Bericht der Bundesregierung und Materialien zur Lage der Nation,* 1971, pp. 118–19, 346–7, 365 (in further text quoted as *Bericht,* 1971).

modernisation[3]) and socio-cultural or rather political-cultural heritage.

The technico-economic level is characterised by Table 1.1. Figures there indicate that, at the beginning of the era of divided Germany, the territory of the FRG was only slightly more urbanised than the territory of the GDR; but the big cities were more represented in the West. In both parts of Germany almost the same percentage of the labour force was employed in secondary production (mining, manufacturing, construction). Primary production (agriculture, forestry and fishing) was better represented in the East and service industries in the West. The rail network was somewhat more dense and *per capita* energy consumption was somewhat higher in the East; but *per capita* living space was virtually the same. Health conditions measured by the availability of doctors and infant mortality rates were better in the West than in the East.

During the subsequent twenty years, 'modernisation' in the technical sense continued. Yet on the strength of indicators in Table 1.1 this occurred at a somewhat faster pace in the FRG than in the GDR.

Only the health indicators improved much more in the East than in the West; the original gap disappeared and in some respects the GDR took the lead. On the whole, however, the 1970 data testify a commensurate level of technico-economic modernisation in both German states.

The commensurability of the technico-economic level in the FRG and GDR has been a matter of industrialisation rather than urbanisation; the corresponding level of industrialisation is in its turn a matter of national averages; within the two German states there are considerable regional differences. Both countries combine highly industrialised areas with still strongly rural areas, but in the West the two types of areas are more or less interwoven. Outside the industrial stronghold in North Rhine Westphalia, there are industrial centres all over the country, especially in the south-west and around the former Hanseatic cities in the North. In the East, the industrial south (formerly Saxony and Thuringia) faces an industrially less developed north.

The main difference between East and West German technical modernisation appears to be that in East Germany the size of settlements has not developed proportionately to the rate of industrialisation. In view of environmentalists' preference for middle-size cities (about 300,000 population considered as optimal), the East German position seems to be rather advantageous.

On the whole the difference in urbanisation seems to be more significant from the socio-cultural point of view. The higher proportion of middle-sized towns in the East is a factor which, in itself, may weaken the tendency towards an ideological polarisation. This might be in a way helpful to the government policy of politico-ideological homogenisation.

There are however some other, more significant, socio- or politico-cultural features which being more or less differently patterned on the territory of the FRG and GDR, partly contribute to the systemic differentiation. They are residues of two turbulent historical processes: dissolution of West European universalism through the Reformation and disruption of the Weimar Republic through political polarisation. Although the ethical contents of these two historical processes differed widely, both produced some similar effects: cleavages within German society.

Yet both these cleavages seem to have vanished or have been super-seded by cleavages with different connotations. The Catholic/Protestant rift was, after two centuries of a more or less peaceful coexistence, largely healed; attitude differences between Protestants and Catholics are gradually becoming less significant. Yet they have not been completely eliminated. The Catholic Church still succeeds in commanding a higher degree of loyalty amongst her members.[4] Catholics are likely to be more conservative than Protestants in questions of family, sex,etc., and also in political attitudes.[5]

So it is not irrelevant to note that whereas in West Germany the population has been almost equally divided between Protestants and Catholics (in 1950, 55·7 per cent Protestants and 44.3 per cent Catholics), in the East there was still a decisive Protestant majority (90 per cent) in 1950.[6]

Less conspicuous but perhaps more significant than the heritage of reformation is the heritage of the Weimar/Nazi confrontation. It cannot be assessed otherwise than by referring to the last free elections before the Nazi take-over, i.e. elections in March 1933. The results are shown in Table 1.2. For the purpose of our analysis the whole territory of 1919—1937 Germany is divided into three areas corresponding to the contemporary FRG, GDR and Polish and Soviet territories.[7] Because of inadequate breakdown of available data, Berlin is also considered separately. Individual political parties are divided into three groups, Nazi-dominated right-wing coalition, democratic centre (including Social Democrats) and the Communist left.

The comparison is revealing; the right-wing parties were strongest and Communists were weakest in territories which as a result of World War Two were annexed by Poland and the USSR. Of all the areas the Right was weakest and the Communists strongest in the city of Berlin. The Centre with 41.3 per cent votes was strongest on the territory of

Table 1.2 Election Results in March 1933 in per cent of total vote

Electoral regions corresponding	Political orientation		
to the present area of:	Right[1]	Centre[2]	Left[3]
Federal Republic of Germany	47.8	41.3	10.8
German Democratic Republic	56.6	28.2	15.2
Berlin (West and East)	40.3	29.6	30.0
Polish and Soviet territories[4]	62.4	29.5	8.1

1. NSDAP (Hitler's National Socialist Party) and Kampffront Schwarz-Weiss-Rot (Conservative Nationalist Party)
2. Social Democrats, Zentrum (Catholics) and all other smaller parties.
3. Communist Party of Germany
4. East Prussia, Silesian regions of Breslau, Liegnitz and Oppeln, half of Pomerania and half of Frankfurt upon Oder region.

Source: Calculated from the *Statistisches Jahrbuch für das Deutsche Reich,* 1933, pp. 540-41.

the contemporary FRG. On the territory of the contemporary GDR, the Centre with 28·2 per cent votes was the weakest of all German areas. Yet neither in Berlin nor in the lost Eastern territories did the percentage of Centre votes exceed the 30 per cent mark. So, the heritage of the Weimar Republic may be expected to be strongest on the present territory of the FRG. However, one must not forget that the influx of Germans from the Polish, Russian and Czech territories strengthened former right-wing elements[8] wherever they settled and this was in most cases ultimately the FRG.

As indicated earlier, different religious affiliation may also have influence on political orientation. In the Weimar Republic Catholics more than Protestants proved immune to extremes, both left and right. Catholic voters of the Zentrum Party held most steadfast against the tide of Nazi-Communist polarisation between 1928 and 1932.[9] In the Second Republic (FRG) the position seems to be as follows: left-wing extremism finds more ground amongst those with a Protestant background, whereas Catholics are more inclined to favour a conservative type of government. In both cases, the polarisation is in favour of more authoritarian solutions.

Yet all these differences, like those in the technico-economic level, indicate only a somewhat different representation or frequency of identical elements. They were, as Dahrendorf put it, 'differences within one society'.[10]

It should also be borne in mind that not only the two German states but also their particular areas differ in a similar way. Such is the case with areas with different levels of urbanisation and industrialisation respectively, with different structure of religious affiliation (especially in the West), and with different political tradition in view of German unity. Although areas with a strong federalist tradition are more represented in the West (Bavaria, Württemberg, Baden, Hanseatic cities etc.), federalist preferences were not wholly absent in the East (Saxony, Thuringia).

Having realised that the main differentiating features of the historical heritage in West and East were not of such intensity as to draw a distinct line across Germany, a line which would in a sense predetermine the systemic dualism in Germany, we may infer that the main differentiation started with the impact of World War Two; or to put it more squarely, with the conquest of Germany by different Allied armies and the ensuing different occupation policy.

This particular event was the decisive factor in putting Germany on different paths of reconstruction and systemic development. Yet it

was not only the new political division in Europe which carried with it
a much deeper division of a civilisational dimension but also the
immediate material impact of this division; this, in addition to the
restraint of sovereignty, put the East into a disadvantageous position
vis-à-vis the West.

The Soviet occupation zone which was later constituted as the GDR
had been more economically weakened than the three Western zones,
the future FRG. First of all, the East suffered greater losses as a result
of the war. Whereas in the FRG direct war damages were evaluated at
DM 2,800 million, on GDR territory they are supposed to have attained
M 3,500 million. Significantly also the share of dismantling was different.
The value was DM 4,400 million in the West and M 6,900 million in the
East. Taking into account that the purchasing power of the Eastern
Mark was at least one quarter less than that of the Western Mark[11] the
difference would be smaller; the DM equivalent of war damages and
dismantling together would be 7,200 million in the West and 7,800
million in the East. On a *per capita* basis this is DM 144 in the West and
DM 424 in the East.[12]

The GDR had also to carry out a heavier programme of reparation
than the FRG. From 1945 to 1961 the FRG paid DM 11,300 million
reparation whereas the GDR paid M 32,400 million. In view of the
lower purchasing power of the Eastern Mark (assuming 25 per cent as
above) the *per capita* reparation burden of the GDR was six times as
much as that of the FRG.

In addition, the FRG received considerable help from the victorious
Allies, help which on the whole more than offset the burden of
reparation. Taking into account the Allied Relief and Rehabilitation
Aid, Marshall Aid and other sources, the FRG received DM 17,600
million in foreign aid.[13]

No parallel action was taken on behalf of the GDR by the Soviet
Union and her allies. Of all the items on the post-war balance sheet only
the aggregate cost of occupation was higher for the FRG, DM 16,000
million than for the GDR, M 10,000.[14] *Per capita,* however, the GDR
had yet to bear a higher cost: in the approximate DM equivalent, about
15 per cent more.

So the FRG had a much better start than the GDR. This is one of
the reasons why the East Germans could not afford an economic boom
on the West German scale. So, the 'objective' situation, i.e. circumstances
which the respective part of Germany had to accept as given from
outside, were more difficult for the GDR not so much because of her
socio-economic system but because of her allies. The FRG received

more generous treatment by her fellow 'capitalists' than the GDR by her 'socialist' friends. It should however be acknowledged that the USSR suffered much more war damage from the hands of Nazi Germany.

Moreover, World War Two had an immense impact on the social mobility, both geographical and vertical, of the whole German nation. After having initiated the mass eviction and deportation of other nationals the Germans themselves eventually had to accept seeing 14 million, i.e. one-fifth of their ethnic community, moving westwards to the densely populated regions between the Alps and the North Sea. Most of them eventually settled in the FRG.

West Germany, however, did not only absorb the tremendous influx of immigrants, but even provided jobs for many more people than those who came to settle down for good. Within five years of recovery West Germany was in need of additional manpower. In mid-1954 73,000 foreign workers earned their livelihood in West Germany. In mid-1971 the number of foreign workers increased to 2,164,000, i.e. 10 per cent of the total employed labour force.[15] Only the recession of 1974—75 brought further recruitment of foreign labour to a halt.

On the other hand the population in that part of Germany which eventually became the GDR drastically declined. Although most of those evicted from Poland, East Prussia and the Baltic countries had to go first to the GDR, only a small fraction stayed there. Most of those expelled came to the FRG and were followed by a mighty stream of GDR residents. Before the establishment of the GDR during Soviet military rule, about one million East Germans escaped to the West. From the establishment of the GDR in 1949 to 1972 another 2,600,000 left for the West. So it happened that the burden of resettling the refugees and finding jobs for them was passed over to West Germany. The liability however soon turned out to be an asset. The expelled and refugees became not mere consumers waiting in refugee camps to return to their own countries but producers helping towards a rapid reconstruction and expansion of the West German economy.

The newcomers gradually became well integrated into West German society. Within twenty years most of them lost interest in returning to their own countries. In the public opinion poll in November 1967, 50 per cent of the expelled and refugees contained in the sample expressed the view that there was no question of them returning. Only 39 per cent would have liked to go back and 11 per cent were undecided. In November 1969, 59 per cent had no desire to return, 29 per cent would have liked to go and 12 per cent were undecided.[16] Of course these data refer only to that generation which experienced the migration; their children do not appear to be at all interested.

With respect to this and with respect to the external help which offset the lower material losses in the West, it is an astonishing fact that the GDR could achieve a commensurate rate of growth with the FRG.[17] Bearing all this in mind we can hardly say whose economic miracle was greater. The GDR had to develop against heavier odds, one of them being her creator and hegemon — the USSR — whom she had to adore and emulate and, last but not least, as far as possible compensate for the immense war damages caused by the Nazi assault and occupation.

More important, however, than all these differences in the material conditions at the beginning of the partition were the political differentiations, dictated by ideological considerations. West Germany was encouraged to remodel herself according to the pattern of Western parliamentary democracies with private enterprise and welfare state as the basic socio-economic parameters. East Germany had to accept the pattern of the USSR in all aspects of her life. This required not only fundamental and drastic changes in her ownership structure but also acceptance of one-party rule with highly concentrated power at the top.

As the victors in World War Two eventually attached the two different parts of Germany to their respective blocs, their contradictory political-cum-ideological concepts became the main factors of the subsequent systemic differentiation of the two 'Germanies'. This differentiation will be considered in more detail in the following study.

Notes

1. In view of the fact that Marxist-Leninist socialism became implemented predominantly in countries where capitalist elements were not fully developed but largely superseded by 'feudal' or 'oriental despotic' features, it is a viable proposition to consider this type of socialism indeed as an alternative to capitalism. Both are different types of 'industrial' society.
2. It is worth remembering in this context that the contemporary border between the FRG and the GDR approximately corresponds (with the only exception of Thuringia) with the ethnic boundary between Slavs and Germans between the sixth and twelfth centuries AD. It might also be interesting to note that Thuringia, although occupied by Western Allies at the end of the war, was exchanged, unfortunately for the West, for West Berlin.
3. Although I am not happy with this colourless and ambiguous term, I am using it as a widely accepted abbreviation for the whole complex of changes which are connected with the industrialisation and secularisation of an increasing number of societal units.
4. In two different public opinion polls in West Germany (Winter 1970—71 and Summer 1972 respectively) 49 per cent Catholics and only 37 per cent

Protestants declared that they were faithful members of their church. *(Jahrbuch der öffentlichen Meinung 1968 bis 1973,* Allensbach and Bonn, 1974 – further quoted as *Demoskopie Jahrbuch,* p. 100). Other indicators such as attendance of services, thoughts about leaving the church etc. point in the same direction.

5. Catholics in West Germany proved less inclined to vote Socialist or become Marxists than was the case with Protestants; in the elections to the Federal diet (Bundestag) held between 1953 and 1972 about 60 per cent of Catholics voted for the Christian Democratic (or Christian Social) Union. Meanwhile the percentage of Catholic voters of the Social Democratic Party increased from 22 to 35 per cent. On the other hand the Protestants' preference for Social Democrats increased from 34 to 54 per cent. The respective losses were at the expense of other parties. *Demoskopie Jahrbuch,* p. 339.

6. The difference in Catholic and Protestant political attitudes, however, is not a general phenomenon; it could similarly be observed only in countries with Protestant supremacy or at least more or less equal position with Catholicism in the past, such as in The Netherlands, Switzerland or East Hungary. In countries where Catholicism has remained the dominant faith as in Italy or Spain, or where Catholic counter-reformation reduced the once powerful Protestants to an insignificant minority as in France or Bohemia, Marxism gained proportionately more converts in the population than in denominationally mixed or predominantly Protestant countries. This can best be illustrated with the case of the Communist vote. Of the Protestant countries only Finland had more than 20 per cent of them, of the Catholic countries only Belgium and Austria have a non-significant Communist Party; yet both have strong and well-established Socialist parties, in Austria with a good deal of the Marxist tradition.

7. Demarcation of the GDR and territories annexed by Poland and the USSR is only approximate, as two electoral regions, Pomerania and Frankfurt upon Oder are supposed to be equally divided between the GDR and Poland.

8. Of the ethnic Germans in Czechoslovakia, 68.2 per cent voted for the Crypto-Nazis (Sudeto-German and Carpatho-German Parties) in 1935. Moreover, the so-called anti-fascist Germans (mainly Social Democrats and Communists) were partly allowed to stay in Czechoslovakia and partly were transferred to the GDR. So the FRG had mainly received former Nazi voters.

9. For empirical evidence of this see S.M. Lipset, *Political Man,* Heinemann, London, reprint 1973, p. 141.

10. Ralf Dahrendorf, *Society and Democracy in Germany,* London, 1968, p. 420.

11. See Chapter 2, section 2d, p. 39 ff.

12. Absolute data from Werner Bröll, *Die Wirtschaft der DDR,* p. 151.

13. ibid.

14. ibid.

15. *Bericht,* 1974, p. 326.

16. *Demoskopie Jahrbuch,* p. 526.

17. See pp. 33–6.

2 INCOME AND WEALTH

2a. Ownership and 'exploitation'

The examination starts with socio-economic issues. There are two reasons for this: firstly, because economic motivations and problems are widely considered, and not only by Marxists, as the most important factors in social relations; secondly, because one particular socio-economic issue, that of ownership of means of production, is widely considered to be most relevant for the contemporary dichotomy of social systems.

As the type of ownership of means of production is the most simple and unambiguous indicator of whether and how far a particular country is supposed to be socialist or capitalist, this issue appears to be the most natural starting point for an intersystemic analysis. Ownership by itself, however, provides only half of the systemic characteristics; the other half is concerned with the way the value of production is appropriated. Consequently, the first chapter deals also with 'exploitation', an issue which the main prophet of the socialism-capitalism dichotomy, Karl Marx, considered the most relevant and also the most abominable consequence of private ownership.

With respect to the ownership criterion, the characteristic of both parts of Germany is clear-cut. In the West, in 1973, about 10 per cent of the working population were employed in the public sector, in the East 93 per cent. At a first glance, this is enough to characterise the Federal Republic of Germany as a capitalist country and the German Democratic Republic as a socialist country. Each of them had only about 10 per cent of alien elements within their respective ownership structure.

There is an additional consideration which may further strengthen this argument. According to the Marxist view, which is the dominant belief of the East, public productive property does not fulfil the requirements of socialist ownership if it operates within the framework of capitalist relationships, i.e., uses capitalist criteria of operation and success (profit motivation), and capitalist techniques, such as free market for goods, services (including labour), capital and land.

Similarly, it can be argued that private ownership within a predominantly socialist framework, commanding allocation of resources and nominal parameters of exchange (wages and prices), does not

23

constitute a genuine capitalist element in the system. Nevertheless, after a comparatively prolonged period when a small but thriving private and mixed sector was allowed to coexist with the 'socialist' one, the GDR leadership decided to reduce the latter to the minimum. From 1971 to 1973 the share of labour force engaged in private business declined from 8.2 per cent to 6.3 per cent and in mixed (semi-state) enterprises from 6.2 per cent to 0.8 per cent. The share of private business in national income decreased from 5.4 per cent to 3.9 per cent, and the share of semi-state enterprises from 8.9 per cent to 0.9 per cent.[1]

Thus, whereas in the East the last vestiges of private ownership are about to disappear, in the West the relationship of the private and public sector in the economy remains fairly stable.

According to Marx, private ownership is the principal cause of the two main vices of class societies, namely of exploitation and alienation. Consequently, substitution of collective for private ownership was for Marx the main means of abolishing exploitation and paving the way for gradual de-alienation.

Any factual analysis aiming either to use, or evaluate, these concepts must first make them operative, that is, if possible, measurable. This is more necessary if one wants to assess practical achievements in this respect, i.e. if one wants to know how far a socialist country has succeeded in fulfilling Marx's expectation.

It is, of course, possible to dismiss this question and make an empirical comparison without too much reference to such vague and emotive concepts as exploitation and alienation. Many Western sociologists, faithful to their ontological and methodological positions, would prefer to do so. It seems to me, however, that this procedure cannot do full justice to the real issues which are at stake in the inter-systemic competition of both parts of Germany. As long as one party in the contest has embraced a certain philosophy or ideology which serves as a model of how to look at, and interpret, reality — and moreover uses this model for justification of its practical measures and very existence — a comparative analyst cannot but take these claims at their face value and evaluate the achievements of that society in the light of these claims and premises. Systems under scrutiny can be studied in terms of their intrinsic ideology or from an extrinsic theoretical position. Therefore, premises of both have to be taken into consideration.

Let us assume that (a) the Marxian concept of exploitation is the main characteristic of a class society, and (b) the rate of exploitation, defined as the ratio of surplus value to the variable capital, can be quantified as the ratio of gross profits, rents, interests and taxes (minus subsidies) to the wage bill in the material branches of national economy. Considering only material branches of economy is in accordance with the Soviet interpretation of Marx's value-producing activities and is an accepted interpretation in all Communist countries, including East Germany.

In order to apply this concept to both parts of Germany, we have (a) to re-calculate the value added in the West German national accounts according to the East German concept, (b) to complete the missing East German data on the basis of indirect evidence and/or substitutive series.

Marxists might, of course, object that in a society with socialist ownership of the means of production, there is no scope for exploitation: all gainfully employed members of the population are either wage or salary earners or co-operative producers; consequently, there is no surplus value; what is needed for further development of productive forces, for sick and old, for administration and defence, is, in essence, another category — surplus product.

This terminological distinction stresses that the difference between the labour value of production on the one hand and workers' labour income on the other is, in a socialist society, not a matter of contradiction. Whereas in the capitalist society the surplus value is appropriated by the capitalist, in a socialist society the surplus product is appropriated by the whole society and used for its benefit. This theoretical presumption has, however, to be tested against facts.

Marx had quite definite views on the use of surplus product in the socialist society, which he expressed in his *Critique of the Gotha Programme of the German Workers (Social Democratic) Party.* Here Marx explained that in the society of his vision workers would get the full equivalent of labour embodied in their products, but partly as an indirect compensation since something has to be left ('deducted' as he put it) for the needs of the society. He expected that these deductions would be from the outset different from those in a capitalist society: the cost of the society's policing and administration will be smaller and the expenditure on culture, health and other social services, pensions and sickness benefits, will be higher.

This programmatic statement of Marx pinpoints one systemic difference between capitalism and socialism. It tackles the 'value appropriation issue' which was central to Marx's concern with the question of ownership. It may be suggested that he saw the change of ownership as the means, whilst the abolition of exploitation was the end. Unfortunately, Marxists are more readily satisfied with the change of ownership than Marx and believe that by using another label and stressing different institutional circumstances they are fulfilling Marx's legacy. Any true Marxian analyst, however, cannot avoid the question of how the produced values are distributed and what is the real extent of appropriation and use of the surplus product by the society as a whole. Surprisingly little has been done to this effect in the Communist countries; from the GDR no hints to this effect are available at all.

Neither do the data from the FRG provide direct evidence for Marx's crucial question. Here, however, a greater supply of data makes it easier to re-calculate the main items necessary for the assessment of the surplus value and its distribution. The West German Institute for Economic Research and the Statistical Office have even attempted to re-calculate some economic aggregates such as gross production and recently also national income[2] to make them comparable with the East German counterparts. The West Germans also re-calculated the East German material national income to a comprehensive gross national product[3] which has shed, paradoxically, more light on the use of surplus value (product) than the official East German sources. Even this comparison, however, provides only the first approximation. A more detailed analysis has to follow, this time on more conventional lines.

There is yet another objection which has to be examined, namely how far the nominal economic values, i.e. prices, wages, etc., reflect the labour value relationships. A lot has already been written on how to bridge the gap between this elusive concept of 'essence' and the tangible concept of 'appearance'; this is not the place to contribute anything to this insoluble question. For operational purposes, it is best to accept the general assumption that the sum of prices equals the sum of labour values, i.e. that the national product in current prices is the quantitative expression of the sum of labour value of that country.

Yet it has to be emphasised that the price/value parity can never be firmly established, as Marx's labour value is essentially a physical or socio-biological term, whereas value expressed in monetary terms such as prices, wages, interest, etc., is a market concept. As the abstract unit of labour value is a non-measurable construction, there will always be some margin for possible dissension on how far the individual prices reflect the respective labour values and, therefore, there will always be room for controversy on a possible amount of 'transferred' surplus.[4]

Some further methodological details connected with the quantification of labour values are discussed in the Appendix, pp. 220–1.

2b. Relative magnitude of the surplus

With all these reservations in mind the practical quantification can now be attempted. For the assessment of the amount of surplus value, or surplus product, the established accounting practice of Communist states will be used. We have, however, to take into consideration that since Marx's time institutional conditions have changed considerably. Not only has 'socialism' become a reality but also 'capitalism' has changed significantly since Marx's day. Workers do not only receive their wage but they also get social benefits, the cost of which is only partly deducted from their wages, the rest being paid for by the employer or the state. If individual workers do not get back what was paid on their behalf to the social insurance institutions, the accumulated money remains at the disposal of the legally guaranteed claims of other workers. Consequently, the social insurance funds can be considered as a kind of capital asset of the working class.

In both East and West there are considerable sums which are taken from the wages in material production and also additionally paid by employers, to be either redistributed to, or kept as a reserve for, the incidence of claims of the same category of workers in cases of sickness, accident or old age. These funds, whether paid by employees or by employers can hardly be included in the surplus value. They have rather to be considered as an addition to variable capital (wage fund). Moreover, as a means of employees' compensation, social benefits are only partly distributed according to the amount of previous work done, and partly awarded according to the claimants' needs. Thus the Communistic principle (in Marx's sense) had found its way into the capitalist establishment long before the socialist state took it over. On the other hand, taxes paid from wages and salaries do not serve a special objective; the state can use them for any purpose. Consequently, they must be considered as a part of surplus value (surplus product). The different treatment of direct taxes and insurance premiums makes the quantitative assessment of national totals more difficult but it has to be undertaken in order to do justice to the original Marxian premises. The respective calculations are reproduced in detail in Appendix A, Tables A.1 and A.2.

Since the available data are limited, some estimates are unavoidable: these take into consideration the main objections which Marxists have raised against the Western concept of value added. Therefore, with respect to the FRG, non-material costs are added in order to increase the surplus value. Moreover, these costs are estimated rather generously whereas the compensation of labour is on the conservative side. The labour income from self-employment is calculated as equal to the average income from employment; it is not equated with the higher incomes of skilled workers or senior employees which, in view of the job in question, would be more appropriate. This more than offsets the fact that some top managers' salaries might be considered as part of profits rather than genuine salaries. On the other hand, the value added in the GDR is taken as it is reported by official sources; compensation for productive work is calculated on the basis of the average income from full-time employment in the socialist sector, which appears to be a fair average income from all types of work.

There may, of course, be some uncertainty as to how far these data represent the true average. Karl Blank mentioned two biases in the averages reported by East German authorities, the magnitude of which can hardly be assessed in his view. Firstly, the East German statistics do not include the wages in the private sector, which seem to be lower than those in the socialist sector. Secondly, they do not include incomes of some high-ranking officials which would make the average higher. One should also bear in mind that, as a matter of principle, they do not include income from co-operative ownership and self-employment which, as will be shown later, was also higher than the average wage and salary.[5]

However, the West German Institute for Economic Research calculated the average gross monthly income from all economic activities, i.e. employment, self-employment and co-operative work, and arrived at a figure 3.2 per cent lower than the reported averages of labour income in the socialist sector.[6] Consequently, if there is any bias in our estimates, it seems to be in favour of what would be the self-image of the GDR rather than of the FRG.

Table 2.1 indicates the approximate relative magnitude of Marxian surplus in both parts of Germany; whether one says 'value' or 'product' is a matter of ideological presupposition, not of factual observation.

As Marx might have expected, the surplus ratio was higher in the 'capitalist' FRG than in the 'socialist' GDR. The development of this ratio, however, points to a diminishing gap between the two countries. Whereas in the West the surplus ratio remained fairly stable or perhaps declined slightly, in the GDR the surplus ratio increased by a half from 1960 to 1973. Should this tendency continue, the GDR surplus ratio will catch up with that in the FRG within a couple of years. This might be considered as an argument in favour of the convergency theory.

For a further evaluation of these figures, we have to take into account the different productivity level and the rate of growth in the two countries. The productivity differences can best be demonstrated

Table 2.1 Surplus Value and Surplus Product Ratios

	Federal Republic of Germany				German Democratic Republic			
	1.	2.	3.	4.	5.	6.	7.	8.
	Calculated net material product (national income produced) in million DM	Calculated labour income in material production net of taxes, in current DM	Surplus value in million current DM (col. 1 − col. 2)	Surplus ratio (col. 3 : col. 2)	Reported national income labour income produced (net of taxes) in material production in million Marks (see note)	Calculated labour income in material production net of taxes in million current Marks	Surplus product in million Marks (col. 5 − col. 6)	Surplus ratio (col. 7 : col. 6)
1960	231,493	130,829	100,664	0.77	71,045	48,860	22,185	0.45
1965	339,595	199,405	140,190	0.70	84,175	53,564	30,611	0.57
1967	352,067	202,975	149,092	0.73	93,043	57,905	35,138	0.61
1970	491,723	275,814	215,909	0.78	108,720	66,123	42,597	0.64
1971	536,038	302,388	233,650	0.77	113,562	69,129	44,434	0.64
1972	581,770*	337,883*	243,887*	0.72*	120,090	72,228	47,862	0.66
1973	645,527*	375,387*	270,140*	0.72*	126,670*	75,332*	51,338*	0.68*

*provisional data

Col. 1: Net market value (value added plus indirect taxes minus subsidies) in material production (i.e. agriculture, fishing, forestry, energy producton, mining, manufacturing, construction, commerce, transport and communication) plus estimated equivalent of non-material costs (included in the net material production according to the Marxist concept).

Col. 2: Reported gross income from employment in material production (as above) net of taxes but not of social insurance premiums paid both by employees and employers, plus estimated labour income from self-employment.

For further details and sources, see Appendix A, Table A.1.

Col. 5: From GDR Statistical Yearbooks: values in 1967 prices; in view of only small changes of implicit price indices over the period (cf. Appendix, Table A.8, line 12) they may be considered as roughly equivalent to the current prices.

Col. 6: According to the average income from employment in socialist sector of the economy, net of taxes but including all social insurance cost on behalf of those in material production.

For further details and sources, see Appendix A, Table A.2.

on the same aggregate which was the basis of our surplus ratio calculations. The net material product per one working person in 1970 was DM 22,579 in the FRG and M 16,224 in the GDR.[7] Without allowing for the different purchasing power of the two currencies, productivity in the GDR was 28 per cent lower than in the FRG. Should the lower purchasing power of the GDR Mark be taken into account, the productivity gap would be still greater.

It has also to be taken into account that during the sixties the respective rates of growth in both parts of Germany were almost the same. Consequently, the above-mentioned difference in productivity can be taken as consistent over the whole period. According to the official data, from 1960 to 1970 the East German 'national income produced' per person employed in its production increased 55.0 per cent and the West German GNP per person employed 58.5 per cent.[8] The 3.5 per cent difference over a decade may well be within the margin of error (especially in view of the different concepts of national aggregates) and, therefore, cannot be considered as significant.

On the other hand, the beginning of the seventies in the GDR has seen a faster rate of growth than the FRG. From 1970 to 1974 the respective national aggregates per person employed increased 23.7 per cent in the East and 14.4 per cent in the West.[9] This gives the GDR a margin for reducing her productivity lag behind the FRG.

In any case, the consumption-inhibiting effect of surplus expressed in comparable monetary units is more burdensome in the GDR with its lower *per capita* income than in the FRG. Under these circumstances, Marx's original assumption that in capitalism the average wage equals the value of labouring power can hardly be taken as still valid. In 1972 the GDR average income from full-time employment (workers and employees in the socialist sector) was M 815 per month.[10] In the same year the West German blue-collar worker received DM 1,190 per month on average and the clerical employee DM 1,532.[11] The net average income from employment in 1972 was M 720 in the GDR and DM 1,170 in the FRG.

Assuming a parity of purchasing power between the two respective currencies[12] the East German worker and employee got 38 per cent less remuneration for his work than his West German counterpart. As the labour productivity in the East was only 28 per cent less than in the West, the surplus in the GDR was of a higher intensity than in the FRG.

In view of these findings, two questions may arise within the Marxian conceptual framework. Firstly, whether there are some objective reasons for the different value of labouring power in the two German states; secondly, whether the increasing surplus ratio in socialist Germany is a necessary corollary of the socialist redistribution of income, i.e. a corollary of the shift from private (personal) consumption to a social, collective one and consequently whether the convergence of the surplus ratios in both parts of Germany is only a matter of coincidence of form (appearance) but not of essence.

A non-Marxist may add a few more questions, namely whether the lower productivity and increasing surplus ratio in the East are the essential factors differentiating a pluralistic, free market society from a 'totalitarian' society with a command economy? Or is it merely a difference in the generosity or acquisitiveness of the one or the other 'Big Brother' whose ally the respective parts of Germany have become?

The first question above can hardly be answered in the affirmative. There is no reason why the abstract unit of labour value should be smaller in the GDR than in the FRG. The other three questions might be more substantiated. The question of the use of surplus product can be tackled immediately: answers to the two other questions are difficult to disentangle. It is virtually impossible to separate the effects of Soviet Russian interference from the effects of the Soviet-type system in the East European countries. In view of East Germany the position is still more complicated by the contradictory policy of the USSR in different periods. At the beginning the Soviet government tried to extract from East Germany as much as possible. Dismantling and reparation played an important role in the Soviet-German economic relationship immediately after the war. Reparation seems to have been significant until 1953 (the year of the Berlin riots). Since then and especially in the sixties, the Soviet authorities have become more considerate. In order not to make the East appear so dreary compared with the thriving West, the GDR was allowed to derive some benefits from the economic co-operation within the Soviet bloc. On the whole, however, some advantages of the more recent period have hardly outweighed the disadvantages of the start.

2c. Disposal of the surplus

However significant the surplus ratio in both parts of Germany may be, the disposal of the surplus may be considered more relevant for the intersystemic comparison. In this respect, however, the official statistics of the GDR are even less revealing than those in the previous inquiry. Unlike other Communist countries, the GDR does not disclose the absolute figures of 'national income utilised' which is roughly the Eastern counterpart of the Western net national product by type of use.

East German statistics contain only percentages of the main components of national income utilised and indices of their respective growth. Absolute data on national income produced which are currently being published in statistical yearbooks of the GDR cannot be used as a key, because the two aggregates differ by an unknown item: national income produced is the 'domestic product' which differs from the national income utilised by the amount of foreign trade balance.[13] Unfortunately, this magnitude is available only in the so-called 'valuta', i.e. exchange Marks which are accounting units of foreign trade and which differ considerably from the Mark used for domestic calculations.[14]

There are apparently serious reasons why the East German authorities conceal the size of their foreign balance in domestic currency. We have to bear in mind that the logic of the net domestic product also requires the inclusion of reparations and other non-requited deliveries. These were of considerable magnitude especially during the early fifties. Only against this background can it be understood that since then the growth of national income used has been faster than that of national income produced.[15]

With respect to the available data, comparative indices of growth will be considered first (Table 2.2). As the West German Institute for Economic Research re-calculated the East German national income series in Western terms, comparison of both parts of Germany becomes easier.[16]

Comparative indices of *per capita* production and consumption growth in Table 2.2 are revealing in several aspects: firstly, from 1960 to 1965 the *per capita* national product grew at an equal pace in both parts of Germany but since then it has grown faster in the GDR than in the FRG. This is shown by both series available for the GDR (the official and the Western one).[17]

Secondly, unlike the GNP, *per capita* private consumption increased faster in the West than in the East between 1960 and 1965. Thereafter the reverse was the case, i.e. faster growth in the East. The shift in the growth rate, however, was not big enough to offset the original advantage of the FRG in the subsequent eight years. Only the 1974–5 recession in the West redressed the balance.

Thirdly, whereas in the West personal consumption grew faster than the GNP, in the GDR personal consumption lagged behind, leaving a greater share at the disposal of the government.

This finding, unfavourable from the point of view of a consumer and citizen, can be countered with the objection that in a socialist society the consumer gets a larger share of benefits through government

Table 2.2 Production and Consumption Growth *per capita* Indices
(constant prices, 1960 = 100)

	Federal Republic of Germany		German Democratic Republic				
	Western Concept		Western Concept (GNP)		Eastern Concept (net material product)		
	GNP	Private consumption	Earlier series	New series	National income produced	Personal consumption	Social consumption
	1.	2.	3.	4.	5.	6.	7.
1961	104.0	104.7	103.9	.	102	103.7	104.7
1962	106.7	109.1	106.5	.	105	103.8	106.9
1963	109.2	111.6	109.6	.	108	104.8	110.6
1964	115.2	116.1	116.3	.	115	109.6	113.9
1965	120.0	112.3	121.8	120.1	120	113.8	116.3
1966	122.2	125.5	127.5	.	126	118.0	123.5
1967	121.4	125.8	134.3	.	132	122.8	129.4
1968	129.4	130.4	141.9	138.2	139	127.2	147.3
1969	138.2	139.1	149.9	145.9	146	134.6	151.5
1970	147.3	149.0	156.7	153.8	155	139.4	154.5
1971	150.1	155.1	.	160.8	162	145.6	161.6
1972	154.3*	159.7*	.	169.7	171	153.7	178.0
1973	161.7*	165.0*	.	179.1	185	164.5	192.7
1974	162.2*	165.1*	.	.	193*	173.0*	211.6*

*Preliminary figures

Sources: Cols. 1 and 2, *Bericht,* 1971, p. 370 and *SJB BRD,* 1975, pp. 37, 49 and
519. Col. 3, *Bericht,* 1971, p. 370 and *Bestandsaufnahme,* 1971, p. 277. Col. 4,
H. Wilkens, 'Das Sozialprodukt der DDR', *Deutschland Archiv,* 1975, p. 603.
Col. 5, 6 and 7, *SJB DDR,* 1975, pp. 3, 13 and 38.

services such as health services, education etc., than in a capitalist one,
thereby offsetting the lower share of personal consumption.
Unfortunately, East German social product and national income data
do not provide an adequate basis for this claim. Although they
distinguish from government consumption a special category 'cultural
and social care of population' (in our table simply 'social consumption')[18]
this category necessarily represents within the material concept of
national income a small percentage (2.5 − 3 per cent of the national
income utilised over the 1950−73 period); it consists of only goods and
material services such as electricity supply, repairs, cleaning, etc. and
not the services of doctors, teachers etc., which are essential for the
assessment of social consumption as a whole.[19] As can be seen from
Table 2.2, the rate of growth of social consumption in the GDR

surpassed the rate of growth of private consumption, and in spite of considerable differences in individual years it rather followed the rate of growth of national income produced.

For a more comprehensive comparison more data have to be collected. This has been done in Table 2.3, compiled from scattered data and fitted into the Western concept of GNP calculated by Herbert Wilkens.

Table 2.3 Total Consumers' Share in per cent of GNP (Western Concept)

	Federal Republic of Germany				German Democratic Republic			
	1965	1968	1969	1970	1965	1968	1969	1970
Private consumption	56.2	55.9	55.0	53.8	56.1	53.8	53.7	53.6
Goods and services from social insurance	4.2	4.8	4.7	4.9	4.0	3.8	3.8	3.8
Government expenditure on education, culture and health	4.8	5.0	5.2	5.6	9.0	8.6	8.6	8.8
New dwellings	6.4	5.6	5.2	5.4	2.1	2.1	2.1	2.1
Total	71.6	71.3	70.1	69.7	71.2	68.3	68.2	68.3

Source: *SJB BRD*, 1972, pp. 523, 524, 398, 379–80; *SJB DDR*, 1971, pp. 150, 316, 317; *Bestandsaufnahme*, 1971, pp. 277, 292; *Bericht*, 1971, pp. 396 and 398. For more details see Appendix, Table A.3.

From Table 2.3 it can be seen that the GDR devotes a higher proportion of national resources to education and health services than the FRG. This gap, however, tended to diminish during the sixties. On the other hand, construction of new dwellings represented a much greater share of GNP in the West than in the East. Also, social insurance benefits in kind were somewhat higher in the West, and unlike the other items, this particular difference tended to increase. On the whole, the consumers' share in gross national expenditure declined somewhat in both parts of Germany during the late sixties. But, in comparison with the middle sixties, the decline was slightly more pronounced in the GDR than in the FRG.

So, even if we take into account the 'socialist redistribution of income' and add all the other items which benefit the final consumer to his private, household consumption, the gap between the FRG and GDR persists. On average, the citizen of the FRG gets from the greater

national cake a slightly larger share than his counterpart in the GDR. So
the relative terms do not redress the balance which is in favour of the
West German consumer in absolute terms.

It can, of course, be objected that this aggregate comparison conceals
the class contradiction. The consumers' share in a 'capitalist' society
necessarily includes also the consumption of the 'capitalists'. To
eliminate this consumption, we have to consider the development of
real wages only. Unfortunately, as previously stated, the statistics in the
GDR do not differentiate between workers and other employees.
Therefore, in order to make a comparison we have to put these categories
together for the West also. The development of average real wages and
salaries is shown in juxtaposition with the production and productivity
growth, in Table 2.4.

Table 2.4 Productivity, Product and Compensation for Work (Constant
prices, indices with different bases)

	FRG				GDR			
	1965	1970	1974	1974	1965	1970	1974	1974
	1960	1965	1970	1960	1960	1965	1970	1960
National Product* per person employed	124.8	127.0	114.4	181.3	121.6	128.0	123.7	191.7
National Product* per capita	120.9	121.9	110.1	162.2	120.0	128.4	125.0	193.3
Average real income from employment (wages and salaries)	129.6	123.5	112.8	180.4	114.1	119.4	113.9	155.0

*In FRG Gross National Product, in GDR National Income Produced; as shown in
Table 2.2 the difference between the growth of the Western and Eastern
concept of national income in the GDR is not so great as to invalidate
comparison on the basis of official data.

Sources: *SJB BRD,* 1974, pp. 21 (GNP per person employed), 508 (*per capita* GNP
in current prices), 518 (GNP price index) and 1975, pp. 37, 508 and 519,
SJB DDR, 1974, pp. 17 (national income *per capita* and per person employed),
19 (nominal income from employment), 328 (retail prices of goods and
services) and 1975, pp. 13 and 15.
For the calculation of real wages and salaries in FRG see Appendix, Table A.4.

In the GDR, the growth of real wages was continuously lagging behind
the growth of national income produced, both *per capita* and per person
employed. In the FRG, the average real income from employment was
well ahead of the *per capita* GNP. But the original lead of real wages
and salaries over the GNP per person employed (productivity growth)

was reversed during the late sixties. Since then productivity continued to grow faster. Taking the period 1960–74 as a whole, the average real wage and salary in the FRG was only a few points behind the growth of the GNP per person employed. On the whole, the span between the productivity and wage growths was much wider in the GDR than in the FRG.

Nevertheless the shift in the respective growth of productivity and real earnings in the FRG is significant. In corroborates the tendency found earlier with respect to the rate of surplus value, but the other way round: in view of the rate of surplus the increasing ratio in the East approached the more or less stable ratio of the West; in the faster growth of productivity over real wages the West approached the more or less stable East.

Comparison of data in Tables 2.1 and 2.4 also reveals that in the GDR the growth rate of surplus ratio was not offset by the higher labour compensation in non-material services. Since the total share of consumers in the gross output of goods and services in the GDR also tended to decline (Table 2.3), it can be concluded that social transfers did not benefit either from the increased surplus. During the late sixties the total cost of social insurance (benefits in money and in kind) was 18.2 per cent of the GNP in the FRG and only 12.4 per cent in the GDR.[20] From 1957 to 1969, the monthly average pensions of statutory social insurance increased much faster in the FRG than in the GDR. In nominal terms the West German old age pension was 46 per cent higher than the old age pension in the GDR in 1957, whereas in 1969 it was 130 per cent higher.[21]

So, whether we look at it from the producers' or consumers' point of view, individuals and their households in the FRG received a larger share of the national cake than those in the GDR. Now, of course, the question of what happens to the surplus not reallocated to the direct benefit of the consumers arises. A comparative review of the respective items in both parts of Germany is given in Table 2.5.

As already shown in Table 2.4, the total consumers' share of the GNP over the period in question was higher in the FRG than in the GDR. If this is so, a Marxist might expect that, in a socialist country, a higher percentage of national resources should be devoted to extended reproduction, i.e. to productive investment. This, however, is not the case; investment in machinery and equipment, together with investment in non-dwelling buildings, absorbed, on average, almost equal percentages of the GNP in both parts of Germany duirng the period under study. Also percentages of additions to stock did not substantially differ

Table 2.5 The Non-Consumers' Share in % of GNP

FRG	1965	1968	1969	1970
1. Machinery and equipment	11.3	9.8	11.1	12.1
2. Buildings other than new dwellings	8.9	7.8	7.9	8.9
3. Additions to stock	2.2	2.1	2.6	2.2
4. Defence	3.8	3.1	3.1	2.9
5. Government consumption other than defence and consumers' services	2.4	2.6	2.7	2.6
6. Net investment abroad	−0.1	3.3	2.5	1.6
7. Total non-consumers' share	28.5	28.7	29.9	30.3

GDR	1965	1968	1969	1970
1. Machinery and equipment	9.6	10.6	11.6	11.9
2. Buildings other than new dwellings	7.1	8.2	9.1	8.7
3. Additions to stock	3.3	0.8	11.1	2.1
4. Defence	)	4.5	4.6*	4.7
5. Government consumption other than defence and consumers' services	)8.8	)7.5	5.5	4.3
6. Net investment abroad	)	)		
7. Total non-consumers' share	28.8	31.6	31.9	31.7

*Interpolated

For sources and calculations see Appendix, Tables A.5 and A.6.

The individual items in this table are so arranged as to exclude all items considered in Table 2.3. This results in a certain underestimation of government consumption other than defence and consumer services (line 5); as the expenditure on education, culture and health investment was not specified, the whole sum spent in these three fields of government concern has been deducted from government consumption and not from fixed domestic investment. Consequently, items in lines 1 and 2 are, on the other hand, slightly over-estimated. As this concerns both parts of Germany equally, this inaccuracy does not invalidate the comparison.

although they varied within a wider range in the GDR than in the FRG.[22] In the late sixties and the early seventies, the gross capital formation — new dwellings excluded — was 21.2 per cent of the GNP in the FRG and 21.4 per cent in the GDR.

The main difference between East and West was in the remaining use of the GNP, namely, in defence, state administration and the balance of trade. These three items together can perhaps best be labelled as administration, security and foreign co-operation cost. Only West German data allow us to follow these items separately. East German statistics lump them together. From scattered evidence, however, the defence expenditure for several years can be assessed.

On the whole, the use of national resources for purposes other than consumer satisfaction and domestic investment has been much higher in the GDR than in the FRG. This is especially the case with defence expenditure: if expressed as a percentage of the GNP, then during the three years 1968–70, the GDR figure was one and a half times greater than that of the FRG.

The other two items were also somewhat higher in the GDR than in the FRG. Here it is difficult to say whether the difference was due more to the higher administration costs or higher international commitments of the GDR than those of the FRG. According to the official foreign trade data, the GDR had, over the ten-year period, 1960–69, a cumulative excess of exports over imports of 6,600 million 'valuta', i.e. exchange Marks. Though these exchange Marks cannot be related to the aggregates in domestic Marks, it is at least possible to compare the importance of the trade balance with that of the FRG.

As shown in Table 2.6, both parts of Germany have achieved, during the sixties, credit trade balances. The West German cumulative excess of exports over imports was about ten per cent of its imports, whereas the East German excess was considerably smaller: over five per cent of its imports only. Over the period 1970–74, however, only the FRG continued to have an excess of exports over imports and this of almost the same magnitude (eleven per cent of the total imports of goods and services); on the other hand, the GDR had a small excess of imports over exports (3.2 per cent of the imports).[23] In terms of the engagement in foreign trade, the West German net investment abroad and/or economic contribution to other countries was, during the whole period under observation, almost four times higher than a similar investment and/or contribution by the GDR. The widening gap in the size of the credit balances in both parts of Germany can hardly be scored as a point against the convergence theory. It rather reflects the growing concern of the GDR for competition with the FRG in living standards. How far the FRG herself subsidises, in different ways, the living standard in the GDR deserves a special inquiry.

Consequently, and in view of what has already been found out on capital formation and defence expenditure, it may be inferred that the main reason for the more extensive 'non-consumer' use of GNP in the GDR was the higher relative level of administration and security costs. To these the core of increasing surplus ratio in the GDR was allocated. In this respect no convergency with the FRG has so far been found. In contrast to the FRG, the GDR continues to use a greater proportion of her resources for purposes which neither benefit the consumer nor increase the country's productive assets.

Table 2.6 Relevance of Foreign Trade Balance (Cumulative Totals)

	FRG			GDR		
	1960—64	1965—69	1970—74	1960—64	1965—69	1970—74
Exports in thousand million DM or M	344.4	567.7	1044.7	52.5	74.3	121.1
Imports in thousand million DM or M	314.6	513.5	942.4	49.6	70.6	125.1
Balance in thousand million DM or M	+29.8	+54.2	+102.3	+2.9	+3.7	—4.0
Balance in per cent of imports	9.5	10.6	10.9	5.9	5.2	—3.2

Sources: *SJB BRD,* 1972, p. 525 and 1973, p. 530 and 1975, p. 519. *Yearbook of National Account Statistics,* 1966, pp. 207 and 233. *SJB DDR,* 1971, pp. 290—91 and 1974, pp. 284—5. *Deutschland Archiv,* 1975, p. 853.

2d. Purchasing power and living standard

To evaluate in absolute terms the impact of changes in the surplus ratios and consumption and wage shares, the different purchasing power of the Western DM and Eastern Mark and changes in their relationship over a period of time have to be taken into account.

Thorough calculations in this respect have been made by the West German Institute for Economic Research with regard to employed persons and pensioners; some results are reproduced in Table 2.7. This table shows a wide discrepancy between the price structure in both parts of Germany. Extremely low rent, fuel and electricity costs in the East are balanced by comparatively high costs of alcohol and tobacco. This surely is a favourable aspect of East German social policy, which, however, finds it less favourable corollary in the scarcity of dwellings available at a low price. Also the relative cost of household goods is much higher in the East than in the West.

On the whole one can realise that although both price structure differences continue to increase rather than decrease, the overall purchasing power of the East German Mark is catching up with the purchasing power of the Western Deutschmark. In terms of the East German consumption pattern, the East German Mark attained, by the turn of 1972—73, purchasing power parity with the Western DM; in terms of the West German consumption pattern it was, however, still about 12 per cent lower.

Calculations of the purchasing power of the 'pensioners' money' indicate a much more favourable ratio for the GDR. In terms of the Western pensioners' consumption basket the Eastern Mark caught up with the Western DM in 1969 and surpassed it by 5 per cent at the turn of 1972—73. In terms of the Eastern pensioners' consumption pattern the Eastern mark was about 25 per cent above the purchasing power of the Western DM. (For details, see Appendix, Table A.7.) This, however, reflects the fact that the East German pensioner with his, on average, very low pension, cannot buy the more expensive goods which his Western counterpart can afford.

Table 2.7 Purchasing Power of the Mark in the GDR as a Percentage of the Purchasing Power of the DM in the FRG

| | Four-Person worker's household Product Mix (consumption basket) | | | | | |
| | in the FRG | | | in the GDR | | |
	1960	1969	1972—3	1960	1969	1972—3
Food	75	82	91	76	89	104
Drink & Tobacco	47	49	50	49	50	55
Rent	133	227	303	133	227	303
Fuel & Electricity	135	189	227	137	189	238
Household goods[1]	66	61	63	67	55	66
Clothing & Footwear[2]	51	65	70	52	67	81
Cleaning Products & Cosmetics	101	83	92	100	100	104
Leisure Activities	96	79	82	105	115	128
Transportation	103	66	74	105	95	103
Total Expenditure	75	83	88	77	89	101

Source: 'Die Kosten der Lebenshaltung in der DDR im Vergleich zur Bundesrepublik an der Jahreswende 1972—73', in *Wochenbericht,* Deutsches Institut für Wirtschaftsforschung, Berlin-West, No. 21, 1973, p. 191, und *Bericht,* 1971, p. 143.

1. Typical Prices in 1970

	FRG DM.	GDR Mark
Electric stove	280	650
Refrigerator	280	1100
Photographic camera	100	100
Television set	500	1750
Car of comparable quality	6000	18000

2. Typical Prices in 1970

	FRG DM.	GDR Mark
Man's suit	130	180
Man's shoes	40	45
Man's shirt	15	50
Ladies' underwear (set)	10	27

Source: *Die Zeit,* 3 September 1971.

The trend towards overall purchasing power parity of both German currencies can also be seen from the development of the respective price indices. Whereas the West German cost of living index was in 1972 46.5 per cent higher than in 1960, the East German cost of living index was reported as virtually stable. This again may be scored as one of the advantages of a command economy. Whatever bias there may be in the calculation of price indices[24] the direct price quotations point in the same direction.[25]

Increase of non-consumer prices, which in the GDR took place during the early sixties, was offset in view of the cost of living index by a ramified system of subsidies. In the late sixties their total weight in the national economy, measured as a percentage of national aggregates, was slightly above one per cent of GNP in the FRG and about 4 per cent of national income produced in the GDR.

In 1960, the average nominal net income in a worker's and employee's household was in the GDR 11 per cent below that in the FRG: 758 Marks and 850 DM respectively. Because of the 25 per cent lower purchasing power of the Eastern Mark, the real income in the East would be about a third below that in the West. In 1970, the respective nominal incomes were 1031 in the GDR and 1665 in the FRG, i.e. the gap to the disadvantage of the GDR was 38 per cent.[26] After allowing for about 10 per cent lower purchasing power of the GDR Mark, the real income would be 44 per cent less than in the West. So over the decade the gap between the living standard in the FRG and the GDR increased to the still greater disadvantage of the latter. Stability of prices did not help the East German workers to catch up with their Western counterparts, ridden by inflationary pressures..

Although there may be some inaccuracy in these figures, the differentials are too large to be invalidated by a possible margin of error. Nevertheless, it is worth while checking these figures by means of some physical indicators, such as consumption of basic food. Although the yearly supply of these foods is calculated per head of population and, therefore, cannot be related to wages alone, it is well known that in developed countries expenditure on food does not significantly differ with respect to the individual socio-economic groups. Therefore, the food consumption *per capita* may also be considered as a fair indication of the workers' standard of living. The absolute increase at the beginning and towards the end of the decade (Table 2.8) shows that in both parts of Germany the situation improved quantitatively and in West Germany also qualitatively. Whereas in 1960 the consumption of meat per head of population was equal in East and West, in 1968 the West Germans were 9 per cent above their Eastern neighbours. The gap widened still more in fresh vegetables and fresh local fruit; only in cereals, sugar and fats was the GDR *per capita* consumption higher than that in the FRG. So, due to a higher consumption of glycid calories (4.3 per cent more) the total calorie intake in the East was, in 1968, 5 per cent higher than in the West. On the other hand, in the GDR, the intake of higher-quality food such as protein was 4.3 per cent lower and that of animal protein 16.9 per cent lower than in the FRG.

In other goods, such as, for example, consumer durables, the gap between East and West Germany is still more obvious. As this is a well-known fact, only a few data indicating the magnitude and orientation of this gap should be mentioned here. In 1969, there were, per 100 households, 14 passenger cars in the GDR but 47 in the FRG; 48 electric washing machines and 48 electric refrigerators in the GDR, but 61 and 84 respectively in the FRG. On the other hand, for television sets the gap was negligible, 66 per 100 households in the GDR and 73 in the FRG; in radio sets there was an almost equal supply of radios in households in both parts of Germany, 92 in the East and 91 in the West. In bicycles, the GDR was in the lead with 40 per 100 households against only 7 per 100 households in the FRG.[27]

These data are significant in two respects. First, they indicate a greater supply of consumer durables in West German households. Second, they show that the difference is smallest in the supply of radio and television sets. This can be explained by the different price structures in the two German countries. In terms of the respective nominal currencies, a refrigerator was, in the GDR, four times more expensive than in the FRG, whereas a television set was only three times, and a radio only 2.3 times more expensive.[28] Apparently, these inter-country differences do not reflect the differences in production cost structures but differences between more or less free market conditions in the FRG and a centrally planned and commanded economy in the GDR. In the latter, the government price policy can deliberately assure a better supply of households with those consumer durables which can also serve another government purpose such as ideological education (indoctrination). The difference in relative supply of cars and bikes reflects mainly the different level of the respective countries' wealth. The less hilly East German countryside can hardly explain the gap in these two complementary indicators.

Within this context, one more physical indicator should be mentioned, namely the living space. During the sixties, the annual increase of dwelling space in square metres per 1000 population was on

Table 2.8 Yearly Supply of Basic Foods per Head of Population

	Unit	FRG		GDR	
		1960	1972/3	1960	1973
Meat & Products of Meat	kg	54.3	79.0	54.3	74.0
Fats (true fat content)	kg	25.1	25.7	27.4	26.5
of which butter =	kg	6.4	6.2	10.4	10.9
Milk	litre	102.7	86.5	94.5	101.6
Eggs	pieces	228	293	197	249
Cereals (incl. rice)	kg	81.7	66.5	101.6	95.0
Potatoes	kg	133.0	93.8	173.9	143.4
Fresh vegetables	kg	45.8	66.6	48.0	70.1
Fresh local fruit	kg	61.2	84.9	61.1	40.9
Citrus & tropical fruit	kg.	18.2	25.4	7.1	17.2
Sugar & sugar products	kg	28.6	33.6	29.3	36.0

Source: *Bericht,* 1971, p. 392; *SJB BRD,* 1975, p. 494; *SJB DDR,* 1974, p. 333.
   Bestandsaufnahme, 1974, pp. 258 and 421.

average three times higher in the FRG than in the GDR. From 1966, however, when the FRG/GDR ratio of the dwelling space increase was at its highest (i.e. 4:1) the difference began to decrease (cf. the declining percentage of new dwellings in the GNP in Table 2.3). In 1970 the ratio was down to 2.62. There is, however, still a long way to go before a suggestion of converging ratios can be made in this respect.[29]

Yet it is not only the supply of goods which matters. It is also the cost, in terms of working time or other effort in obtaining them. That is to say, (a) what is the purchasing power of earning for a unit of time, and (b) how easily accessible are goods and services offered to the consumer?

There is no doubt that in both these respects the record of the FRG is more favourable than that of the GDR. In the FRG a worker can obtain for his average hourly wage a larger quantity of goods and services than his East German counterpart. His or his wife's shopping facilities and services provided for households are more plentiful and superior in quality.

These as all other differences in the level of consumption, are sometimes dismissed for ideological reasons; they are considered to be 'consumeristic' preoccupations of a 'one-dimensional' man. Yet, whatever might be the philosopher's dream, however he might want to reform the common man's 'false consciousness', no one with socialist consciousness can dismiss the comparison of effort-reward relationship as irrelevant to the evaluation of quality of socio-economic systems.

Therefore, it is appropriate to mention some results of such a comparison.

Of a sample of about 60 current consumer goods and services, the cost of which is reproduced in Appendix, Table A.9, only a few items were, in mid-1971, cheaper in terms of working time in the GDR than in the FRG: rye bread, potatoes, pickled herring, white cabbage, lignite briquets and weekly rail fares. Margarine, ordinary sausage and soap cost almost an equal amount of working time. All the other food and especially industrial goods were obtainable in the GDR for a price requiring a much longer working time than in the FRG. In these terms, most staple food and also textile products, excluding the items previously mentioned, were one and a half to two and a half times dearer in the GDR than in the FRG. Imported commodities, such as coffee, chocolate and lemons were five to eight times dearer, and consumer durables three to six times dearer in the GDR than in the FRG.

So, not only is the West German socio-economic system more productive (efficient) than the Eastern one, but also it can afford a higher ratio of profit or surplus ratio. This potentiality, however, is not fully exploited; the West German capitalists and/or government content themselves with a lower suplus value than the value of labouring power would admit. Surplus ratio (measured on the basis of material product) in the FRG in 1973 was only 6 per cent higher than in the GDR (see Table 2.1) and overall profit ratio, measured on the output of all goods and services (see Table 2.20 further on), was virtually equal in both parts of Germany. In this respect 'late capitalism' does not differ from what is supposed to be a 'developed socialism'. In view of the use of surplus, however, the late capitalism fulfils more of Marx's expectations than its supposedly socialist counterpart.

2e. Income distribution by size

So far, only national aggregates or averages have been compared and it might be rightly objected that they do not reflect the different degree of income inequality in the two German states. This is the most widely used argument put forward by GDR sympathisers. Oddly enough, East German statistics do not provide enough evidence to support this thesis. Whereas income inequality in the West can be studied in considerable detail and also with respect to the population as a whole, for the GDR there are data available only for the households of workers and employees lumped together. With respect to other social groups we have to be satisfied with averages in the main socio-economic groups.

Table 2.9 Income Differentials by Socio-Economic Groups

	Average monthly net income in DM or M per income recipient				1972 in % of 1960	Ratios — (lowest category = 1.00)			
FRG	1960	1965	1970	1972		1960	1965	1970	1972
1. Employed	476	710	974	1170	246	1.47	1.50	1.54	1.50
2. Self-employed	1154	1661	2829	3770	327	3.56	3.50	4.48	4.83
3. Pensioners	324	474	632	780	241	1.00	1.00	1.00	1.00
GDR									
4. Employed	485	554	663	720	148	3.39	3.44	3.42	3.26
5. Co-operative members	661	786	858	958	145	4.62	4.88	4.42	4.32
6. Self-employed	1650	1925	2220	2025	123	11.54	11.96	11.44	9.16
7. Pensioners	143	161	194	221	155	1.00	1.00	1.00	1.00

Source: Heinz Vortmann, 'Einkommensverteilung in der DDR', *Deutschland Archiv,* 1974, No. 3, p. 275.

Figures in Table 2.9 reveal some expected and also some unexpected features. First, concerning the inter-group comparisons : the difference between the highest income (from self-employment) and the lowest income (pension) was, throughout the whole period under study, much wider in the East than in the West. Only in the seventies did the gap begin to diminish. From 1960 to 1972 the differential between the average income in the highest and lowest type of income increased from 3.6 to 4.8 in the FRG, whereas in the GDR it declined from 11.5 to 9.2. In 1960, the average income from self-employment in the FRG was 2.4 times higher than the average income from employment, but 3.4 times higher in the GDR. In 1972 the differential was 3.2 in the West and 2.8 in the East. On the other hand, the average pension in the FRG was continuously about two-thirds of the net average income from employment, whereas the average pension in the GDR hardly attained one-third of such an income.

During the sixties, average income in all the three Western and all the four Eastern socio-economic groups grew at approximately the same pace. In both parts of Germany income from employment growth was slightly ahead, whereas self-employed people were at the bottom in the West, as were members of co-operatives in the East. The difference between the highest and the lowest type of income was almost steady, i.e. three and a half times in the West and between eleven and twelve times in the East. With the beginning of the seventies, the growth of income from self-employment accelerated in the West and decelerated in the East. In the West it seems that this resulted partly from the higher rate of inflation and partly, as will be shown later, from lower taxation. In the East, the deceleration was due to the new nationalisation drive which apparently affected 'big business' first. So, whereas in 1960 the range of income differentials in the GDR was 3.2 times wider than in the FRG, in 1972 it was down to 1.9. This may be considered another case for the convergency theory.

It is amazing that throughout the whole of the sixties the difference between an average income from self-employment and income from employment was higher in the GDR than in the FRG. This is apparently due to the fact that among the self-employed in the West there are a lot of small firms, artisans, shopkeepers and farms, the low income of which pulls the average down. On the other hand, in the East a typical self-employed person would be a craftsman in the strongly understaffed repair services and/or building trades, where the supply/demand relationship enabled comfortable earnings to be obtained.

According to available data, only a complete liquidation of the private sector may bring the group income differentials in the GDR within the range of those in the FRG, namely, to the tune of 4.5 : 1. Is it not strange that a socialist country has to abolish its last vestiges of private enterprise in order to narrow her income differentials by socio-economic groups to those of a capitalist country?

Income distribution among income recipients of all types is available solely for West Germany. Only income distribution from employment can be compared with the East (Table 2.10). Both West and East German data reveal a similar tendency; decline of income recipients in the three lowest brackets and increase in the three upper brackets. In the medium bracket there was a moderate decline in the East, but a considerable increase in the West.

The continuous improvement shown by a steady drive from lower to higher income brackets has, however, to be checked by the corresponding changes in the purchasing power of the respective currencies. A comparison of equivalent ranges of living standard has to take into account different price levels in both countries.

As was shown earlier (Table 2.7), in 1960 the purchasing power of the East German Mark was about three-quarters of that of the West German Deutschmark (and this was in terms of consumption patterns both in East and West). Consequently, we have to lower the East German incomes by about one quarter in order to make them comparable with incomes in Western Deutschmarks. In 1969 the

Table 2.10 Income Distribution of Households of Workers and Salaried
           Employees

Nominal net income	FRG				GDR			
	Percentage of Households							
DM or Mark per month	1960	1964	1967	1970	1960	1964	1967	1970
All households less less than 400	13.1	4.0	2.1	0.8	10.4	8.1	4.9	3.1
400 − 600	25.1	13.8	8.8	4.9	23.8	20.4	16.0	11.9
600 − 800	21.1	19.1	14.8	9.3	25.2	23.6	19.1	14.3
800 − 1000	12.4	16.6	16.2	11.6	21.9	24.4	24.1	19.0
1000 − 1200	9.5	12.3	13.3	12.4	10.8	13.8	19.8	22.0
1200 − 1500	9.3	13.2	14.8	16.9	5.6	6.8	11.6	19.2
1500 & over	9.5	21.0	30.0	44.2	2.4	2.9	4.5	10.6

Source: *Bestandsaufnahme,* 1971, p. 332; 1974, p. 411 (also *SJB DDR* 1974,
       p. 340).

purchasing power of the East German Mark was about 10 per cent lower
than that of the Western Deutschmark.

Making an allowance for these purchasing power differences the real
income distribution in both parts of Germany appears as shown in
Table 2.11. The upper limit of the lowest bracket can be considered as
the poverty level or the monetary equivalent of Marx's value of
labouring power, i.e. the price equivalent of goods and services
necessary for reproduction of physical and mental strength required for
a simple type of work. In that sense it can be considered as an abstract
unit of the value of labouring power. Unfortunately it is not possible to
assess the monetary equivalent of the basic standard with respect to
some physiological or socio-cultural considerations.[30] We have to make
use of available income brackets which are comparable in both parts of
Germany. This leads us to the DM 600 of purchasing power in 1960
(about DM 800 in 1970) per household, which in both parts of Germany
was almost of the same size.[31] Of the West German households, 38 per
cent were below that level in 1960 and 15 per cent in 1969. Of the East
German households 59 per cent were below that level in 1960 and
29 per cent in 1970.

To show in concrete terms which households this living standard
may concern, we have to look for scattered information on earnings in
individual professions or enterprises. Comparisons of a salary scale in
West and East Germany published in *Die Zeit* may illustrate the case

Table 2.11   Real Income Distribution of Workers' and Salaried
Employees' Households in Purchasing Power of 1960

DM of 1960	FRG		GDR	
	1960	1970	1960	1970
Less than 600 DM	38.2	15.0	59.4	29.3
600 — 1200 DM	43.0	40.8	38.2	60.1
Over 1200 DM	18.8	44.2	2.4	10.6

Calculated from data in Table 2.7 with respect to the following purchasing
power equivalents adjusted to the available income brackets: in 1960, 1 DM =
0.75 M; in 1970, 1 DM = 1 M; 1 DM of 1970 = 0.78 DM of 1960.

(Table 2.12). For further information on East German salaries see also
Table 2.13. As these data refer to the year 1970, the DM 600 standard
has to be put up to the amount of the price increase — (600 x 128.5 =
DM 771, i.e. approximately DM 800 purchasing power in 1970). East
German purchasing power equivalent would then be about 900 Marks.
Hence, whereas in 1970 the basic standard was attained by junior
typists in the West, in the East clerical workers or grammar-school
teachers were still below this mark.

On the other hand, the range of differentials was much broader in
the West. The director's salary was, in the given example, ten times
higher than the messenger's salary in the West and only 8.7 times
higher in the East. Yet this is not the end of the story. A West German
President of the Board had thirty-three times as much as a messenger.
Although no direct analogy with this function can be drawn in the
East, an equivalent might be a Minister or Deputy Minister within the
highly specialised state economy administration. As seen in Table 2.13,
his salary was estimated at 4,500 Marks, which is more than thirteen
times the messenger's salary.

As these salaries are before tax, differences in the rates of taxation
have to be taken into account. In the FRG the tax progression is
much steeper than in the GDR. Lower incomes are taxed less and
higher incomes taxed more in the West than in the East. Also tax
allowances for children are more substantial in the FRG. The West
German tax rate in class no. 1 starts with 5.5 per cent of DM 400
monthly income, and at DM 2000 income attains 21.8 per cent. The
East German tax rates for the corresponding levels of income are 9.5
per cent and 20 per cent respectively. In higher income brackets the

Table 2.12 Gross Monthly Earnings in Industrial Enterprises of
   Comparable Size in 1970

Profession	FRG A joint-stock company, yearly turnover approx. 1 million DM DM	GDR A union of nationalised enterprises, yearly gross output approx. 1 million Marks M	Ratio — (col. 1 : col. 2)
Messenger	600	340	1.8
Junior Typist	800	450	1.8
Secretary	1,400	650	2.2
Clerical Worker (no diploma required)	2,000	800	2.5
Staff Member (university level)	2,800	1,100	2.5
Group Leader	3,500	1,350	2.6
Department Chief	5,000	1,650	3.0
Manager (sales & external relations)	—	2,000	
'Prokurist' ('fondé de pouvoir')	6,000	—	
General Director	—	3,000	
Director	8,000	—	
Member of the Board	15,000	—	
President of the Board	20,000	—	

Source: Frank Gratz, 'Extras für die Bosse in der DDR', *Die Zeit,* 3 September
   1971.

tax rate further increases in the FRG whereas in the GDR it remains on
the same percentage level.[32]
   In the middle sixties a married man with one child was liable to wage
tax when his salary exceeded DM 550 per month, whilst in the GDR a
salary of over M 300 was taxable. In a family with two children the
threshold was DM 700 in the West, but M 350 in the East; for families
with three children the thresholds were DM 900 and M 400 respectively
Comparative tax rates from monthly wage or salary of DM or M 1000
were higher in the GDR than in the FRG in the following way: for
bachelors 1.39 times higher, married without children 1.67 times higher,
married with one child 1.90 times higher, married with two children,
2.52 times higher, married with three children 4.25 times higher,
married with four children 21.12 times higher. In this last case the West
German income recipient paid only a token tax of DM 6.50 from

Table 2.13   Earnings in Selected Professions in the GDR in 1970

Profession	Average gross monthly earnings in Marks	Index
Clergyman (Vicar)	550	72.8
Secondary (Grammar-school) Teacher	800	106.0
Engineer (graduated)	1,300	172.2
Economist (graduated)	1,300	172.2
Senior Doctor in a teaching hospital	1,600	211.9
University Lecturer	1,800	238.4
Plant Manager (in a plant with labour force of 1500)	2,400	317.9
University Professor	2,900	384.1
General Manager of an industrial holding	3,500	463.6
Minister	4,500	596.0
Average earnings of full-time manual or clerical worker in socialised sector	755	100.0

Source: Frank Gratz, 'Extras für die Bosse in der DDR', *Die Zeit,* 3 September 1971. *Statistisches Taschenbuch der DDR,* Berlin 1973, p. 123.

DM 1000. A married man with five children paid no tax at all in the FRG whereas in the GDR the tax on M 1000 was M 126.[33]

The higher tax progression in the FRG, both with respect to the level of income and number of dependents, considerably diminishes the gross income differences of individual professions in Tables 2.12 and 2.13.

There are still some additional factors which make the income distribution in the GDR steeper than may be inferred from salary scales only: first, the gainful employment of spouses of top management personnel is not uncommon in the GDR, whilst it is rather exceptional in the FRG. Second, in the GDR some non-publicised advantages for people on a higher level of the power hierarchy have to be added. Purchases in special shops, preferential allocation of flats, cars and other scarce goods provide additional income in kind. This appreciably reduces the differences in real living standard between Eastern and Western managers' households. It also, to a considerable extent, offsets the steeper income differentiation in the West where everybody has to rely more on his monetary income. Hence, data indicating wider income differences in the FRG than in the GDR have to be interpreted with these qualifications in mind.

The overall view can best be illustrated by the quintile distribution of wages and salaries in both parts of Germany and the quintile

distribution of income from all sources in the FRG alone (Table 2.14).
In the light of these data, the East German distribution of income from
employment appears to be more equal than in the West. As the data are
reported on households and not on individual income recipients the
different intensity of employment per household has to be taken into
account. In 1968, three out of five women in the age group 22—65
were gainfully occupied in the GDR, whilst there were only two out of
five in the FRG. So, the number of two-'breadwinner'-households was
significantly higher in the GDR than in the FRG.

Although the distribution of income from all sources is reported
only from the FRG, it is possible to draw from it some conclusions for
our comparison. As can be expected, this distribution is much steeper
than distribution of income from employment (wages and salaries).
From what has been found on income differentials by socio-economic
groups in the West and East, it may be assumed that in the GDR the
overall income distribution would be steeper than the distribution of
income from employment.

It has, however, to be borne in mind that the self-employed,
especially those in liberal professions, have greater opportunity for tax
evasion than other groups. So the statistical picture rather understates
the incomes of the self-employed. Tax evasion is, of course, a matter of
guesswork, but it might be to some degree facilitated by the overall
liberal attitude of the state in the West. On the other hand, silence of
East German sources on this topic, in contrast with the widely
publicised wage and salary income structure, is also significant.

Table 2.14 Household Income Distribution by Size in 1970: Percentages
of the Sum of Net Disposable Income

	Households of Wage-Earners and Salaried Employees		All Households	
	FRG	GDR	FRG	GDR
Lowest fifth	8.3	10.4	5.9	n.a.
Second fifth	12.7	15.8	10.4	n.a.
Third fifth	16.8	19.8	15.6	n.a.
Fourth fifth	22.3	23.3	22.5	n.a.
Highest fifth	39.9	30.7	45.6	n.a.

Source: *Bestandsaufnahme,* 1974, p. 248; *Bericht,* 1974, p. 430.

On the whole, the differences of income distribution in the FRG and the GDR do not seem to be as spectacular as might be expected. Although there has been much more levelling of income from employment in the GDR than in the FRG, pensioners' incomes have been brought closer to the average income from employment in the FRG than in the GDR. Similarly, the average income from self-employment in the FRG deviated less from the average wage and salary than in the GDR. Although these group differentials may not offset the differentiation of individual incomes, they nevertheless remind us not to consider the income distribution from employment as being representative of the income distribution as a whole.

So, all the three income flow aspects, namely, that of surplus ratio, the use of surplus, and income distribution by size, do not indicate the theoretically expected difference between a capitalist and a socialist country. First of all, the surplus ratio tends to converge; second, the lower share of private consumption in the GDR is only partly offset by higher government spending for the benefit of the consumer. On the whole, the consumer in the West gets a larger proportion of a bigger national product. Only the income distribution appears to be more equalised in the GDR than in the FRG, especially if the disappearance of the private sector in the GDR is anticipated; however, very low pensions in the GDR on the one hand and additional income in kind for leading party and government officials on the other, make this difference considerably smaller, if not cancelling it out altogether.

2f. Distribution of wealth and production units

Bearing in mind that virtually all substantial means of production in the GDR have been socialised since 1972 and that in the FRG only 10 per cent of those gainfully employed were in the public sector, we can proceed to examine the structure of all other sorts of wealth, as far as possible, in both parts of Germany. As can be expected, West Germany offers more opportunity for such an inquiry.

According to an estimate on the basis of representative data in 1969, 88 per cent of West German citizens' households had a savings deposit, about 76 per cent had life insurance, 40 per cent owned a house or landed property, 23 per cent had a contracted saving with a building society, 20 per cent had bonds or equities. So with the exception of savings and insurance most of the households were without property. Yet a comparatively high percentage owned real estate. Considering only those who owned some of these types of property, we find that savings were distributed most evenly among them (concentration ratio 0.278);

second were those with landed property (0.415). Most uneven was the distribution of bonds and equities (concentration ratio 0.571).[34]

According to tax statistics, there were in 1969 in the FRG, 413,197 property owners with taxable property of DM 84,436 million. Thirty-eight per cent of them, with assets below DM 100,000 each, owned 8.2 per cent of the total taxable property; 36.3 per cent with assets between DM 100,000 and 250,000 owned 18.3 per cent; 20.4 per cent with assets between DM 250,000 and 1,000,000 owned 28.0 per cent; 4.5 per cent of owners with more than DM 1,000,000 almost 45.5 per cent of the total taxable property.[35]

According to another source, 73.5 per cent of non-agricultural assets were owned by 1.72 per cent of private households in 1966.[36]

Unfortunately, there are no comprehensive data on the process of concentration of private property; only some isolated evidence is available. From 1949 to 1971, the number of farms in the FRG decreased by 40 per cent but the cultivated area by only 9 per cent. So the average size of a holding increased from 7.0 to 10.6 hectares; the proportion of farms with more than 10 hectares increased from 20 per cent to 38 per cent.[37]

In the FRG, the concentration proceeded at a much slower pace in industry than in agriculture. During the sixties, the average number of persons working in enterprises with more than 1000 people remained virtually stable (40.1 in 1961 and 40.2 in 1970). The number of enterprises in mining and manufacturing increased by 5.1 per cent.[38]

Also in the GDR, the size of productive units continued to increase and their number to decline; this happened not only in agriculture as in the FRG, but — in contrast to the FRG — also in industry. In 1960, the average size of a state farm was 591 hectares and in 1970, 866 hectares. Meanwhile, the number of state farms declined from 669 to 511. The drop in agricultural co-operatives was still more conspicuous — from 19,331 in 1960 to 9,009 in 1970. The average size of a co-operative farm increased from 280 hectares to almost 600 hectares. The membership dropped only slightly (from 901,000 to 891,000). In 1974, there were 5,764 co-operatives with a total membership of 871,000. The average size was 935 hectares. The number of industrial enterprises in the GDR decreased from 16,038 in 1960 to 12,067 in 1970. The average number of people employed in one enterprise increased from 173.5 to 233.6. The percentage of industrial labour force in enterprises with more than 1,000 employed increased from 50 per cent to 60.6 per cent.[39]

So in the GDR there was not only a large-scale concentration of ownership in state hands,[40] but also an administrative-technical concentration of production units which proceeded faster than in the FRG. In 1970 enterprises with more than 1,000 employees represented 4.7 per cent of all industrial enterprises in the GDR but only 1.3 per cent in the FRG. As we have already seen, in such big enterprises 60.6 per cent of all industrial labour force was employed in the GDR, but only 40.2 per cent in the FRG. In agriculture the disparity was still greater with 600 hectares per agricultural co-operative in the GDR against 10.5 hectares per individual farm in the West.[41]

We must not, of course, overestimate the economico-political meaning of these figures. They leave out the possible 'conglomerates' and other links which might considerably reduce the enterprises' independence. Nevertheless, they have some technico-economic meaning which in its turn has some reflection in the lower echelons of the power structure.

Concentration of ownership and management of the means of production is usually considered to enhance economic efficiency. It does not seem, however, that the GDR took any particular advantage from the higher degree of concentration and the consequent economy of scale. Productivity, both per labour and per capital or land unit was higher in the FRG. Only in certain areas was this gap being narrowed.

According to the calculations of the German Institute for Economic Research, the labour productivity in industry of the GDR was, in 1960, 66.6 per cent of that in the FRG. In 1968 the ratio was 68.4 per cent, i.e. a slight improvement for the GDR. In the so-called productivity or, better, efficiency of capital, the GDR was at 76.2 per cent of the FRG in 1960 and 85.7 per cent in 1968,[42] i.e. a still more remarkable improvement of the GDR.

In contrast to industry, the productivity of agriculture in the GDR lagged behind that of the FRG to a degree that remained almost constant. The gap was most striking in view of the labour productivity. In 1968–69 the labour productivity in agriculture in the GDR was 39 per cent below that in the FRG. This is most surprising as the aim of collectivisation in the Communist countries was, *inter alia*, to achieve higher productivity of labour. The magnitude of this gap is the more striking as the productivity per land unit (hectare) was in the GDR only 12 per cent lower than in the FRG and the productivity per livestock unit 16 per cent lower.[43]

The gap in the productivity of labour in agriculture would appear to be still greater, if the 'voluntary' help by townspeople and school-children on collective farms at harvest-time (often on Saturdays and

Sundays) were accounted for.

Of course, the low productivity in collective agriculture has a
sociological explanation, namely, (a) the 'no-control – no responsibility'
attitude of the collective farmers, (b) the fact that most chairmen of
collective farms were rather 'parachuted' from the towns, that is, from
the district Party secretariats, than genuinely elected from among the
peasants, and thus were excellent for transmitting orders but had hardly
any farming experience.

Another comparison of wealth in both parts of Germany is possible
in relation to liquid assets (Table 2.15). In the early seventies, there was
in the GDR 5,300 million Marks of 'quasi-capitalist' assets (securities
and bonds) which constituted 7 per cent of the total value of liquid
assets in that country. In the FRG there were DM 123,000 million in
comparable property, i.e. 22 per cent of the total value of liquid assets.
This is perhaps another indicator of the relevance of capitalist elements,
i.e. in the technical sense, in both parts of Germany respectively.

Otherwise, the difference is less striking. In the East, the savings
deposits were 84 per cent, in the West, 60 per cent; the insurance assets
were 9 per cent in the East, 18 per cent in the West of the total assets
value. In the West the nominal *per capita* savings deposit was 55 per
cent higher than in the East. In real terms (purchasing power) the
difference would be still greater. In the West, insurance assets per head
were nominally four times as high as in the East.

Within this context it may be relevant to ask how far individual
social groups or classes participated in the accumulation of wealth. Or,
to put it the other way round, what is their capacity to produce wealth
from income? Relevant figures are available only with respect to the
FRG (Table 2.16).

According to these data, the savings capacity of an average worker
was less than an average pensioner's. The latter's average holding was
higher than that of all wage and salary earners together. This is
apparently due to the greater social differentiation within the
pensioner's group. Unfortunately this category is not subdivided
according to the former position of pensioners. From the fact that
only 9 per cent of pensioners held assets, it can be inferred that there
are not many wealthy pensioners; however, when they were wealthy,
they tend to be very wealthy indeed. Also the fact that among the
self-employed only 30 per cent were asset holders points to a high
differentiation of wealth in this category. On the whole, 80 per cent of
savings deposits in 1964 were below DM 3,000, a sum which can
scarcely be said to represent any wealth at all. So, as might be

be expected, the wealth-producing capacity of income recipients was limited to a small number.

Table 2.15 Structure of Savings, end of 1972

	FRG			GDR		
	Total in thousand million D Marks	per cent	DM per head of population	Total in thousand million Marks	per cent	M per head of population
Savings deposits	337	60	5,452	60,0	84	3,527
Bonds and securities	123	22	1,990	5,3*	7	312
Insurance assets	98	18	1,586	6,6	9	388
Total	558	100	9,028	71,9	100	4,227

*end of 1969
Source: *Bestandsaufnahme,* 1974, p. 420.

Table 2.16 Capacity to Produce Wealth from Income in the FRG

	1. Net Income per month per household DM 1972	2. Saving in % of monthly net income in 1959	3. Average savings deposit in 1964	4. Average holding of bonds &equities DM 1972	5. Bond & Equity owners in % of households in the group
Self-employed	4,492	16.1	2,439	42,263	30
White-collar employees	2,056	10.8	1,305	)11,338	18
Workers	1,784	4.3	1,071	)	
Pensioners	1,120	4.7	n.a.	16,938	9

Sources: Col. 1, 4 & 5 — *Die Angestelltenversicherung,* 1974, No. 2, p. 93; Col. 2 & 3, *Classens, Klönne, Tschöpe, Sozialkunde der BRD,* pp. 262 and 263.

The opposite question, however, deserves to be examined, namely, the extent to which wealth (both as consumers' property and productive assets) is a source of income. The consumers' wealth produces services which can be considered as income in kind which, however, diminishes with wear and tear. In view of the income and expenditure aggregates which have already been discussed, we have to bear in mind that of all the consumers' wealth only the services from dwelling houses enter the national and personal income accounts. A comparison of the intensity and quality of this particular service is reproduced in more tangible terms in Table 2.17.

There are a few significant facts shown in this table. First of all, the consistently higher number of dwellings per 1000 population in the GDR than in the FRG. This is particularly striking in view of the much more extensive construction of new dwellings in the FRG than in the GDR. If we take into account that from 1948–1970 the GDR population decreased by 10 per cent, whereas in the FRG there was a considerable population increase, i.e., by 25 per cent, we understand that in this particular respect the GDR population drain has brought at least some benefit for those who remained.

Table 2.17 Supply and Quality of Dwellings

	FRG		GDR	
	1961	1968	1961	1968
1. Number of dwellings (flats, apartments) per 1000 population	292	325	327	352
2. Floor space per dwelling (in square metres)	67	71	53	53
3. Floor space per head (in sq. m.)	19.7	23.0	17.2	18.6
4. Age of dwellings in % of number of dwellings built before 1919;	41	32	65	58
built 1919–1945 or 1948[1]	22	17	25	22
built after 1945 or 1948[1]	37	51	10	20
5. Equipped with (in % of number of dwellings):				
Lavatory within dwelling	67	n.a.	33	n.a.
Bath	47	n.a.	22	n.a.
Central heating	12	n.a.	3	n.a.
6. Rent as % of disposable income of average household (of workers & employees)	9.0[2]	12.5	4.6[2]	3.9
7. Rent increase index (1962 = 100)	100[2]	148.4	100[2]	101.1

1. 1945 for the GDR, 1948 for FRG.
2. 1962.

Source: *Bericht,* 1971, pp. 365–7.

More dwellings, however, do not mean larger living space. Here the FRG is better off as in all other qualitative indicators, such as inside lavatories, baths, central heating and the period over which the dwellings are being used. In the GDR, 80 per cent of dwellings which were used in 1968 were built before World War Two and 58 per cent before World War One. In the FRG, 51 per cent of the dwellings were constructed after 1948 and only 32 per cent before World War One.

Secondly, rent is much lower in the GDR than in the FRG. In 1968 it accounted for almost 13 per cent of disposable income from employment in the West but only 4 per cent in the East. Also the rent in the GDR remains fairly stable, whereas in the FRG it leads the general price increase.

So, on the whole, the comparative position is as follows: the East Germans enjoy a somewhat higher number of dwellings, but these dwellings are smaller and predominantly in old buildings and, consequently, not so well-equipped as dwellings in the FRG. Dwellings in the GDR are also obtainable at a lower rent than in the FRG; yet this is less due to their lower quality than to the particular price/cost relationship practised in all Communist countries. As construction of new houses is much more expensive than any potential level of rent, acquisition of new flats depends either on political position or on extra voluntary brigade work or on a special amount of purchase money.

As for other types of property as a source of income, the information is available only for the FRG. The West German Institute of Economic Research found that between 1950 and 1960 the proportion of self-employed on income from property increased from 50 per cent to 55 per cent of the total income from property. Then from 1960 to 1970 this share dropped again to 49.6 per cent. The share of salaried employees on income from property increased from 16.7 per cent in 1950 to 21.1 per cent in 1955, and then declined to slightly above 20 per cent where it remained also in 1970. On the other hand the share of pensioners and annuitants first declined: from 16.6 per cent in 1950 to 8.2 per cent in 1960 and then again increased to 12.9 per cent in 1970. Only the share of workers' households on income from property remained fairly static: 16.7 per cent in 1950, 16.3 per cent in 1960 and 17.3 per cent in 1970.[44]

An investigation into the increase of property between 1950 and 1969 brought somewhat different results. According to this the share of self-employed in the ownership of private property declined from 64 per cent in 1963 to 53 per cent in 1969. All the other socio-economic groups have increased their percentage, especially the salaried employees (from 11 per cent to 16 per cent), and workers' participation in private wealth slightly increased (from 10 per cent to 12 per cent).[45]

On the other hand a sample investigation in 1969 revealed that only a quarter of income from enterprise and property was received by other than self-employed.[46]

In view of considerable differences in the data, it is difficult to draw an unambiguous conclusion. Only one tendency seems to stand out clearly from the inconsistent results, namely that the socio-economic group of salaried employees increased its share in total property privately held and also improved its share in income generated by this holding.

This appears plausible. Managerial staff are in the best position to acquire bonds and equities whether on the market or from new emissions. Also the so-called Volksaktien (people's shares) seem to have been sold mainly to managerial employees. According to the opinion poll undertaken by the Institute for Demoscopy in 1969 the highest percentage of buyers of Volksaktien was amongst the leading salaried employees(33 per cent); second were the self-employed including professionals (29 per cent), of the lower salaried staff only 16 per cent and of the skilled workers only 8 per cent reported that they ever bought any Volksaktien. Among the unskilled workers and farmers the percentage of buyers was negligible (4 per cent and 2 per cent respectively).[47]

2g. National income by distributive shares

In this chapter, our analysis of aggregate income distribution undertaken at the beginning of this section (2a) from the point of view of Marxian concept of value will be checked from the point of view of factor cost according to the classical theory of value. This, however, is possible only with respect to West Germany. East German data provide no clue to comparable computation of national income by distributive shares. So the contents of this chapter will be focused on the FRG. Only towards the end will an attempt be made to compare the aggregates of net cost of labour, of capital and of social transfers in both parts of Germany.

West German data on national income by distributive shares are reproduced in Table 2.18. They indicate several significant features: on a gross income basis the relative weight of labour compensation increased continuously during the last decade at the expense of capital and self-employment compensation. From 1960 to 1974, the total gross income from employment increased from 60.6 per cent to 71.6 per cent of national income at factor cost and the gross income from enterprise and property decreased from 39.4 per cent to 28.4 per cent respectively.

This seems to be in contradiction to two of our previous findings: those concerning the surplus value ratio, and the *per capita* GNP and average real wage growth.

With respect to the first point, we have to bear in mind that when quantifying the surplus ratio we considered only the income from material production, whereas here incomes from the total production of goods and services are taken into account. The continuous relative increase of the tertiary sector absorbs a good deal of surplus value, which, in its turn, is used on an increasing scale for wages and salaries in that sector. So, what from the point of view of the Marxian concept of value appears to be a part of surplus, from the Western concept of value appears as a compensation of labour within the primary division of national income.

With respect to the second point (wage and GNP growth), the present data shed more light on the appropriation of the fruits of labour. After deduction of wage tax and employees' contribution to social insurance, the share of wages and salaries remained remarkably stable; after a slight increase in the middle sixties (from 44.5 per cent in 1960 to over 47 per cent in 1965–67) it dropped to the previous level, i.e. about 44 per cent of national income at factor cost in 1973. The share of social transfers followed the same development. Also the percentage of net income from self-employment and corporate profits distributed to individuals barely increased; it was, in most years of that period, between 20 and 21 per cent of national income at factor cost. On the other hand, the share of non-distributed profits declined considerably and also the share of profits accruing to the state somewhat declined. In striking contradiction to this, the payment on behalf of labour not distributed in net wages, salaries and transfer payments increased enormously: from 0.1 per cent in 1960 to 9.1 per per cent of national income at factor cost in 1973. This means that the bulk of the increase of the gross income from employment went into the forced savings which, whether they accrued to the state or to social insurance funds, eventually helped to offset the decline in business savings. So, labour in the FRG contributes, on an increasing scale, to finance the capital expansion.

In comparing these shares we have to remember that the relative number of persons living predominantly either from wages and salaries or from profits changed. From 1960 to 1973 the number of wage and salary earners increased from 77.5 to 85.0 per cent of the gainfully employed population, whereas the self-employed declined from 22.5 to 15.0 per cent of that total. The share of profits in national income

Table 2.18 National Income by Distributive Shares in the Federal Republic of Germany

	Per cent of National Income at Factor Cost										
	1960	1965	1966	1967	1968	1969	1970	1971	1972	1973	1974
1. Total gross income from employment	60.6	64.7	65.7	65.9	63.9	65.2	66.7	68.3	68.6	69.5	71.6
2. Of which: net wages and salaries	44.5	47.4	47.4	47.3	45.0	44.9	44.8	44.8	44.7	43.4	43.9
3. income from social insurance and government pensions	16.0	16.6	17.1	18.9	17.8	17.4	16.4	16.6	17.2	17.2	18.6
4. balance (line 1 minus lines 2 and 3)	0.1	0.7	1.2	−0.3	1.1	2.9	5.5	7.0	6.7	9.0	9.1
5. Total gross income from enterprise and property	39.4	35.3	34.3	34.1	36.1	34.8	33.3	31.7	31.4	30.5	28.4
6. Of which: tax and other obligatory payments	8.9	8.2	8.0	7.9	7.8	7.8	6.6	6.3	6.2	6.9	6.7
7. distributed profits accruing to private households	19.8	20.1	19.9	20.6	20.7	21.7	21.1	21.3	22.2	21.5	21.3
8. distributed profits accruing to the government	1.2	1.1	1.0	0.8	0.9	0.9	0.8	0.8	0.5	0.6	0.3
9. non-distributed profits	9.5	5.9	5.4	4.7	6.8	4.4	4.8	3.2	2.4	1.5	0.1

Source: *SJB BRD*, 1972, pp. 520 and 521; *SJB BRD*, 1973, pp. 527 and 528; *SJB BRD*, 1975, pp. 508, 515, 516.

For absolute data, see Appendix, Table A.10.
Column totals may not add to 100.0 due to rounding.

is, however, not commensurate with the percentage of self-employed people. In this respect, only distributed profits of non-incorporated enterprises can be taken into consideration. The share of these profits declined less than the percentage of self-employed.

This finding is consistent with the data in Table 2.9, indicating a faster growth of nominal income from self-employment than from employment. This development is due to two circumstances: firstly, the taxation of profits was declining (see Table 2.18, line 6), whereas the taxation of income from employment was increasing (the average rate of the wage tax increased from 6.4 per cent in 1960 to 13.4 per cent in 1971[48]); secondly, out of the profits an increasing share was being distributed to individuals whilst the percentage of undistributed profits was sharply diminishing. This gave the individual profit shares a double benefit, both at the expense of the state and of the business sector. It might be expected that this would have led to the decline of capital formation; this, however, did not happen. Data in Table 2.5 indicate a stable percentage of gross fixed investment in the GNP. Also the ratio of net fixed investment in net national product was comparatively stable: 16.9 per cent in 1960, 18.4 per cent in 1965, 17.5 per cent in 1970 and 16.6 per cent in 1972.

This development is explained by data on financial sources of net capital formation (Table 2.19) indicating that the business sector, while retaining less and less of its proceeds, had, for new investment, to rely more on borrowing than re-investing its own profits. From 1960 to 1970 only the government's share in the net capital formation remained comparatively stable. The percentage of profits declined by more than a third and the percentage of savings increased by about a quarter. It has, however, to be emphasised that the latter had happened already in the first half of the decade.

Table 2.19 Financing Sources of Net Capital Formation in the FRG

	1960	1965	1970
Profits	30.1	22.4	18.7
Taxes	29.2	24.8	30.0
Savings	40.7	52.8	51.3
Total	100.0	100.0	100.0

Source: Calculated from data in national accounts in *SJB BRD,* 1972, pp. 507, 511 and 513.

For the absolute figures, see Appendix, Table A.11.

What conclusion can be drawn from these data? Paradoxically, a contradictory one: in terms of individual *per capita* net income, the income-producing capacity of productive assets increased more than the earning power of labour. In terms of net national aggregates, the income generating capacity of the productive assets developed at equal pace with the earning power of labour. In terms of gross national aggregates the relative share of labour increased at the expense of that of capital. So, whereas in the economy as a whole the relevance of capital gains declined and that of remuneration of hired workers increased, individual owners of productive assets received an increasing share of the accruing profits. Moreover, they did not use this increased income for consumer purposes, but saved or re-invested it for further possible profit.

The socio-economic implication of these findings also seems to corroborate the theory of convergency. However well individual capitalists in the FRG may do in the struggle for a greater share in the national cake and however they might be occasionally supported by the taxation system, the share of capital gains in national income and also the proportion of capitalists themselves in the population is declining. Although in the FRG this happens at a much slower pace than had happened in the GDR, the trend is quite clear-cut.

There is yet still another surprising feature in this development. The sharp increase of forced savings from payments on behalf of gross income from employment and the most significant drop in the share of undistributed profits and also in the share of profit tax occurred either in, or immediately after, 1969. This was the year when, as a result of general elections, the Social Democratic and Free Democratic parties formed a coalition government which then ruled the country for all the subsequent years of our survey.

An outside observer must find it difficult to evaluate how far the government policy has contributed to this development. It seems, however, that it was rather the cumulative effect of previous legislation and economic development which produced such a conspicuous statistical shift towards the end of the sixties. The West German Institute for Economic Research explains the reduced tax from profits and ownership by the ampler use of investment and amortisation allowances admitted since 1958, and by the fact that numerous tax-payers reached the highest possible income tax bracket.[49]

It remains to be seen how much the unintended shift in favour of *per capita* disposable employers' income will be affected by the recent tax reform planned as a major redistributive device and effective since

1 January 1975.

Meanwhile, it may be worth while trying to find out whether there is any possibility of comparison with the GDR. As no data on national income by distributive shares are available, one has to be content with some indirect evidence. It is possible to juxtapose national income produced (net material product) with the sum of labour income in the whole economy and the sum of social transfers and to assess the 'surplus' as the residue (Table 2.20). In this juxtaposition labour income is calculated as the product of the reported average wage and salary and the number of workers, employees and active members of production co-operatives in both productive and non-productive branches; social transfers are assessed as the total expenditure of social insurance. Income from ownership and enterprise is the residual item.

It should be borne in mind that this is only a very rough comparison. East German labour income does not include salaries in the non-reported sector, such as the army, police, party apparat etc.,[50] but it does include income from co-operative work (important mainly in agriculture). The West German data on the other hand have a comprehensive coverage of wages and salaries but no attempt was made to include the labour income of small farmers, artisans and shopkeepers. The inclusion of salaries from the non-reported sector in the GDR would increase the net labour income by 5–10 per cent. The inclusion of the labour income of small farmers and other producers into the labour income in the FRG would increase this item by 10–20 per cent.[51]

Table 2.20 Approximate Distributive Shares in per cent of Net Material Product at Market Prices

	FRG			GDR		
	1960	1970	1972	1960	1970	1972
Net income from hired and co-operative work	45.3	48.2	49.2	58.1	54.2	52.4
Income from social insurance	16.2	17.6	18.9	13.5	13.8	14.8
Income from owner-ship and enterprise	38.5	34.2	31.9	28.4	32.0	32.8

Sources: FRG see Appendix, Table A.1, line 10 (material product) and A.10, lines 2 and 3 (net income from employment and social insurance). GDR see Appendix, Table A.12.

This juxtaposition reveals a still more striking contradiction between the GDR and the FRG than was evident with respect to the surplus value (surplus product) ratio. In that comparison, the surplus ratio in the GDR increased, whereas in the FRG it was comparatively stable. In this comparison the share of net labour income in the FRG increased, whereas in the GDR it declined. The percentage of income from social insurance increased in both parts of Germany, however in the FRG at a much faster pace. Consequently, the share of the income from socialist ownership in the GDR caught up in 1972 with the share of income from predominantly private property in the FRG. Realising the ascending line of the former and the declining ratio of the latter, we cannot but conclude with a paradoxical statement: the capacity of capital to generate income (profits) was better guaranteed under conditions of state 'socialist', rather than private 'capitalist', ownership.

Another paradox has been discovered with respect to the FRG: the system of income redistribution, devised, in a welfare state, as a means of equalisation, operated, at the turn of the decade, in favour of capital rather than of labour.

2h. Summary

In this section, the main justification for the socialist transformation of society (abolition of exploitation) has been subjected to the scrutiny of quantification on the basis of the experience of divided Germany. At the outset, an attempt has been made to assess how much workers and employees derive from the labour value of production. Calculations were undertaken on the basis of both Marxian and classical concepts of labour value.

In view of the Marxian labour value, the scrutiny confirmed first that the Marxian concept of reified labour can be quantified only when accepting simplifying assumptions. Secondly, its analytical use is limited; it leaves out a considerable amount of the labour force, the importance of which is continuously growing in the process of what Marxists themselves call the scientific technical revolution.

Be that as it may, surplus ratio, calculated on the basis of reified labour value according to statistical practice in the Communist states, indicates a stable magnitude in the FRG and a rapid growth in the GDR. In 1973, the respective ratios were 0.72 in the FRG and 0.68 in the GDR. In this respect, the East is catching up with the West.

Taking into account the whole tertiary sector of which only a part is included in the reified labour value, the development since 1960 in the two German states was quite different. In the GDR real income from employment continuously lagged behind productivity. The gap was considerable and of a fairly constant magnitude: productivity increased about one and a half times as fast. In the FRG, the relative development of productivity and real earnings was uneven. In the early sixties real income from employment grew faster, but after that productivity took the lead; from 1960 to 1974 both increased almost equally by some 80 per cent.

Looking at the development from the point of view of the final use of national output of goods and services, the citizen as a consumer obtained a larger share of the national cake in the FRG than in the GDR. This was so, even if benefits from social insurance and government expenditure on education, health and social care were added to private consumption and construction of new dwellings. Seen from this angle, the surplus ratio, i.e. non-consumers' share of the GNP, was higher in the East than in the West. The reason for this, however, was not, as might be expected, a higher investment or aid to other countries; higher surplus in the GDR than in the FRG had to cover higher administration and security costs. The rate of investment was, in both parts of Germany, almost the same. The excess of exports over imports was considerably higher in the FRG.

At the beginning of the seventies, the average real income from employment in the FRG was two-thirds higher than in the GDR. Yet, these incomes in the GDR tended to deviate less sharply from the average than in the FRG. But the greater levelling of gross incomes in the GDR was partly offset by additional amenities in kind (preferential supply of scarce goods and services) for the top employees and by the more progressive taxation in the FRG.

Taking into account income recipients other than wage and salary earners, the income structure does not seem more equal in the GDR than in the FRG. Extremely low pensions on one side and surprisingly high income from self-employment on the other, were reasons for a much wider range of income differentials by socio-economic groups in the GDR than in the FRG.

Distribution of wealth rather than income made East German society more egalitarian than West German society. This was most apparent with regard to the productive assets which in West Germany were largely in private ownership. In the middle sixties almost three-quarters of non-agricultural productive assets were owned by less than 2 per cent of households. Since the private ownership of the means of production is in the process of disappearing in the GDR, there will be no question of inequality in that sector of wealth. On the other hand, there is a continuing inequality of consumer wealth the extent of which, unfortunately, cannot be quantified.

Irrespective of ownership, there was a continuous process of concentration of production units. In the FRG this was the case mainly in agriculture. In the GDR, the concentration also affected industry and on the whole proceeded at a much faster pace than in the FRG. Nevertheless, both the productivity of labour and the efficiency of capital in the GDR still lagged behind that in the FRG. A certain catching up could be observed in industry — especially in view of capital efficiency — but not in agriculture.

Further data from the FRG indicate a wide-ranging difference in the average capacity of income to produce wealth, especially by individual socio-economic groups. Information on development of distribution of wealth and income from property is, however, not conclusive. On the other hand, data on national income at factor cost indicate that in the FRG the combined earning capacity of labour (gross incomes and social insurance funds) grew on the whole faster than the income-producing capacity of capital (gross profits). Yet after tax the development was uneven. In the early sixties there was an increase of the share of net wages in national income; then a decline set in. At the same time the *per capita* net profits started to grow faster than net wages. A new tax system was introduced as from the beginning of 1975 to offset this development.

In the GDR, where almost all productive assets were in state or co-operative ownership, the nationalised means of production were returning profits at a faster pace than was that of the remuneration of labour. So, whereas in the 'capitalist' FRG private capital as a source of income kept a precarious balance *vis-à-vis* the earning power of labour, in the 'socialist' GDR the relative role of state capital in producing income was — in relationship to the share of labour — increasing.

Notes

1. *Statistisches Jahrbuch der Deutschen Demokratischen Republik* (further quoted as *SJB DDR*), 1974, pp. 39 and 53. *Statistisches Jahrbuch für die Bundesrepublik Deutschland* is further quoted as *SJB BRD*.
2. *DDR Wirtschaft, eine Bestandsaufnahme*, Frankfurt am Main, 1974 (further quoted as *Bestandsaufnahme*, 1974); pp. 111 ff.
3. *Bericht der Bundesregierung und Materialien zur Lage der Nation* (further quoted as *Bericht*), 1971, pp. 310–11 and 368–9.
4. This is a label which to my knowledge first emerged among the Polish

Marxists, 'produkt przewlastniony'.
5. Karl Blank, *Beiträge zum innerdeutschen Gewerkschaftsdialog,* Bonn-Bad Godesberg, 1971, Vol. I, pp. 252–3.
6. *Bericht,* 1971, p. 130, and *DDR-Wirtschaft, eine Bestandsaufnahme,* 1971 (further quoted as *Bestandsaufnahme,* 1971); p. 192.
7. Apprentices are not included in these figures.
8. Unfortunately, the magnitude of the West German net material product could only be estimated in current prices. Recalculations by means of the average of wholesale and retail prices indices indicate, however, a faster growth than that of the GNP. This would make the West German position still more favourable in comparison to the GDR.
9. *SJB DDR,* 1975, p. 13, and *SJB BRD,* 1975, p. 37.
10. *SJB DDR,*1973, p. 19.
11. *Angestelltenversicherung,* 3/74, p. 93.
12. As will be shown later, this is a realistic assumption only with respect to the East German consumption pattern; on the West German consumption basis, the purchasing power of the Eastern Mark was still a good 10 per cent below the Western Deutschmark (for more details see pp. 39 ff).
13. In other Communist countries there is still another item which makes the difference between the national income produced and the national income used, namely, the losses. Yet the East German statistical yearbooks do not mention this item in their methodical notes. The West German sources however, mention this item as included in the aggregate.
14. Czechoslovak export and import data have since 1967 been published both in exchange and domestic crowns. The latter is about three times higher than the former. For more details, see J. Krejci, 'Measurement of Aggregate Efficiency in Czechoslovak Economy', *Soviet Studies,* 1974, p. 599.
15. On the basis of scattered data, the West German Institut für Wirtschaftsforschung (Berlin-Bonn) calculated the absolute magnitudes of the national income utilised from 1960 to 1973 (*Bestandsaufnahme,* 1974, p. 354), but with the warning that these data are not comparable with the series of national income produced. So this exercise is of little help for our purpose. According to these recalculations national income produced was in all years of the period in question higher than national income utilised in 1960–62 by a negligible magnitude; from 1963 to 1969 by about 5 per cent, for 1970 to 1973 by less than 3 per cent. The decrease of the difference since 1970 is consistent with the drop of the export surplus reported by the trade statistics (cf. Table 2.6 on p. 39).
16. Calculations of Herbert Wilkens in *Bestandsaufnahme,* 1971, pp. 275–7 and *Deutschland Archiv,* 1975, pp. 601–8. Recently the gross domestic product of the FRG was recalculated also according to the Eastern concept (*Bestandsaufnahme,* 1974, pp. 111 and ff.). Although results obtained by the latter calculation might be more accurate, omission of the greater part of the tertiary sector, the importance of which is growing with technological progress, makes this approach less useful for intersystemic comparison.
17. This may seem to contradict our previous finding, namely, that the GNP per person employed increased at an equal pace in both parts of Germany between 1960 and 1970. The reason for the difference is that in the GDR the proportion of the labour force including the self-employed in the total population slightly increased (according to the official statistics, excluding armed forces, party officials etc.) from 44.6 per cent in 1960 to 45.5 per cent in 1970), whereas in the FRG the corresponding ratio declined (from 47.3 per cent to 44.9 per cent of the whole population).
18. The earlier label was 'social consumption affecting the living standard'

(lebensstandardwirksame gesellschaftliche Konsumtion), col. 7 in Table 2.2.
19. Oddly enough, the East Germans have not even attempted so far to substitute this deficiency of the Marxist concept of national income by additional national accounts as, for example, the Czechs did, or by alternative calculations of comprehensive GNP, as has become the Hungarian practice.
20. *Bericht,* 1971, p. 398.
21. *Bestandsaufnahme,* 1971, p. 187.
   It is difficult, however, to compare the impact of income redistribution on individual socio-economic groups. According to a juxtaposition calculated by the West German Institute for Economic Research for the late sixties, the average wage and salary earner had to pay in taxes and social insurance premiums 18.3 per cent of his income from employment, and whilst still active got back in social insurance benefits 7.3 per cent of his income, so that his net payment to the redistribution account was 11 per cent of his income. In the GDR the respective percentages were 13.7 and 7.7, the net payment being 6.0 per cent only. In the FRG a self-employed person and a member of a co-operative had to pay 18 per cent and got back 9.7 per cent; the net payment being 19.8 per cent in the FRG and 8.3 per cent in the GDR (*Bericht,* 1971, p. 398). On the strength of these data, income was redistributed more extensively in the FRG than in the GDR and the brunt of it was borne more by the self-employed population than by the wage and salary earners.
22. This is in contradiction to other Communist states where the additions to stock absorb a much higher proportion of national income, and thus diminish the volume of functionally utilised production.
23. The trade balance in the FRG is taken from national accounts where services and also some income are included. Although the trade data of the GDR include only a part of services such as projection work, services for airports and ports, geological and technological research, buying and selling of licences and services connected with the delivery of merchandise to the border, the comparison with the FRG data can be considered adequate: the missing items are not expected to be as important as in the trade of the FRG where the invisible imports play a more substantial role.
24. It is well known that the cost of living indices especially exclude as a rule the more expensive goods and services, the prices of which are liable to faster increases than the other commodities.
25. For the development of individual price indices in juxtaposition with the weight of subsidies, see Appendix, Table A.8.
26. Nominal data from *Bestandsaufnahme,* 1971, p. 197.
27. *Bestandsaufnahme,* 1971, p. 211.
28. ibid., p. 335.
29. Data from *Bericht,* 1971, p. 364, *SJB BRD,* 1972, pp. 252 and 25, *SJB DDR,* 1971, pp. 158 and 3.
30. If it were possible to construct a scale of labouring power values for individual jobs or professions then we would be able to compare that average with monetary incomes in these jobs or professions and arrive at the approximate rates of exploitation. As this is not the case, the rate of exploitation can only be assessed in the aggregate way shown in Table 2.1.
31. At the beginning of the sixties there were 2.88 persons per household in the FRG and 2.84 persons in the GDR. In 1970 these ratios were 2.74 and 2.97 respectively. *SJB BRD,* 1972, p. 38; W. Bröll, *Die Wirtschaft der DDR,* p. 185.
32. Karl Blank, *Beiträge zum innerdeutschen Gewerkschaftsdialog,* Vol. 1, p. 257.
33. *Bericht,* 1971, pp. 378–9.
34. Estimates by the Seminar for Social Politics at the Frankfurt University, quoted in *Bericht,* 1974, p. 439.

35. *SJB BRD*, 1975, p. 418.
36. J. Siebke, *Die Vermögensbildung der privaten Haushaulte in der Bundes-Republik Deutschland* (Forschungsbericht für das Bundesministerium für Arbeit und Sozialordnung), Bonn, 1971.
37. Calculated from *SJB BRD*, 1972, p. 141.
38. *SJB BRD*, 1962, pp. 226–7 and 1972, pp. 204–5.
39. *SJB DDR*, 1962, p. 266 and 1971, p. 110.
40. Unfortunately, GDR statistics do not give breakdowns of fixed assets according to ownership. Only labour force and production are sub-divided with respect to this variable.
41. Calculated from *SJB DDR*, 1968, p. 18. The aforementioned data were calculated from the *SJB DDR*, 1971, pp. 182 and 110, from *SJB BRD*, 1972, pp. 141 and 204–5, and Statistical Pocket Book of the GDR, 1975, p. 63.
42. *Bericht*, 1971, pp. 324 and 325. Unfortunately, the productivity both of labour and capital are measured per gross production which includes a good deal of double counting; this flaw, however, invalidates the inter-sectoral rather than inter-country comparison.
43. *Bericht*, 1971, pp. 104 and 334. Calculations of the Institut für Agrarpolitik und Agrarstatistik der Technischen Universität, Berlin.
44. *Bericht*, 1974, p. 444.
45. W. Krelle, J. Schunk, J. Siebke, 'Überbetriebliche Ertragsbeteiligung der Arbeitnehmer', Tübingen 1968, Band II, S.326, quoted in *Bericht*, 1974, p. 438.
46. ibid.
47. *Demoskopie Jahrbuch*, p. 356.
48. *Bestandsaufnahme*, 1974, p. 408.
49. Deutsches Institut fur Wirtschaftsforschung (further quoted as DIW), *Wochenbericht*, 25, 1973, pp. 219 and 221.
50. In our calculation of surplus value (Table 2.1) it was not necessary to take into account this item because, there, only employees in material production were envisaged. In this sector, the percentage of non-reported labour force may be considered as insignificant for our calculation.
51. Results with respect to the FRG are of course not comparable with data of national income by distributive shares reproduced in Table 2.18. In this table national income is conceived at factor cost, i.e. including both material and non-material services but not indirect taxes net of subsidies. In Table 2.20 national income is conceived as net material product at market prices.

3 STRATIFICATION AND MOBILITY

3a. Complex schemes and evaluations

Since the study of society ceased to be a matter of speculative induction on the basis of partial empirical evidence, and became a matter of systematic factual analysis, the simplifying concept of social classes has been gradually substituted by the concept of social strata. It took, however, some time before this concept was freed from the one-dimensional heritage of medieval estates and Marxian philosophy, and social stratification became conceived as a multi-dimensional pattern. It has to be borne in mind that this development largely reflected the continuing changes in relevance of individual distinctions within the social structure: the estate society, prevalent on the European continent until the eighteenth century, gave way in the nineteenth century to a society where socio-economic differences related to industrial ownership became more important. In the second quarter of the twentieth century wealth and power started to dissociate and in a few countries the extra economic power re-emerged as a rigid backbone of societal structure.

In spite of the growing variety of graduation scales the tendency to conceive stratification as a unitary scheme framed in neutral terms of gradation (upper, middle, lower) still persists. It is preserved paradoxically more in the West than in the East. In the Communist countries, the official postulatory principle of non-existence of contradictory classes virtually closed the door for any universal stratification and pushed sociologists into the open; only a few of them, however, dared to take the opportunity to bury the concept of classes under the multi-dimensional approach to social stratification. Unfortunately this trend has bypassed East Germany up to now so that here the work has to be done by outsiders.

In West Germany, social stratification and social mobility have been subject to intensive exploration for many decades. There is a long list of detailed studies devoted to particular aspects of this topic; synthetic literature is, however, less prolific. Moreover, the general conclusions, particularly those of Helmut Schelsky and Ralf Dahrendorf, are quite contradictory. Schelsky found that West Germany society is becoming more open to vertical mobility and consequently less stratified, that a greater proportion of her population is clustered around the middle and that this tendency is paralleled by a general upward move of living and cultural standards.[1] On the other hand Dahrendorf, although not denying the increase in living standard, found West Germany society not only highly differentiated but also horizontally divided by barely surmountable barriers.[2]

Both Schelsky and Dahrendorf seem to agree on the incongruence of social status components in principle, although Schelsky's position implies that the incongruence is more general than that of Dahrendorf. The latter's barriers in vertical mobility point to some quite far-reaching congruence at least at certain critical levels of stratification.

Before passing our own judgement on this controversial issue it seems expedient to confront these positions in more detail and to refer to less committed views in the matter.

Schelsky's views can be summarised as follows:

In the German society of the last two generations, there were extensive social upward and downward movements. There was firstly a collective upward ascent of industrial workers and secondly, a more individual, however also significant, ascent of technical and administrative personnel into the new middle class. The upward mobility was somewhat counter-balanced by the downward movements beginning during World War One, culminating after 1945. This enhanced upward and downward mobility resulted in the attenuation of class contradictions and in the development of a comparatively unitary stratum which is as much proletarian as bourgeois. Also the increasing expansion of social policy and progressive taxation contributed to this development.

The levelling of real economic and political status has been followed by far-reaching simplification of social and cultural forms of behaviour; the groups concerned were those groups characterised as lower middle. The universal consumption of mass-produced industrial goods and publications provides almost everybody with the opportunity to feel that he is not completely at the bottom but that he can participate in the luxuries of existence (*Luxus des Daseins*). Not only living style but also social needs are being levelled.

Social mobility within German society can no longer be understood as a 're-stratification' (*Umschichtung*) but as a 'de-stratification' (*Entschichtung*) process. What happens in effect is that social mobility becomes more and more detached from the established stratification patterns and acquires other, more dynamic criteria. It is understandable that in levelled middle-class society analysis of social stratification can still be carried on according to earlier criteria because their hallmark has not completely disappeared. It is, however, questionable whether groups with specific needs and interests still exist in such a way. Although it can be maintained that German society is still basically divided into three groups (employees, pensioners and self-employed, the quantitative relationship being 3:1:1) only the first of these groups can be considered as decisive, whereas the other two are of only marginal importance.

So, according to Schelsky, with respect to West Germany society, the concept of stratification remains relevant only in so far as one form of social behaviour has not, until now, been subject to the levelling process: namely the social prestige and social self-consciousness of individuals. The social self-consciousness of a petty bourgeois and middle-class man abhors nothing more than social status without rank and assertion; therefore in this levelled society the prestige grades of the old class society continue to be adhered to.[3]

Unfortunately Schelsky does not give any quantitative evidence for supporting his views. He apparently assumes that processes described by him are well known and can be taken for granted. Yet, other sociologists, looking more closely at empirical data, were more reserved in their evaluation of the 'middle-class society'.

So, for instance, Morris Janowitz, while reporting on one sample survey of 1955, found among the respondents more subjective acquiescence in the existing differentiation than in the levelling itself. He said:

> The weight of the evidence rests on the side of the conclusion that the consequences of social stratification and social mobility are now operating to decrease traditional class consciousness and to increase social consensus concerning internal matters.

The reason for this is the greater importance of education for upward mobility and this in its turn is being accepted as more justified than any other prerequisite: 'As Germany becomes more and more an achievement-orientated society, access to education emerges as a crucial factor in social mobility and thereby on social consensus.' Janowitz also realised that income differentiation upset remaining estate prejudices: 'The patterns of income distribution reveal considerable overlap between the top of the working class and the bottom of the middle class.' On the other hand there is virtually a continuum of differences throughout all individual strata. 'Sharp social differentiation operates as between the upper-middle and the lower-lower strata.'[4]

Similarly, Karl M. Bolte[5] found a lot of overlapping between the types of employment (workers, salaried employees, officials and self-employed) and social status; this was derived from research in 1960 on self-identification within seven status strata characterised by typical vocations.[6] From top to bottom individual strata had the following percentages: upper, 1 per cent; upper-middle, 5 per cent; middle-middle, 15 per cent; lower-middle, 30 per cent; upper-lower, 28 per cent; lower-lower, 17 per cent; and socially despised, 4 per cent.

In the lowest two strata there were only workers. In the third stratum from the bottom (upper-lower stratum) there were predominantly workers. In the medium lower-middle stratum which comprised 30 per cent of the whole of the population there were mainly salaried employees; self-employed and workers were almost equally represented. The three upper strata were predominantly composed of salaried employees. In Bolte's graphical presentation they also appear to be the main group within the 1 per cent top élite. Apparently the top élite was composed mainly of managerial staff and not as much of officials and self-employed entrepreneurs.

As the strata were characterised by vocations and this mainly in view of their relative social prestige, their overlapping with the type of employment seems to be a matter of definition rather than of combination of two independent variables such as the type of employment and income (see below, section 3d).[7]

Concerning the acuteness and awareness of stratification, Schelsky arrived at the conclusion that stratification in West Germany is a matter of subjective rather than objective evaluation, whereas Janowitz saw just the opposite: the existing stratification became influenced more by reputable criteria (education) and therefore acquired wider consensus and became less resented.

Unlike Schelsky and Janowitz, Dahrendorf was less concerned with consciousness than with upward mobility prospects. From this point of view he saw society divided into two or three zones of relative seclusion. Although the barrier between them is not as a matter of principle insurmountable it is rarely crossed. In his own words the position is as follows:

German society is stratified in such a way as to create three barriers. Two of these are medium-sized and may, therefore, be overcome with some effort by those who reach them; similar barriers may be found in any modern society. In the German case, these are, first, the borderline between the elites and the adjoining reaches of service class[8] and middle class; and, second, the boundary between the lower class and the adjoining lower ranks of the working class and the false middle class.

But there is a third barrier, and this is very much harder to overcome. It divides an Above from a Below — namely, approximately the upper third of the edifice of stratification from the lower two-thirds — and it runs (to remain within the spatial metaphor) from the lower end of the service class along the line between the working class and the middle class. On either side of this line, social mobility is not uncommon. But so far as movement across the border, and therefore belonging to one of the two sides is concerned, we have to conclude that class positions are still largely ascribed to German society.

Whether an individual stands on one side of the barrier or the other, is a position falling to him without his doing, and one he can escape only in the exceptional case. In this sense, German society continues to be a divided society; divided into an Above that knows little of the Below, and a Below that knows equally little of the Above. Only psychoanalytic theories could explain why a society split in this fashion systematically compensates for its internal divisions by ideologies of the community of the German people and of national unity.[9]

Dahrendorf's main argument for the almost insurmountable third barrier cutting across the whole nation was the extremely low percentage of lower-class descendants among the student population.[10] This seems to be substantiated by Janowitz's findings that education, at least among the male population, 'serves most critically as a pre-condition of mobility.'[11] Also Janowitz's other suggestion, namely, that 'only a university education is insurance against downward social mobility',[12] has some bearing on Dahrendorf's proof.

As ten years have already elapsed since Dahrendorf's summary of findings on West German social structure and stratification, some more recent evidence has to be collected if the contemporary position is to be assessed, both with respect to reality and to its images.

A particular difficulty arises if the position in the GDR has also to be ascertained. As was stated earlier, information from that part of Germany is scarce. Nevertheless it might be worth while making an approximate comparison using whatever information is available in comprehensive terms. Such a comparison is shown in Table 3.1. The West German picture is taken from Dahrendorf, the East German from

Kurt Lungwitz who derived it from East German official statistics; to follow Dahrendorf's retrospective view, Theodor Geiger's social structure of Weimar Germany is included as well.[13]

In all three schemes the stratification is conceptualised from different angles which consequently do not permit assessment of the comparable magnitudes. Whereas Geiger's stratification is, in principle, a socio-economic one, and reflects the notion of classes, Dahrendorf's strata take more into account the multiplicity of social status components. Moreover, Dahrendorf envisages the hierarchy of strata down to the

Table 3.1 Social Stratification in the Three German Societies (in per cent of total population)

	1.	2.	3.
	Weimar Republic	FRG 1959/1960	GDR 1960
1. Capitalists	0.92	—	0.6
2. "Elites"	—	less than 1.0	—
3. "Intelligentsia"[1]	—	—	4.6
4. "Service Class' (bureaucracy)	—	12.0	—
5. Middle Class "Old"[2]	17.77)	20.0	5.0[6]
"New"[3]	17.95)		
6. Working-class élite	—	5.0	—
7. Co-operative producers (farmers and craftsmen)	—	—	13.6
8. "Proletaroid strata"[4]	12.65	—	—
9. "False middle class"[5]	—	12.0	—
10. Undifferentiated working class	50.71	—	76.2
11. Working class proper	—	45.0	—
12. Lowest strata	—	5.0	—
Total	100.0	100.0	100.0

1. mainly employed; 2. mainly self-employed; 3. mainly salaried employees; 4. self-employed poor (in handicraft, commerce, services and agriculture); 5. rank and file employees in tertiary sector; 6. including 0.4 per cent self-employed farmers.

Sources: Column 1: Theodor Geiger, *Die Soziale Schichtung des Deutschen Volkes,* Stuttgart, 1967 (reprint), p. 73. Column 2: Ralf Dahrendorf, op. cit., p. 118. Column 3: Kurt Lungwitz, *Über die Klassenstruktur in der Deutschen Demokratischen Republik,* Berlin (Ost), 1962, p. 162.

For a more detailed estimate of the class structure in the GDR see Appendix, Table A.13.

bottom and thinks in terms of élites irrespective of their socio-economic or legal status. From Dahrendorf's graphic presentation, which does

a more structured view can be obtained.
p (hardly 1 per cent of the population)
l,   _ntly recruited from, the middle class (20
pe   _ class (12 per cent). The latter can also perhaps be
lab   _reaucracy'. Dahrendorf accepts Geiger's division of the
middle class into the old middle class (mainly self-employed and the
new (white-collar employees). Between the middle class and working
class and partly parallel with both of them is the 'workers' élite' (5 per
cent). Parallel with the working class, and with possible access to the
middle and service classes, is the false middle class (12 per cent)
including mainly workers in the tertiary sector such as shop assistants,
waiters, postmen, conductors, petrol station attendants etc. The
working class proper, containing almost half of all the population is in
itself highly differentiated; though in view of a good deal of common
mentality and consciousness, Dahrendorf found it expedient to
consider it as one, albeit differentiated, stratum.[14] Right at the bottom
are the socially despised without any general characteristics and
common mentality, such as people evading work, life-long criminals,
semi-literates etc. Dahrendorf's estimate puts these people at 5 per cent
of the whole population.[15]

So, as Dahrendorf himself points out, his stratification scheme
includes (a) groups with certain common mentality or consciousness,
(b) groups without such cohesiveness. In the former, self-conscious
groups, he puts the service class (bureaucrats), workers' élite, and the
core of the middle class and working class. On the other hand, neither
the top élite nor the bottom and the fringe (false middle class) can in
his view be considered as self-conscious groupings (classes 'for
themselves' in Marx's terminology).

In envisaging as strata groupings with different degrees of collective
consciousness (individual sense of belonging), Dahrendorf provides an
additional argument for a multi-dimensional approach to social
stratification, an approach in which the consciousness itself can be
considered as one of the variables.

The East German data in Table 3.1 reflect the ideological motivation:
blue- and white-collar workers are lumped together: only the
intelligentsia slips out of the group; according to a more detailed
breakdown (see Appendix, Table A.13), 92 per cent of the intelligentsia
are salaried employees whereas the rest are professionals, members of
farmers' co-operatives and of solicitors' boards.

On the whole, the East German categories are not conceived as
strata, but as classes. They reflect the 'objective' relationship to the

means of production; a specific class consciou.
stressed. Different types of ownership are supp
of early socialism. There are still remnants of th
there are two kinds of socialist ownership, the n.
belonging either to the nation as a whole (*Volkse.   *e*) or to the
co-operative producers (*Produktionsgenossenschaj*   ere are also
some mixed enterprises (private with state participation).

The concept of a political élite based on differentiation of power
instead of ownership, a concept which takes into account not only top
management of the means of production but also the command of the
'means of education' and 'means of compulsion', still seems to be taboo
amongst East German sociologists. The breakthrough of Polish
sociologists, who by the recognition of 'inegalitarian classlessness'
opened a new field for Marxist theory,[16] has not yet been exploited in
the GDR.

So with respect to both parts of Germany new data have to be
collected and possibly some preliminary spadework undertaken. Bearing
in mind the multi-dimensional character of social stratification, the
inquiry has to be directed towards the following main issues: (a) the
grades of stratification with respect to individual components (elements)
of social status; (b) the possible degree of congruence or divergence
between these separate lines of stratification; (c) the frequency of
vertical mobility within the gradation pattern of individual components
of social status (lines of stratification); although in one's own lifetime
such a change (intragenerational change) may be rare, it may more
easily happen in view of subsequent generations (intergenerational
change). The possibility of such moves indicates the degree of openness
or closeness of the stratification structure.

3b. Stratification by type of work and employment

To facilitate a quantitative picture of stratification by type of work
and employment (socio-economic groups) we have first to complete
the data missing in the over-all statistics for East Germany: we have to
attempt a breakdown of wage and salary earners into white- and
blue-collar workers. The reason for lumping these categories together in
official statistics is partly ideological and partly pragmatic. In the GDR,
it is supposed that all working people in socialist enterprises are
co-owners of all the socialist assets and that all work in them has an
equal social value. Therefore legal provisions such as those on working
time, holidays, social insurance, payment intervals, etc., make no
difference between blue- and white-collar workers.

Unlike in the GDR, the traditional differentiation between workers and employees in the FRG is not only a matter of prestige but of some legal and factual discrimination concerning working hours, length of holidays, periods of payments, periods of notice and social insurance. Moreover, West German law makes yet another difference, namely between the clerical staff in the business sector (*Angestellte*) and in the government service (*Beamte*). Both these categories still preserve the aforementioned advantages or privileges *vis-à-vis* manual workers. Moreover the 'Beamte' enjoy added privileges such as tenure, higher pensions etc.

No doubt in this particular case the comparison is to the advantage of the GDR. The comment of an official West German source referring to the FRG reads as follows:

> Employees are distinguished into workers (*Arbeiter*) and clerical staff (*Angestellte*). Ascription of individuals to these categories is performed according to the actual type of work. The meaning of this difference has been overcome by technical development and is being rightly criticised as out of date. The former differences such as those concerning old age and health insurance have largely been abolished through the recent legislature. The Trade Unions in the FRG consider this differentiation as a harmful split in their struggle for social improvements of working conditions.[17]

The West German legislature is gradually abolishing the remaining differences. So, for instance, since 1 January 1970 not only sick clerical staff but also sick workers in the FRG receive their full wage (salary) during the first six weeks of their sickness.[18] Only then do social insurance benefits start. On the other hand medical care is still somewhat different. This however is a matter of vocational differences and particular contracts rather than social discrimination.

A significant difference which still persists in the FRG is the different period over which earnings are paid; workers' wages are as a rule paid weekly whilst white-collar workers are paid monthly; the period of time of notice (firing) is scaled accordingly. This latter discrimination however is mitigated by the circumstance that under the Protection Against Notice Act, notice is ineffective if it is socially unjustified; conditions of such a justification are partly regulated by law and partly decided by workers' committees generally introduced as from January 1972.[19]

In view of the legal provisions, the obliteration of separate statistical accounting of blue- and white-collar workers in the GDR seems to be substantiated. Yet it is worth while noting that this distinction is respected in other Communist countries such as Poland and Czechoslovakia, where similar legal equalisation of workers and employees took place. It is supposed that such distinction is relevant for technico-economic and socio-cultural reasons. The relevant amount of white-collar work is supposed to indicate the degree of technical progress. Yet there are some serious doubts whether this is the main reason. The so-called Parkinson's Law in the West and the concept of 'bureaucratic hydrocephal' in the East reveal that administration may be self-generating irrespective of its usefulness to those whom it is supposed to serve.

It has also to be borne in mind that administrative and other white-collar work is more often than not cleaner, in more pleasant surroundings and provides greater opportunities for cultural consumption than blue-collar work. Consequently, it may be assumed that white-collar workers are less likely to become alienated from their work in Marx's sense. Only some more or less manual work in the distributive trades, which is usually also classified as white-collar work, does not fit this characteristic.

Also, the East German authorities themselves have not completely abolished reporting on manual and non-manual workers separately. They do so with respect to political representation, i.e. in local and national assemblies, and in the Communist Party membership. Also data on students' social origin distinguish between the family background of workers and non-manual employees. It is hardly possible to draw proper conclusions from this sporadic data, unless one gets at least an approximate image of the proportion of white- and blue-collar workers in the labour force as a whole. Scattered data concerning individual sectors of production may provide a key for such an attempt.

First of all, East German industrial statistics concerning mining and manufacturing single out production workers from the total industrial labour force. The remainder are mainly clerical staff, but also some auxiliary blue-collar workers as well. In the building industry, blue- and white-collar workers are reported separately as technical, economic, administrative and accounting personnel, without including auxiliary workers. So it is possible to find out that in 1970, in nationalised construction enterprises (*Volkseigene Betriebe*) there were 1.8 production workers per 1.0 white-collar employee.[20] The ratio between production workers and other employees in mining and manufacturing was almost identical with the above ratio and this not only in the GDR but also in the FRG.

It may be worth while to digress a little and review the long-term development. Whereas in 1882 there were 21 workers per one clerical worker in German industry, in 1907 this ratio was 9:1 and in 1925 only 4:1, but the faster relative growth of clerical staff thereafter stopped. In 1939, the ratio of blue- to white-collar workers was 3:1. After World War Two, when the second phase of the industrial revolution began, the ratio again started to change quickly. In 1945 there were 3.6 workers per one clerical worker in West German industry and in 1965 only 1.8.[21] In 1970 the ratio in the GDR was 1.9:1.[22]

Data from other economic sectors allow only approximate assessments of the proportion of manual and non-manual labour force. Sources and results of this investigation are summarised in Table 3.2.

Comparison with the West and with pre-war Germany is drawn in Table 3.3. These data reveal a lower proportion of manual workers in the GDR than in the FRG. This is all the more striking, as before the war there was a higher proportion of manual workers in what is now GDR territory. Apparently, many of them worked in agriculture from which they disappeared under the impact of a two-fold change: rationalisation and socialisation.

Before the war the number of salaried employees was slightly higher in the West. In 1970, however, they comprised about 39 per cent of the labour force in the East and 37 per cent in the West. The proportions of blue-collar workers were 45 and 47 respectively. The proportion of the others in the labour force was virtually identical, 16 per cent. The only difference was that in the GDR the others were mainly members of production co-operatives, whereas in the West they were either self-employed or helping family members.

In interpreting these figures we have to take into account that in the GDR not all people employed are accounted for. As in other Communist countries, the so-called non-planned sector, containing the army, police and party apparatus is left out. Workers in uranium mines are also thought to have been excluded in the reported totals.

Nevertheless, it is possible to get a rough idea of the magnitude of this predominantly masculine sector by comparing the male population of working age with the reported number of employed and student population. In 1970 there were 4,860,000 men of working age (i.e. between 15 and 64).[23] Of the working age male population there were 4,020,000 reported as actually working and 248,000 apprentices. As the number of male students was not reported for all types of schools, partial evidence allows only for an estimate, about 450,000. It has also

Table 3.2 Calculation and/or Estimate of Manual and Non-manual Labour Force in the GDR in 1970

	in thousand		
	Total Labour Force[1]	Manual Workers	Non-manual employees
Industry	2,838	1,962[2]	876R
Handicraft	404	404E	–
Construction	572	474R	98[3]
Agriculture and forestry	997	957R	40[4]
Transport and communication	564	311[5]	253R
Commerce	858	103[6]	755R
Other material branches	181	181E	–
Non-material services	1,355	135[7]	1,220R
Total	7,769	4,527	3,242
of which:			
Members of production co-operatives	1,008	980R	28[8]
Private farmers and craftsmen	150	150R	–
Private traders and professionals	79[9]	–	79E
Other self-employed	38	–	38E
Workers and employees	6,494[10]	3,397R	3,097R

Notes: R = residual item. E = estimate; figures in further notes indicate pages of *SJB DDR*, 1971.
1. Breakdown by industry, p. 57; by type of employment, p. 52.
2. Production workers (1,862,000; p. 124) plus estimated number of auxiliary workers.
3. Clerical staff in bigger enterprises, p. 144.
4. Persons with completed higher or secondary education, p. 195.
5. Production workers in the sector excluding post; this is supposed to be fully served by non-manual employees, p. 259.
6. According to the percentage of transport personnel in the wholesale trade with consumer goods, p. 268.
7. Estimated 10 per cent according to the authors' experience from Civil Service.
8. Persons with completed higher or secondary education in farmers' co-operatives.
9. Including complementary and commission traders.
10. Excluding the 448 thousand apprentices who are not included in the breakdown by industries.

to be borne in mind that many pensioners, i.e. men over 64, continue working (either part- or full-time) and consequently, their number is included in the working population. This means that the number of unaccounted men of working age is larger than the 140,000 which is the

Table 3.3 Structure by Socio-Economic Groups (in per cent of total
population)

Socio-economic group	FRG			GDR	
	1939	1950	1971	1939	1970
Workers	48.3	50.7	46.7	56.4	44.6
White-collar employees (including government officials)	18.3	20.1	36.8	17.7	39.0
Co-operative producers	—	—	—	—	13.0
Self-employed	14.9	(14.0)	10.2	12.6)	3.4
Helping family members	18.5	(15.2)	6.3	13.3)	

Sources: 1939, Dieter Sterbeck, *Soziale Struktur in Mitteldeutschland,* p. 150.
1950, FRG, D. Claessens et al., *Sozialkunde,* p. 185. 1971, FRG, *SJB BRD,* 1972,
p. 123. 1970, GDR, calculated from data in *SJB DDR,* 1972, pp. 52, 57, 124,
144, 259 and 268 (for more details see Table 3.2).

residual item of the above calculation.

West German sources evaluate the strength of the GDR army at
171,000 and that of the police at 29,000; together 200,000 in 1971.[24]
The same sources evaluate the total labour force (male and female) in 1971
at 8,600,000, i.e. 350,000 more than official data, including apprentices.

The additionally estimated labour force would increase the number
of wage and salary earners in the GDR, without, however, any hint of
how to divide it into manual workers, privates etc. (lower status) and
non-manual officials, officers etc. (higher status).

3c. Stratification by level of education

Although not always accompanied by adequate wealth or power, higher
educational level enjoys particular respect in Germany. The prestige
scale quoted by Dahrendorf is headed by a university professor, second
is a physician, and only third is an economic boss (manager). The fact
that this scale of prestige was ascertained in 1951 (it is taken over from
K. M. Bolte, *Sozialer Aufstieg und Abstieg,* Stuttgart, 1955, pp. 38–50)
is no reason for its lesser relevance. A public opinion poll undertaken in
January 1968 by the Institute for Demoscopy revealed a similar
preference for university professors in the field of politics. A sample of
1,700 were asked whom they would prefer as a candidate for national
elections: a university professor, or alternatively a doctor, a self-
employed business man, a business employee or a worker. In all cases,
university professors won. Closest contest was with the business man;

they obtained 34 and 21 per cent of the poll respectively.[25]

It was partly the high esteem of government service which required a higher education as a prerequisite, partly a predilection for titles, whether aristocratic or academic, but partly also a genuine respect for books and those dealing with them which contributed to the fact that a successful academic and professional career was as a rule valued more highly than business achievement. This mood might have abated during the continuous post-war economic boom which brought economic successes to the forefront of public attention. As Almond and Verba found in 1959, in the absence of other spectacular successes, the economic achievement of the FRG became the most popular feature in West Germany.[26] In spite of that, the traditional valuation still seems to dominate the scale of prestige.

Although in the GDR there is no investigation parallel to this scale of prestige, inquiries in youth occupational preferences may provide some orientation in this respect. A sample of a hundred 20 year-old boys and girls in the district of Gera in 1964 showed preference for technical professions among the boys and for medical and educational professions among the girls. Although the typically prestigious professions such as professor, doctor, scientist, and writer scored only 11 per cent of top preferences, together with other highly qualified jobs such as official, laboratory worker, agronomist or music director, the category of occupations requiring higher education was heavily represented in the poll. (For more details see Appendix, Table A.14.)[27]

It is of course difficult to weigh the relevance of different polls such as that on the pride of economic achievement with those of occupational prestige. As the new generation gradually takes over, the love for titles becomes less apparent. But this does not mean that the valuation shifts towards a greater appraisal of economic achievement. The result is rather a new set of values which gradually emerge. Nevertheless in the GDR the predilection for titles continues to flourish. They may be brand new titles such as Hero of Socialist Work, Master of Industry, Master of Agriculture, but titles they are, whether performance or qualification orientated.

In view of this value orientation in both parts of Germany, data on stratification according to the level of education and vocational training are most needed.

Contrary to previous investigations, data on educational level are more complete in the GDR than in the FRG. In the GDR, the main types of education and training level are ascertained by the population censuses; data on people with completed higher education are continuously reported by the annual labour statistics. In the FRG, there are only a few data: in the last decade there was the micro-census of 1964, a sample survey of the Institute of Demoscopy in January 1969. and data on school education (not other vocational training) in the 1970 census.

Table 3.4 Labour Force with Higher Education by Economic Sectors in 1964 (in per cent of labour force in respective sectors)

	with completed college graduation		with completed technical school graduation	
	FRG	GDR	FRG	GDR
Agriculture and forestry	0.2	0.5	5.4	2.1
Mining, manufacturing and public utilities	1.2	0.8	3.4	3.2
Construction	0.6	0.5	2.9	3.0
Trade	1.5	0.5	2.7	1.2
Transport and communication	0.6	0.6	4.8	2.6
Other services	11.6	9.0	5.1	10.9
All branches	3.4	2.3	4.0	4.3

Source: *Bericht,* 1971, pp. 300–301.

Figures in Table 3.4 show a considerably higher percentage of labour force with completed college education in the FRG and a slightly higher percentage with completed technical education in the GDR. This, as will be shown later on, reflects the general orientation of education in the two parts of Germany: more technical vocational training in the East, more academic education in the West.

There was also a significant difference in individual economic sectors. Primary production was better staffed with technically qualified people in the FRG, but the share of the college educated was higher in the GDR. Mining, manufacturing and trade were better supplied with both types of qualified labour in the West than in the East. In the construction industry the position was virtually equal in both parts of Germany. Transport and communication in the FRG were also better supplied with technical school graduates than in the GDR (almost twice as many per equal number of employed). On the other hand, other services in the GDR had twice as many staff per 100 with completed technical education as the FRG, whereas in view of college education the FRG had only a slight lead.

On the whole the percentage of labour force with a technical education in the GDR was almost twice as high as that with a college education; in the FRG this difference was negligible.

From 1964 onwards only the East German development can be followed. In 1973, 5.2 per cent of the working population had completed a college education and 8.4 per cent were with a completed technical education.[28] Thus the gap between the two types of education somewhat narrowed. Between 1964 and 1973 the numbers of the labour force with an academic education increased by 126 per cent and with a technical education by 95 per cent. This is a remarkable expansion duly stressed and advertised by East German authorities.

Meanwhile, the FRG had not remained stationary. As the data comparable with the GDR are not available, some idea of the development can be derived from the statistics of yearly graduations. From 1964 to 1972 the number of college graduates per year increased by 53.0 per cent in the FRG and by 33.4 per cent in the GDR. With respect to the total population which in the period in question increased by 6.4 per cent in the FRG and only by 0.4 per cent in the GDR, the comparative increases were: 44 per cent in the FRG and 33 per cent in the GDR, respectively.[29]

The division of population by all the main types of education can be compared on the basis of only partly commensurate data: there is a sample survey in the FRG and census data in the GDR. The juxtaposition is reproduced in Table 3.5.

Table 3.5 Social Structure by Level of Education (per cent)

	FRG January 1969	GDR 1 January 1971
With college graduation	3.8	4.0
With technical school graduation)		6.9
With foreman qualification)	15.2	4.9
With other completed vocational training	56.0	50.0
Without completed vocational training	25.0	34.2
Total working population	100.0	100.0

Source: FRG, *Demoskopie Jahrbuch,* p. 374; recalculated to 100 per cent basis
   and checked against data on school education in 1970 (*SJB BRD,* 1974, p. 82);
   GDR calculated from absolute figures in Statistical Pocket Book of the GDR
   1973, p. 131 (also *SJB DDR,* 1973, p. 433).

In view of the less reliable nature of West German data, the FRG lead in medium educational levels should not be exaggerated. Nevertheless, the difference is big enough to show that the GDR did not catch up or even overtake the FRG with respect to the educational qualifications of her working population. Unlike the comparison in 1964, the 1969—71 data indicate a higher technical qualification in the FRG than in the GDR. This hardly seems to be consistent with the trends in educational patterns in both parts of Germany.

In the GDR the whole educational system is based on the polytechnic type of education devised for vocational training. In 1970, only about one-eighth of the pupils in secondary schools attended the so-called Extended Polytechnics which, while adding two more years to the general ten-year (basic and polytechnic) education, provide greater scope for general education. On the other hand, in the FRG about two-thirds of the secondary school population attended the 'Gymnasium' (which emphasises the humanities) whereas only one-third were in the schools with prevalent technical orientation.

In the GDR in 1972, 41.5 per cent of students in higher education establishments studied technical branches, whereas in the FRG (in 1971) only 18.1 per cent did the same. In the GDR, technical training is, in addition to political qualification, the most rewarding condition for advancement on the scale of income and, in a way, also on the scale of power. In the FRG, the qualification which provides the widest opportunities is the study of law. The jurists are abundantly represented in all top positions whether in government or business service. According to the data reviewed by Dahrendorf, more than half of all higher civil servants were lawyers, but also, more than half of all German lawyers were civil servants; of the members of parliament at least 20 per cent were lawyers.[30] Among the business élite the percentage of lawyers was still larger; it was discovered that law graduates were preferred for promotion to top management by comparison with those from other disciplines.[31] Graduates of the economic faculties, whether of political economy (*Volkswirtschaftslehre*) or of the firm economy (*Betriebswirtschaftslehre*) type were less successful in the drive for power positions.

Recently, new academic disciplines, such as sociology and political science (*Politologie*) began to attract the attention of that part of the younger generation which is interested in social change rather than simply in promotion within the existing power structure. In the FRG, faculties of sociology and political science largely became centres of intellectual opposition to the system, and thus, in a sense, institutional bases of counter-élite.

In contrast to the West, the East has not only a uniform ideology but also a more prolonged uniform basic education. Both these circumstances contribute to the greater homogeneity of the society in the East. In the West, basic, comprehensive education (*Grundschule*) lasts, as a rule, for four years whereas in the East (*allgemeinbildende polytechnische Oberschule*) it lasts 8 or 10 years. After completing their basic education, young people in West Germany have three possibilities: either 8 years Gymnasium (humanistic-type education), or 5 years Realschule (technical type education) or 4 years Hauptschule (equivalent of the secondary modern school in the UK). In the GDR the young can, after 8 years of basic comprehensive school, become either apprentices (as a rule 3 years' training in work combined with part-time school attendance) or can attend the comprehensive school for two further years. Only then can specialisation begin and explicit conditions for further stratification set in.[32]

3d. Stratification by level of income

This type of stratification has already been tackled in section 2e in connection with income distribution. At this point more has to be said on the impact of the level of income on the scheme of stratification. It seems that in Germany, as in other Central European countries, occupational prestige is more relevant for self-identification than different amounts of income within individual occupations. The relative position of individual occupations on the general income scale seems to be of greater importance. However considerable the range of income distribution within the occupational groups may be, it would be easier to overcome this by years of service, additional vocational training or higher performance, than to try to increase one's income by shifting from one occupation to another. Income differentials within one and the same occupation may also be better substantiated, i.e. they may more adequately reflect the objectively assessable level of performance or time of practice than the inter-occupational relativities.

Bearing this in mind, we shall try to find out whether and how far the main socio-economic groups have changed their respective positions within the scale of income. Here adequate data are available only from the FRG, especially concerning wage- and salary-earners, male and female. Comparison of workers' and white-collar employees' incomes can be followed from 1957 on the basis of gross weekly earnings of workers in industry and gross monthly salaries of employees in industry, commerce, banking and insurance.

The ratio between the earnings of these two groups, separately for each sex (Table 3.6), indicates two significant features: firstly, a comparatively small difference between white-collar and blue-collar earnings, secondly, only a small fluctuation of this ratio over a period of time. Although there was a clear-cut reversal of the equalising trend between 1962 and 1967, in 1972 the difference between the average salary and the average wage was smaller than in 1957.

Table 3.6 Workers' and Employees' Earnings Differentials in the Federal Republic of Germany

Salary/Wage ratios:	1957	1962	1967	1972
Men	1.28	1.23	1.26	1.23
Women	1.29	1.17	1.20	1.19

Ratios indicate the range between the average gross salary of white-collar employees in industry, commerce, banking and insurance and the average gross earning of industrial workers. Monthly salaries and weekly wages are recalculated to the year basis.
Source: *SJB BRD,* 1962, 1973 and 1974, pp. 470 and 477.

The ratio between earnings from self-employment on the one hand and income from employment on the other has been shown already in Table 2.9. According to these figures, the aforementioned ratio throughout the sixties was virtually stable (approximately 2.4:1.0), but towards the end of the decade, the disparity increased and attained a range of 3.2:1.0 in 1972. As indicated earlier, the main reason for this opening of the 'income scissors' was partly the increase in prices, partly the impact of direct taxation.

Now we have to consider two more questions; firstly, the possible differentiation of income within the individual socio-economic groups; secondly, the possible differentiation of two main branches of self-employed sectors; the urban, industrial-commercial on one side and the rural, agricultural on the other.

Investigation of consumption in a West German sample of households in 1969 also revealed the proportion of households in different income brackets. The result is reproduced in Table 3.7. These figures indicate, among others, the degree of incongruence between stratification by level of income and by type of employment (by socio-economic groups). Income in all socio-economic groups was widely diffused around the average, thus corroborating Janowitz's findings from 1955, namely a considerable overlap between what is roughly described as the 'working class' and the 'middle class'.

Although all socio-economic groups participated in this overlapping, there were some significant differences in the scale of the dispersion. The group of government officials (*Beamte*) was the most homogeneous. Almost 40 per cent of officials' households had monthly incomes of DM 2000—3000 and more than a third incomes of DM 1200—2000.[33]

On the other hand the least homogeneous group was that of those not employed who were mainly pensioners or those living from capital.[34] On the whole this group was represented mainly in lower income brackets; about 25 per cent had incomes between DM 600—900 per month, which also corresponds to the average in that group.

Salaried employees' households, although with a somewhat lower average income than officials' households, were more differentiated. Workers' households were represented in all but the bottom and top brackets. Almost one-third of them were between DM 1500 and 2000 and 27 per cent between DM 2000 and 3000, and 6 per cent had even over DM 3000. In absolute terms there were as many workers' households with income between DM 2000 and 3000 as officials and salaried employees together.

The incomes of the self-employed, both in primary and other sectors, were more differentiated; however, only the self-employed, other than farmers, were represented in the highest income bracket, with almost 8 per cent of their households. On the other hand farmers were represented in the lower brackets more than blue-collar workers. Whereas there were only 4.9 per cent of the workers' families with less than DM 900 per month, of the farmers' households there were 7.1 per cent below this mark. Of the other self-employed 4.8 per cent, i.e. the same percentage as of workers' households, had a monthly income below DM 900.

Farmers did comparatively well in this juxtaposition. More than one-third of their households had an income between DM 2000—3000 and almost 17 per cent had still higher income. Even if we take into account that farmers' households have on average more members than other households, it may be assumed that according to this data almost a half of farmers' households enjoyed a good middle-class living standard. Another third of farmers' households had an income between DM 1200—2000 which could still be considered as a lower middle-class standard.

A more recent inquiry by the German Institute for Economic Research corroborates the findings arrived at by the 1969 sample

Table 3.7 Households by Socio-economic Groups and Level of Disposable Income in the FRG in 1969*

Socio-economic groups	Average disposable income per household per month	Households in 1000	per cent of each group in 'net' income brackets (DM per month and household)											
			-300	300-400	400-600	600-900	900-1200	1200-1500	1500-2000	2000-3000	3000-10000	over 10000
Farmers	2,029	765	0.0	0.8	2.6	3.7	8.6	11.9	21.1	34.6	16.7	0.0
Other self-employed	3,888	1,568	0.0	0.6	0.8	3.4	4.5	7.0	13.2	25.1	37.7	7.7
Officials	1,954	1,229	0.0	0.2	0.2	0.4	3.0	11.0	24.8	37.4	23.0	0.0
Salaried employees	1,840	3,576	0.0	0.0	0.2	1.5	5.7	10.9	23.2	36.1	22.3	0.1
Workers	1,355	6,323	0.0	0.4	0.7	3.8	10.5	18.5	32.4	27.3	6.4	0.0
Not employed	873	7,079	0.8	13.1	21.5	24.5	14.3	8.4	8.3	6.6	2.5	0.0
Total	n.a.	20,540	0.3	4.7	7.8	10.3	10.0	12.1	20.1	22.4	11.7	0.6

Sources: *Bericht*, 1974, pp. 434 and 435; *SJB BRD*, 1973, p. 503.
*Not including foreigners' households and people accommodated in institutions.

concerning the comparatively good position of the farmers. According to a testing sample of 7016 farms, the average farmer's net household income in the 1972—73 farm year surpassed not only the manual worker's but also the white-collar worker's household income, and was nearly 50 per cent above the national average. On a *per capita* basis, however, farmers' households were still slightly lower than the national average. It has also to be borne in mind that the farmers' household income did not come exclusively from agriculture, but to a certain extent from private capital, from letting and leasing, from employment outside the farm business, and last but not least, from pensions and other social benefits.[35]

It should be remembered in this context that during the sixties the amount of social benefits to farmers increased much more than social benefits as a whole, and also that the growth of social benefits surpassed the production growth. Between 1960 and 1971 the gross national product of the FRG increased more than twice (index 227), the total of social benefits almost three times (index 268) and the amount of social benefits to farmers more than four times (index 415).[36]

If the sample data on farmers' income are fairly representative, and if this development is a long-term one, and if it can be corroborated by findings in other countries with a similar level of modernisation (economic maturity), it might be suggested that the upward shift of farmers on the stratification scale is one of the features of the second industrial revolution, or, as Marxists prefer to say, technical-scientific revolution.[37]

From the point of view of household income, the whole West German society in 1969 could be divided into four strata: upper stratum with monthly incomes of over DM 3000; upper-middle stratum with DM 2000—3000; lower-middle stratum with DM 1200—2000; and lower stratum with incomes below that level. The percentages of all households in these groups were 12.3, 22.4, 32.2 and 33.1 respectively.

The upper stratum was composed of the following socio-economic groups: 31.6 per cent salaried employees, 29.1 per cent self-employed (not including farmers), 16.0 per cent workers, 11.2 per cent officials, 7.0 per cent non-employed and 5.1 per cent farmers.

In the upper-middle stratum there were 37.5 per cent workers' households, 28.0 per cent salaried employees' households, 10.1 per cent non-employed households, 10.0 per cent officials' households, 8.6 per cent self-employed outside agriculture and 5.8 per cent farmers' households.

Almost half of the lower-middle income stratum was made up of workers (48.6 per cent); 18.4 per cent salaried employees; 17.8 per cent non-employed, 6.6 per cent officials; 4.8 per cent non-farmer self-employed and 3.8 per cent farmers.

The lowest income stratum was made up mainly of non-employed people (77.2 per cent). Of the other groups there were 14.3 per cent workers, 3.9 per cent salaried employees, 2.1 per cent self-employed outside agriculture, 1.8 per cent farmers and 0.7 per cent officials.

The lowest income per household seems to have been DM 400 for employed, and DM 300 for non-employed people (percentages of households below that level were negligible). At the upper end of the scale, only self-employed other than farmers significantly exceeded the DM 10,000 mark.

So, in spite of significant differences between average households' disposable income in individual socio-economic groups, there was, as Janowitz has already pointed out, a wide overlapping with respect to individual income brackets. Defined by the amount of income, both the upper and lower middle strata were composed of large numbers from all socio-economic groups. These groups cut across all income strata in such a way that neither of these variables (type of employment and amount of income) can be properly used for the assessment of social stratification. In view of this both Schelsky's position and Dahrendorf's pyramid may be better understood.

On the whole, the juxtaposition of the type of employment with the level of income indicates how difficult it might be to demarcate, in tangible terms, categories which became widely accepted as meaningful entities such as the working class and the middle class. Dahrendorf's specification of officials, workers' élite and the false middle class appears to be more useful, except that the quantification may look slightly different, partly as a result of recent changes, partly as a matter of definition. In particular the working élite appears to be an elastic concept. On the strength of 1969 income data it might be larger than Dahrendorf's 5 per cent. Also the proportion of population in the false middle class might be greater if low-paid salaried employees were to be included.

Considering the development of West German income distribution by size, there seems on the whole to have been no significant change during the last twenty years. According to comprehensive data, the distribution of income of private households has not appreciably changed between 1950 and 1970. As the calculations of the German

Institute for Economic Research, reproduced in Table 3.8, indicate, the growth of average real income was not accompanied by a significant narrowing of differentials. A modest levelling tendency prevailed during the fifties but from 1964 a reversal set in. In 1970 the sum of absolute deviations from equal income distribution was the same as in 1950. (Two similar waves can be seen with income differentials by socio-economic groups in Table 2.9; decrease of differentials between 1960 and 1965 and increase between 1965 and 1970–72.)

Table 3.8 Quintile Distribution of Income of Private Households in the FRG

	1	2	3	4	5	Quintile deviation
1950*	5.4	10.7	15.9	22.8	45.2	0.560
1955*	5.8	10.7	16.2	23.2	44.1	0.548
1960	6.0	10.8	16.2	23.1	43.9	0.541
1964	6.1	10.8	16.1	22.9	44.1	0.541
1968	6.2	10.5	15.7	22.5	45.1	0.552
1970	5.9	10.4	15.6	22.5	45.6	0.560

*Excluding West Berlin and Saarland.
Source: *Bericht,* 1974, p. 430.

A comparatively constant pattern of quintile distribution of income does not, however, exclude shifts within the income stratification. The data on salary/wage ratio (Table 3.6) indicate a slow, but on the whole continuous, narrowing of differentials between white- and blue-collar workers.

This and other similar or contrary developments might have been important for subjective evaluation of the individual's position within the stratified pattern. As long as individuals were satisfied with the general increase of real income and were not disturbed at lagging behind others, there might have been greater satisfaction with the development.

According to an opinion poll by the Institute for Demoscopy this tendency seems to have prevailed during the sixties. Although the survey covers only the period between 1964 to 1972, i.e. the period when again the de-levelling trend set in, some relevant conclusions may be drawn from it. To the question whether the economic conditions (i.e. what people own and earn) are considered to be just, the following answers were given: in August 1964, 42 per cent considered the conditions as just, 38 per cent as unjust, 20 per cent were undecided.

In October 1970 the percentage of those who considered the conditions as just increased to 46 per cent and the percentage for 'unjust' remained unchanged. The number of undecided dropped to 16 per cent. Since then however the trend has reversed. In February 1973 only 44 per cent found the economic conditions just and 42 per cent unjust and 14 per cent were undecided.[38] These results seem to reflect the already stated shift within the distributive shares of national income, namely the higher increase of *per capita* income from self-employment than from employment after 1969.

Unfortunately with respect to the GDR no more data are available than those referred to in the chapter on income and wealth. The income distribution of the workers and salaried employees' households which in the GDR is being ascertained in regular intervals, does not differentiate between blue- and white-collar workers. As these two categories constitute 85 per cent of total labour force both in the GDR and FRG, any juxtaposition lumping together these two socio-economic groups would be hardly satisfactory for a comparative analysis of a two-dimensional stratification. Neither is the income distribution for the population as a whole available for the GDR. So in view of stratification by level of income, we cannot but reiterate what has already been shown in Chapter 2, Table 2.11, p. 48, namely the real income distribution of workers and salaried employees' households in 1960 and 1970: these data indicate that in 1969—70 the proportion of employed population with an inadequate income per household (i.e. below the equivalent of DM 800 of 1970 purchasing power) was twice as high in the GDR as in the FRG.

3e. Upward mobility through the educational channel

As social stratification is a multiple (multi-dimensional) phenomenon, so too are the channels of vertical mobility: better training or education, business (money-making) dexterity and political or trade union careers are the main alternatives. Concerning vertical mobility through training and education there are fortunately fairly comparable data from both parts of Germany. As the GDR data on students' social origin distinguish between workers and white-collar employees, it is possible to relate these figures to our estimate of blue- and white-collar personnel in section 3b.; the result is given in Table 3.9. Moreover, it is possible to follow the development in the GDR during the sixties (Table 3.10).

Concerning the inter-country comparison reproduced in Table 3.9, the figures confirm the East German claim that in the GDR the

Table 3.9 Students' Origin and Working Population by Socio-Economic Groups in 1967 (Students in Higher Education Establishments)

Groups in the FRG	Students' Parents	Working Population	Ratio	Students' Parents	Working Population	Ratio	Groups in the GDR
	FRG			GDR			
Workers	6.7	47.3	0.14	38.2	44.5	0.86	Workers
Salaried employees	31.1	28.2	1.10	23.5	30.9	0.76	Salaried employees
Government officials	29.5	5.4	5.45	20.4	7.8	2.62	Intelligentsia
Farmers	3.3	3.4	0.97	7.8	13.0	0.60	Co-operative farmers, craftsmen etc.
Other self-employed	26.7	7.8	3.42	7.1	3.8	1.87	Self-employed
Others and unspecified	2.7	7.9	0.34	3.0	—	—	Unspecified
Total	100.0	100.0		100.0	100.0		

Source: *Zahlenspiegel,* Bonn, 1973, p. 18.
In the GDR, the category of workers and salaried employees is divided according to the ratio in Table 3.3; intelligentsia is deducted and equals the labour force with completed higher or secondary education (*SJB DDR,* 1971, p. 56).

Table 3.10 Students by Social Origin in the GDR (in per cent of the whole student population of the respective type of education in 1960 and 1967)

	University Level				Secondary Level			
	Full time Students		Part time Students		Full time Students		Part time Students	
Social Group	1960	1967	1960	1967	1960	1967	1960	1967
Workers	50.3	38.2	7.3	11.9	58.4	52.0	43.5	31.0
Salaried employees	19.2	23.5	61.8	30.8	18.6	20.5	41.6	61.2
Members of co-operatives	4.2	7.8	0.8	1.8	9.3	11.7	8.7	5.1
Intelligentsia	15.6	20.4	27.9	53.8	5.9	8.9	3.1	1.9
Self-employed	8.0	7.1	2.0	1.4	6.8	4.9	2.0	0.3
Others	2.7	3.0	0.2	0.3	1.0	2.0	1.1	0.5

Source: Peter C. Ludz, 'Die Entwicklung der DDR', in *Das 198. Jahrzehnt, Eine Team-Prognose für 1970—1980,* München, 1972, pp. 243—4.

educational channel of vertical upward mobility is much more open than in the FRG. Although in the GDR students of workers' families were in the year in question slightly under-represented and students from families of the intelligentsia strongly over-represented the disparity was not so great as in the FRG. Whereas in the GDR, the range of disparity between the highest and the lowest frequency of student recruitment (between intelligentsia and farmers) was 5, in the FRG the range of disparity between the highest and lowest frequency of such a recruitment (between officials and workers) was 39. Barriers against intergenerational upward mobility through the educational channel were eight times higher in the FRG than in the GDR.

Figures on the development in the GDR (Table 3.10) are revealing in several respects. They indicate that the workers' families' representation in the student population declined in all but one reported type of education; only amongst the part-time university students, where students from workers' families were heavily under-represented, had their proportion increased. On the other hand, the drop of worker origin in the full-time university student body was considerable. The decline in secondary education was less conspicuous.

The proportion of full-time student population from salaried employees', intelligentsia and co-operative producers' families increased both at the university and secondary level. Regarding part-time students, the development was uneven and partly even contradictory but on the whole the white-collar workers and co-operative producers' families increased their representation. Ludz explained these developments as the sign of reconsolidation of those strata from which the proportion of student population increased, namely the salaried employees, intelligentsia and co-operative producers.[39]

Only the representation of the self-employed declined in all the four types of education. It is, however, to be borne in mind that their proportion in the working population declined also: from 5.5 per cent in 1960 to 3.8 per cent in 1967. So, paradoxically, in full-time university education, this group was more over-represented in 1967 than in 1960. It is, of course, not possible to qualify this fact as reconsolidation as in the previous groups. It was rather an outcome of natural pressure of achievement in the lower stages of education and of determined efforts on the part of the students or their parents. In so far as they were willing to co-operate on the political plane, their class origin was less objectionable.

Something similar may be said of the other strata; the stress on catching up with, and possibly overtaking the West, helped to open the way for able, efficient people. This seems to have been, from the early sixties, one of the pillars of Walter Ulbricht's policy of accelerated technico-economic modernisation within political and cultural stabilisation, or rather stiffening. Ulbricht's fall in May 1971 opened the door for the reappraisal of the whole policy which eventually re-emphasised the class aspect of the socialist development. This resulted not only in a new wave of nationalisation of enterprises but also brought about a greater stress on class requirements for admission to higher and secondary education.[40] How far this policy was reflected in facts and how far the consolidation of non-manual strata was jeopardised is difficult to assess. In the long run, however, it seems hardly probable that those who were promoted from worker status to that of clerical staff, government officials or intelligentsia would want to see their children relapse into the previous position of their fathers. It is also more difficult to discriminate against the descendants of members of those strata in a similar way as was possible with the descendants of 'bourgeois' families. The tendency towards over-representation of the new upper strata in the student population can hardly be expected to abate.

Although there can be little doubt that education is the main channel of upward mobility, it has to be realised that it need not necessarily affect all components of social status. The most likely success is in obtaining a more prestigious type of employment but not always a higher income. The income distribution by type of employment (Table 3.7) has amply demonstrated this. The supply/demand relationship seemed to be still more important for the amount of income distribution than the level of education.

Neither is the educational level in direct relationship to income in those occupations where higher education is more or less a necessary prerequisite. A sample survey in Nordrhein-Westfalen in 1964, reproduced here in Table 3.11, has revealed no particular income advantage for employees with a university education over those with a lower education within the same job category. The average differential was only 8 per cent. The remarkable exception was attained by older employees (born before 1931) whose university education gave them a 25 per cent lead over the others. Performance of parents did not appear to be significant for income differentials. In most groups in the sample people from more successful families attained a somewhat higher salary than those from less successful families, but on average only by 4 per cent. The most relevant variable

Table 3.11 Influence of Age, Intelligence, Social Origin and Formal Education on the Salaries of Employees (sample survey, Land of Nordrhein-Westfalen, FRG, 1964)

Columns 1	2	3	4	5	6
			Salary in DM per month		
Lines Age	Intelligence	Social origin	University education	Other education	Ratio (col. 4:5)
1		successful families	2,397	1,919	1.25
2	superior	less successful families	2,212	2,023	1.09
3 born 1931 and before		successful families	1,989	1,927	1.03
4	average	less successful families	1,911	1,828	1.05
5		successful families	1,872	1,470	1.27
6	superior	less successful families	1,693	1,637	1.03
7 born 1932–1935		successful families	1,614	1,520	1.06
8	average	less successful families	1,556	1,470	1.06
9		successful families	1,430	1,612	0.89
10	superior	less successful families	1,381	1,305	1.06
11 born 1936 and after		successful families	1,300	1,289	1.01
12	average	less successful families	1,400	1,223	1.14

Source: Gerhard Brinkmann, *Berufsausbildung und Arbeitseinkommen,* Duncker and Humblot, Berlin, 1967, p. 98.

for income differentiation appeared to be age. There the differentials between the highest and lowest income were 1.84 in view of employees with university education and 1.57 for employees with other education. Neither of the scales of income was directly dependent upon age.

So, the white-collar sample in the richest West German Land (Table 3.11) points to a lesser rather than a greater congruence of education level with the amount of income.

Concerning the GDR, it is extremely difficult to evaluate the possible correlation between individual components of social status.

The only tendency which seems to result clearly from scattered evidence is the increasing requirement of higher education for a political career. As in all other Communist-dominated countries, members of the Party and state apparats are encouraged to improve their qualifications by part-time courses. A higher level of education is now more than ever before required of the new recruits.

An illustration of this trend can be seen in the structure of the People's Chamber (*Volkskammer*) by the level of education. Unfortunately these data are only available for the most recent 'election' periods (1967 and 1971). Within these four years the proportion of deputies with higher education (including professors) increased from 24.0 to 36.8 per cent and of those with completed secondary education from 18 to 21 per cent.[41]

This is a significant change for such a short period of time. Whatever standard these levels of education might reach, the data support the previous observation that higher education is increasingly required as a prerequisite for a political career. It appears that at least with respect to two components of social status, namely education level and political career, there is a tendency toward congruence of social status in the GDR.

3f. Upward mobility through the economic and political channels

When the so-called capitalist class emerged in Germany, it did not take power directly from the aristocracy but, by developing industry and trade and financial services, built a new source of influence which eventually restricted the range of the traditional seats of authority. It was entrepreneurial and commercial success which opened the way to those of lower birth and also to those with a lower level of education. Only gradually was higher education required as an additional qualification for a business career. Nevertheless, an investigation of 978 top economic bosses in West Germany, reported by H. Marcus, indicates that in the middle sixties, 51 per cent of entrepreneurs, 35 per cent of bankers and 29 per cent of managers in that group were without higher education.[42]

Table 3.12 reproduces results of an inquiry into the education level of a sample of 536 top managers and their ancestors in the FRG in 1965. This inquiry shows that whereas 62.5 per cent of respondents had a high level of education, of their fathers only 21.7 per cent and their grandfathers only 8.8 per cent had achieved that level of education. Apparently, a certain level of education became increasingly required as a prerequisite for business careers. In that sense, the

tendency towards the decomposition of social status seems to have
been reversed. The quoted data indicate a growing congruence between
the level of education and economic position which implies both
wealth and power.

From the point of view of social origin defined according to the
subjective evaluation of respondents, the results were as follows: only
16.2 per cent of the respondents' fathers considered themselves as
belonging to the upper-middle class, whereas 49.5 per cent identified
themselves as of lower-middle class; in the grandfathers' generation
the proportions were 4.3 per cent and 62.9 per cent respectively. From

Table 3.12 Social Mobility in the FRG. Educational Level and Social
Origin of West German Top Managers. Sample Survey (n = 536)
around 1965; percentages

A. *Managers' and general education level*

	education level of managers	of general population
Elementary	5.8	79
Secondary	5.6	16
Any post-secondary	88.6	5
Total	100	100

B. *Managers', their fathers' and grandfathers' education level*

Education level	Respondents to the questionnaire	Their fathers	Their grandfathers
Elementary and Secondary	11.4	46.7	68.7
Post-secondary non-university	26.1	31.3	17.2
University or Technical University	62.5	21.7	8.8
Unknown	—	0.3	5.3
Total	100.0	100.0	100.0

C. *Social Origin of top managers*

Social stratum or class	Fathers	Grandfathers
Upper class	16.2	4.3
Upper middle class	29.2	21.4
Lower middle class	49.5	62.9
Lower strata	5.1	11.4
Total	100.0	100.0

Source: Stephanie Münke, *Die Mobile Gesellschaft,* Stuttgart, 1967, pp. 146, 147,
quoting M. Jungblut: 'Die "Clique" an der Spitze — Woher kommen
Deutschlands Managers?' in *Die Zeit,* No. 52, 23 December 1966, p. 32 and
Helge Pross, *Manager und Aktionäre in Deutschland,* Frankfurt a.M., 1965.

the lowest strata, i.e. from below the critical line stressed by Dahrendorf, only 5.1 per cent were fathers and 11.4 per cent grandfathers of the top managers. This supports the thesis that, for a business career, there was also a clear-cut 'opportunity barrier' cutting across West German society.

Yet there is still another channel of upward social mobility in the West and in the East alike: that of the political and trade union career. According to a biographical manual reporting on 801 politicians in 1921 Germany, 20 per cent of those covered by the survey were of workers', 20 per cent of farmers', and 21 per cent of petty craftsmen and traders' families. Fathers of 8 per cent in the sample were low-ranking government officials and primary school teachers and 2 per cent business employees. This leaves only 29 per cent of politicians originating from upper or upper-middle strata: most of their fathers were landlords (11 per cent), then came industrialists (6 per cent), professionals (5 per cent), officers and aristocrats (3 per cent), high-ranking government officials (2 per cent) and academics (1 per cent).[43]

A comparison of the social origin of three different types of élite in the FRG in Table 3.13 indicates that only the political and not the administrative or economic career provides a sufficiently far-reaching means of overcoming the critical Dahrendorfian barrier in social mobility. Yet even this channel was not broad enough to bring an adequate number of workers to the top. If only the number of those whose social origin is known are taken into account, workers had a 10 per cent representation among the political élite.

In the GDR much more than in the FRG, political qualification can make good the lack of vocational training. Comparison of the educational level of technical and political élite in 1960 has shown that of 528 East German technical managers, 40 per cent had the basic education only, of the 86 political managers 79 per cent were on that educational level. On the other hand, 51 per cent of technical managers and only 17 per cent of political managers had some sort of lower-secondary education (*Mittlere Bildung*). The number of managers with upper-secondary (*Abitur*) or higher education was negligible in both groups: 9.5 per cent among the technical and 4 per cent among the political managers.[44]

Similar proportions could be ascertained between 'political' and 'operational' officers in 1954. Of the former, 88.2 per cent had basic education only, of the latter 58.6 per cent. Persons with lower-secondary education were represented by 4.1 per cent among the political, 12.4 per cent among the operational officers, persons with upper-secondary

Table 3.13 Social Origin of Leading Groups in the FRG in 1955 (absolute figures)

Type of Elite	Fathers' occupation											
	Officers	Entre-preneurs	Profes-sionals	Teachers	High-ranking officials	Low-ranking officials	Self-employ-ed middle-class	Crafts-men	Employ-ees	Farmers	Workers	No inform-ation
Political (n = 60)	2	2	5	2	6	8	4	2	3	5	4	17
Administrative (n = 60)	4	1	6	9	11	3	0	2	2	1	0	21
Economic (n = 52)	0	14	5	3	1	2	1	0	1	1	0	24

Source: W. Zapf, *Wandlungen der Deutschen Elite*, p. 181.

education (*Abitur*) by 6.5 per cent and 28 per cent respectively; only 1.2 per cent or 1.0 per cent respectively had university education.[45]

It is clear that both in the civil and military service of the GDR, a political career was more open to those without higher or secondary education than was the professional (technical) career. Also in the latter, however, political qualification was more important than the educational level.

There is no doubt that in comparison with the FRG, the political channel of upward mobility in the GDR is much broader. As was said earlier and shown in Table 3.13, the workers' sons' participation in the West German political élite was only 10 per cent and in the West German élite as a whole hardly 4 per cent, whilst there were well above 40 per cent workers in the total working population.

A similar under-representation can be seen in the membership of the lower Chamber of the Parliament (Bundestag) — the top political body in the FRG. Table 3.14 shows the structure of the Bundestag according to its members' occupation.

Table 3.14 Social Composition of the FRG Bundestag Membership in 1965 in per cent

Entrepreneurs and top managers	6.2
Other managers	7.5
Middle Class	5.0
Farmers and officials of their associations	8.1
Employees and workers	8.1
Officials of political parties	7.1
Trade union officials	8.9
Lawyers and economic advisers	7.3
Scientists, priests, doctors and architects	4.4
Publishers, journalists	6.4
Government officials	28.7
Housewives	2.3
Total	100.0

Source: D. Claessens, A. Klönne, A. Tschoepe, *Sozialkunde der Bundesrepublik Deutschland,* Düsseldorf-Köln, 1968, p. 51.

Although categories in this table are not consistent, it is quite clear that, in the Lower Chamber, the upper strata were over-represented and the lower strata under-represented. The middle strata seem to have been represented adequately. Employment in the trade unions and political parties, however, provided an additional channel for the lower strata.

In the GDR the Volkskammer is formally analogical to the West

German Bundestag. Significantly, the social structure of this body's membership is not reported according to actual occupation or status, but according to social origin, i.e. occupation of the father or one's own first occupation when starting working life. So, in 1970 workers scored 57.4 per cent, co-operative farmers 8.8 per cent, co-operative craftsmen and tradesmen 10.4 per cent, employees 14.2 per cent, intelligentsia 6.8 per cent and others 2.4 per cent of Volkskammer membership.[46]

Fortunately, social comparison according to the actual occupation of membership is, in the GDR, known of a much more relevant body than the Volkskammer, namely of the Central Committe of the Communist Party (Sozialistische Einheitspartei Deutschlands). The relevant data are reported in Table 3.15. They indicate that workers

Table 3.15 Occupational Structure of the Central Committee of the SED (GDR) in 1971, in per cent

Officials of Central Party Apparat	18.5
Regional Party officials	19.6
Central Government officials	23.3
Local Government officials	1.6
Economic officials	9.0
Scientists, artists, research workers and officials of their organisations	12.2
Mass organisations' officials	7.4
Other workers	4.7
Party veterans	3.7
Total	100.0

Source: *Neues Deutschland* of 20 June 1971, quoted in *Bericht,* 1972, p. 39.

cannot get to the top in the GDR as workers, but as party, government, or mass organisation officials; in brief, as apparatchiks. Rank and file workers are not better represented in the supreme body of the GDR than in that of the FRG.

Of course, most of the 'apparatchiks' are of workers' origin — many of them were for a long time manual workers themselves. They can still have emotional ties with their past, they can better understand the interests of their former fellows than anybody else. But do they really behave like that? Do they defend first of all workers' interests? Or have they developed special interests, interests of the new ruling stratum?

There are several important issues on which actual interests of the 'toiling masses' and of their leadership diverge. A faster growth of productivity than that of real wages and the growing surplus resulting from it seem to be the main reason for dissatisfaction among the rank and file. But there are also other issues such as the ban on spontaneous associations, interference in non-political activities and interest of authorities in private matters which often become viewed differently by those Above and those Below.

3g. Downward mobility

So far we have envisaged only the upward channels of vertical mobility. However in both parts of Germany there has been enough evidence of the reverse trend, especially as a result of the wars. Schelsky mentioned such downward mobility as a special contribution to the general levelling of German society. He has in mind people affected either by health and/or loss of property, the expelled and refugees who in both parts of Germany had virtually to restart their lives. The number of these people was considerable. In the FRG there were four million people who were eligible for government care because they were physically affected by war and 3.4 million people who suffered losses from the air raids. Moreover the FRG absorbed over 13 million expelled people and refugees of which, significantly, 3.6 million came from the GDR.[47]

This means that about 20 million people or approximately 40 per cent of the population living between 1950 and 1960 in the FRG were somehow endangered by downward mobility. This, however, did not fully materialise; if they did not all drop in relation to others, or if they dropped only temporarily, it was due to two particular circumstances. First, the West German authorities took special care of all the above-mentioned categories of people. Second, the economic upsurge which took place in West Germany helped not only in financing government support but, and this was still more important, enabled many of these people affected to regain their socio-economic status. In the case of the expelled and the refugees, many attained a higher living standard and prestige than they would have had if they had remained in their original countries.

In 1950 the government of the FRG unified the previous legislature concerning the care of the wounded and mutilated (*Bundesversorgungsgesetz*). In 1969, 2.6 million people were still obtaining benfits through this channel.[48] In 1952 a special law was passed concerning the social equalisation of burdens (*Lastenausgleich*). It was based on the idea that the casualties and ravages of war usually hit some people more than others and that it is a matter of social justice that those who succeeded in escaping the worst or even surviving without damage had to compensate those who were unfortunate. This idea was effectively realised and from 1952 to the end of 1970 over DM 73,000 million, i.e. more than 10 per cent of the 1970 gross national product, was paid off on behalf of those people. The yearly benefits from these sources are still running at more than DM 4,000 million. It is supposed that most of the claims will not be finalised until 1979 but the benefits are supposed to be paid until well after this date and it is expected that the arrangement will be terminated in the year 2015. The total expenditure until then will attain DM 110,000 million.[49]

In the GDR, there was no special arrangement of a similar type to that of the West German *Lastenausgleich*. People concerned could claim for help or compensation, but only through the general channels of a social insurance system within the category of war victims (*Kriegsopfer*) or social support (*Sozialhilfe*). In 1955 benefits on behalf of these two categories amounted to 7.4 per cent of the total expenditure on social benefits in the GDR.

Consequently in the GDR there was greater scope for downward mobility as a result of the war. This was the case in spite of the greater intake of refugees and those expelled by the FRG, and in spite of the fact that almost 20 per cent of GDR residents joined the westward migration.

Further, there were large-scale changes in ownership in the East which resulted in the decline of many former self-employed people both on the scale of living standard and prestige. Also children of former 'capitalists' and their 'helpers' had to bear the consequences of their class origin. As a rule, they were barred from access to higher education and the career prospects offered by such an education. It is difficult to ascertain the intensity of these shifts because not all the expropriated suffered a permanent reduction in their living standard. In the absence of adequate information we can only list the change of ownership and discrimination against the descendants of former 'upper strata' as additional causes of downward mobility.

Economic or professional failures can also be considered as a similar channel of downward mobility in the FRG; their extent can be roughly estimated by the number of bankruptcies, running up to between two to three thousand per year, i.e. less than 0.1 per cent of private enterprises between 1965 and 1971.[50] Also the selling up of non-profitable farms can be considered up to a point as an indication of downward mobility but only in cases where the farmer does not find a compensatory job elsewhere. The magnitude of these failures is difficult to assess.

A more widespread form of downward mobility in a basically free market economy like the West German one can occur if there is an economic recession; then within individual professions and types of employment there can be a considerable decrease in income. This can become socially significant if the recession lasts for a long period.[51]

After World War Two nothing like that happened. The latest lean year so far was 1967: unemployment which otherwise during the decade was negligible (between 0.6 and 0.8 per cent) rose to 2.1 per cent (and in 1968 fell only to 1.5 per cent). The gross domestic product declined by 0.2 per cent; this setback was reflected mainly in investment (there was a decline by 9 per cent) and in bankruptcies (increase by 50 per cent over 1965) but not in consumption, the aggregate volume of which increased by 0.6 per cent.[52] In all other years until 1973 the continuous *per capita* increase of the aggregate production provided a climate favourable for upward rather than downward mobility. Only in 1974 a wider scope for unemployment and failures re-emerged. With a stagnating output unemployment rose to 3.5 per cent and many foreign workers' labour contracts were not renewed on expiry.[53] It remains to be seen whether the 1974–5 setback will be like that of 1967 but of short duration, or whether in view of some structural changes in the society this recession may introduce some more permanent features in the socio-economic framework of the Western world.

Similarly, growth in the GDR was not always even. Here however it was rather the consumer who had to bear the brunt of decelerated growth. Between the years 1961, 1962 and 1963 the produced national income increased by 2.3 per cent and 3 per cent respectively. National income utilised in the country increased by 1 per cent in 1961, 3 per cent in 1962 and declined by 1 per cent in 1963. Private consumption increased by 3 per cent in 1961, stagnated in 1962 and went up by less than 1 per cent in 1963.[54] The East German 'command' economy was unable to assure a continuous growth with uninterrupted prospects for catching up with the West German living standard.

There is yet another possible channel of downward mobility: conviction and punishment for crime or major offences. In this respect the FRG seems to provide a more ample framework for backsliding than the GDR. In spite of a much wider concept of criminal activity against the state in the GDR, the relative number of ascertained legal offences continues to be much higher in the FRG than in the GDR (Table 3.16). The difference is so high that it can hardly be fully

Table 3.16 Frequency of Criminal Offences known to the Police per 100,000 population

Year	FRG	GDR
1957	3140	967
1958	3175	1072
1959	3547	907
1960	3660	806
1961	3775	867
1962	3699	949
1963	2914	956
1964	2998	814
1965	3031	756
1966	3213	730
1967	3465	680
1968	3588	586
1969	3645	620
1970	3924	640

Source: *Bericht,* 1972, p. 236.

explained by different methods of assessment. According to the hints in East German literature[55] it seems that, in the middle sixties, the GDR ceased to consider some minor offences as criminal acts and trusted the local authorities or mass organisations with rehabilitation of such offenders. This however only explains the temporary drop in the number of offences and not their lower ratio in comparison with the FRG. It can rather be assumed that the tighter control and supervision of individuals in the East, either by means of political screening or government-sponsored neighbourly interest or direct police action, provide a considerably less conducive climate for delinquency than a liberal, permissive society. The latter respects more, as a matter of principle, individual predilections irrespective of their possible social impact. A liberal society is also loath to embark on preventive measures.

Freedom is in a sense indivisible. Unless checked by the widespread acceptance of common ethos and responsibility, institutional guarantees of individual freedom seem to provide a greater scope not only for unhampered political and intellectual activity, but also greater opportunity for crime. On the other hand less freedom does not exclude, but rather induces, organised crime by government; Germany herself experienced during the Nazi times a most horrible example of such a reversal of roles. Neither can the shooting of refugees by the GDR border-guards be considered as something different. As the author himself experienced, both strong and weak governments may be in an awkward position with their alienated subjects. A strong government may be tempted to enforce their conformity by terrorist methods. A weak government may itself become an object of terror.

3h. Mobility and what else?

There is yet another aspect of the stratification/mobility pattern, namely, whether the enhanced vertical mobility brings about a better position to those Below in the social stratification, or whether it is a matter of individual promotion only, a promotion which might be beneficent for those Above rather than those Below. As Vilfredo Pareto has already realised, a broader recruitment basis is one of the best means of preserving established élites.

Concerning the relative position of upper and lower strata, the inidicators discussed so far are not unequivocal. In the GDR workers are treated more equally with white-collar employees in matters concerning working time, holidays, social insurance, firing conditions etc. There also seems to be a greater equality of wages *vis-à-vis* salaries in the GDR. On the other hand, the GDR, like other Communist states, abides by the principle of a faster growth rate of productivity than that of real wages. This opens a gap between performance and rewards which, if it develops too fast, cannot be concealed from those concerned. Also, as will be shown in the subsequent chapter, the self-assertion of workers within enterprises in the GDR is less pronounced than in the FRG. Although, or rather because, workers in the GDR are formally co-owners, they are subject to stricter discipline, regulations and responsibility than their West German counterparts. Trade unions are, according to the GDR Labour Code (*Gesetzbuch der Arbeit*) supposed to contribute continuously to the strengthening of socialist working morale and the discipline of work.[56] Also the workers' legal responsibility is much higher in the GDR than in the FRG.[57]

In circumstances where individual objective indicators point to diverging directions, much depends on how the workers themselves evaluate the situation. Do they appreciate their status of greater equality with the white-collar employees more strongly than they resent the growing disparity between the growth of productivity and real wages? Do they really possess the supposed higher social consciousness of disciplined co-owners of the means of production, a consciousness ready to make sacrifices for the sake of future generations? Unfortunately there has so far been no research into these questions in the GDR.

The normative statements are supposed to be followed by reality. It is assumed that workers in the GDR need not strike because factories belong to them, because they enjoy better treatment, freely elect their representatives who bargain their wages with the management; if they settle down with a lower wage than their West German counterparts, it is because they bargain with 'their' socialist management, and because of their higher social consciousness and responsibility.

In reality there might be some real bargaining about minor matters, such as splitting the end of the year bonus between different uses or achieving a fair balance between piece rates for single tasks, but the major decisions concerning wages are not the result of bargaining, they are the outcome of the planning, i.e. the macro-balances set by the State Planning Commission.

As long as there is no possibility of asking workers in the GDR what they really think about their positions, all these suppositions are a matter of subjective belief or disbelief, but not of an objectively verifiable assessment. Personal experience may be too personal. Only a judgement acquired analogically by comparison with a known situation in similar conditions elsewhere may perhaps be helpful. In neighbouring Czechoslovakia a genuine research in social stratification was undertaken in November 1967.[58] Its results concerning those Above and those Below can be summarised as follows:

> The question whether, in Czechoslovak society, social differences do exist was answered by 74.9 per cent in the affirmative, and by only 9.5 per cent in the negative. The question whether classes or strata existed was answered by 56.5 per cent in the affirmative; 17.2 per cent denied this kind of differentiation. Answers to more detailed and complex questions were analysed and distributed into seven groups. Of these, four, totalling 44 per cent of the sample, were basically of a dichotomic type: mass and élite; one of a more complex hierarchical model received 20 per cent, and one of non-hierarchical concept, 25 per cent; the official concept of the three harmoniously co-operating social groups (workers, co-operative farmers and intelligentsia) was held by only 11 per cent of the respondents.[59]

Although it may be misleading to compare the experience of another Communist country with the East German one, it would not be prudent in view of so many similarities in the political and economic structure, to reject a judgement by analogy altogether.

Also the fact that so many industrial managers in Czechoslovakia and in the GDR joined the Communist Party and attained a good career in it, should be borne in mind. More than once in post-war days the author of this study has heard from people of this particular group that only Communists can harness the workers and bring them back to the badly needed discipline. And so it happened both within the CSSR and the GDR. Also, the author of this study has heard from the workers, amongst whom he spent many years of his life, the complaint that they are not better off than their fellow workers in capitalist countries. As an old German saying puts it:

'Es kommt nichts besseres nach.' (Nothing better comes after.)

On the other hand, in the FRG where workers are subject to less discipline and are able to demand higher wages by means of strikes, their satisfaction with their position may also be questioned. Although they are not experiencing a similar gap between productivity and real wages as is the case in the GDR, they are more exposed to traditional inequalities, especially with respect to white- and blue-collar employees. As job security depends on economic prosperity, it is also a matter for concern. Although during the 10 years 1963–1972, with the exception of one particular year (1967) there were more vacancies than people seeking jobs,[60] there is no guarantee built in to the system that the situation will last forever. Data for 1974 and 1975 indicate that the comfortable surplus of vacancies has disappeared. It is only the government's moral and political duty to take care of economic development, a duty expressed in the first paragraph of the Law for Promoting Stability and Economic Growth from 1969: 'The Government is obliged to take anti-depression measures, to care for evasion of the danger of employment and to provide for retraining and resettlement of those who might have lost their jobs because of the structural changes in the economy.'[61]

When we say this, we have of course to look more closely at the position in the East. Neither can the GDR, in spite of her command economy, guaranteeing in her Constitution the right of work for everybody, proclaim also the reverse side of the coin, namely the duty to work. Only under such a juxtaposition is it possible to make such a law really binding. The right to work does not mean work according to one's qualification or training, and/or in the place of one's domicile, but work in general. The practical consequence is that in the FRG, there is a highly structured network of labour exchanges headed by the Bundesanstalt für Arbeit in Nuremberg, while in the GDR the matching of employment seekers and vacancies is a minor activity within the local administrative bodies.

In view of this, Article 24 of the Constitution of the GDR which
proclaims the right of a free choice of jobs, adds not only a subjective
condition (corresponding to one's qualification) but also an objective
one (according to social needs). This means that individual persons may
be directed to particular jobs. As compulsory allocation (*Zuweisung*)
has been abolished, this direction has to take voluntary forms. Workers
have to be persuaded; the Party and trade union discipline play a
substantial role in this.[62]

Discipline in a traditionally law-abiding nation, especially if coupled
with a certain feeling of security, may be accepted with more comfort
than the embarrassment of a free choice among alternatives which in
their turn may depend on relationships beyond the grasp of the
people concerned. As the preference for either more social security and
less freedom or more freedom coupled with more risk, depends not
only on social background and cultural tradition but also on type of
personality, any balanced evaluation of a respective feeling of those
below a certain level of power and/or wealth is extremely difficult.

In this respect, as in many others, more information is available from
West Germany than from East Germany. There are findings of German
sociologists quoted by Dahrendorf which, on the whole, testify a rather
passive acquiescence or resigned acceptance of the situation of those
Below.[63]

Then there are Almond's and Verba's findings on the comparatively
high 'subject (administrative) competence' and low 'citizen (political)
competence' in the FRG in comparison with the other four countries
under study i.e. the US, the UK, Italy and Mexico. It may be inferred
from these comparisons that in the FRG many more people than in the
other four countries expect serious consideration by their government
and police for their requirements and that they do not need to take
action against an unjust law either on a national level or on a local
level.[64]

L.W. Edinger found that the sense of subject or administrative
competence strengthened rather than weakened during the time:

> Whereas in 1950 only 21 per cent of a representative cross-section
> of citizens of the Federal Republic expressed trust in their civil
> servants, by 1965, 50 per cent believed that civil servants could neither
> be influenced nor corrupted, and only 29 per cent expressed explicit
> doubts on this score. Another study, in 1960, found that 70 per cent
> of adult West Germans could not imagine a strike by their civil
> servants, and this included 73 per cent of the government bureaucrats

in the sample.[65]

Almond and Verba describe the German situation as follows:

> The pattern of political and administrative competence in Germany contrasts sharply with that of the United States. Germany seems to be a nation in which the subject orientation is relatively frequent, as against the citizen orientation. Consider the treatment Germans expect in Government offices or from the police. In both cases, they (after the British) most frequently expect serious consideration for their point of view. In contrast to this is their response to unjust legislative activity. In connection with an unjust local regulation, they rank third in the frequency with which individuals feel they can do something to redress such an act; in connection with an unjust national law, they rank fourth — slightly below the Mexicans. It is only in Germany that more respondents could be described as administrative competents rather than political competents. However, that pattern appears to apply especially to those Germans of lower educational attainment. Just as important as the number who say they can influence an unjust law are the strategies they report. Relatively few would attempt to form groups for these purposes, the German respondents frequently talk of contacting administrative officials.[66]

Yet fifteen years have elapsed since the 5,000 interviewers provided the basis of Almond and Verba's conclusions, and ten years since Edinger found their corroboration. Did, meanwhile, the West Germans become less 'subject' and more 'citizen competent' or did they embark on another way of change?

Information on the German development viewed from another angle, but pertinent to these particular aspects of German civic culture, is provided by two public opinion polls undertaken within 21 years by the Institute of Demoscopy in Allensbach. A sample of 2,000 persons over 16 years of age was asked identical questions in June 1950 and in December 1971 — 'Do you consider the class struggle harmful or necessary?' The responses were as follows:

	1950	1971
'class struggle is harmful'	45%	32%
'class struggle is necessary'	21%	28%
'undecided'	22%	25%
'never heard of class struggle'	12%	15%

Among the male respondents the shift from those against class struggle
to those seeing it as necessary was still more conspicuous: whereas in
1950 the respective scores were 51 per cent and 27 per cent, in 1971,
the percentages were almost equal, 35 per cent against 33 per cent. In
1971, of the age group between 16 and 29, 40 per cent considered the
class struggle as necessary, 24 per cent as harmful.

Of individual occupational groups, skilled workers were most
favourably disposed to the class struggle (32 per cent for and 28 per
cent against). Also respondents with higher education were more
favourably disposed to the class struggle (37 per cent) than those with
basic education only (25 per cent). In the breakdown according to the
level of income, class struggle was favoured most by those in the second
income bracket from the top; here 32 per cent considered class struggle
as harmful; and 33 per cent as necessary.

It is not surprising that the least appreciation of class struggle was
in the villages and the highest in the great cities; in the latter 33 per
cent considered the class struggle necessary and 31 per cent harmful,
in the former 23 per cent gave a positive answer and 35 per cent a
negative answer. Also, as can be expected, a higher percentage of
answers in favour of the class struggle came from the followers of the
Social Democratic Party (39 per cent against 25 per cent) whereas
among the Christian Democrats the scores were reversed (19 per cent
positive and 42 per cent negative answers). Surprisingly, the followers
of the Free Democratic Party were best informed (only 5 per cent said
that they had never heard about the class struggle) and 43 per cent
considered it necessary, whereas 32 per cent harmful![67]

Although the individual percentages may suffer from the
inaccuracies of a sample which was too small for so many breakdowns,
the general tendencies expressed in this poll are consistent with the
results of other polls and also with other indicators.

As was shown earlier (p. 95) the trend towards an increasing
satisfaction with the economic conditions in the FRG (with what
people own and earn) was reversed after 1970. The changing mood
has been found also by two surveys on the right to strike. In December
1967, 52 per cent of the poll expressed the view that the trade unions
have threatened to strike too often; 19 per cent were content with
their practice and only 8 per cent considered them not militant enough;
21 per cent were undecided.[68]

In December 1971 a similar sample was asked for their opinion on a
particular wage struggle in Baden-Württemberg. To the question whether
the metal-workers were right to strike there were almost as many

affirmative as negative answers, for both sexes 37 pros and 38 cons. Of the male respondents however, 47 per cent approved of the strike, and only 36 per cent disapproved, 14 per cent were undecided and only 3 per cent had never heard about that particular strike.[69]

Turning from attitudes to actions, i.e. considering actual industrial disputes (strikes and lock-outs), the development shows a similar tendency. As Table 3.17 indicates, both the number of workers involved in industrial disputes and the number of days lost considerably fluctuated from year to year. The peaks in 1963 and 1971 were followed by a considerable calm in the subsequent years. In spite of the very sharp fluctuation, during the last 15 years there has been a tendency towards increasing involvement in industrial disputes. The index of sliding five years' averages of workers involved in industrial disputes increased from 100 (average for 1958–1962) to 251 (average for 1968–1972); the index of similar averages of days lost went up in the same period from 100 to 351. Meanwhile employment increased only by about 10 per cent and unemployment remained at a low ebb.[70] It remains to be seen how the position may change during the 1974–5 recession.

Table 3.17 Industrial Disputes and Unemployment in the FRG

	Number of workers involved	Thousands of days lost	Percentage of unemployed out of the labour force
1950	79,270	38,100	10.2
1955	597,353	846,600	4.0
1958	202,614	782,254	3.5
1959	21,648	61,825	2.4
1960	17,065	37,723	1.2
1961	20,363	60,907	0.8
1962	79,777	450,948	0.7
1963	316,397	1,846,025	0.8
1964	5,629	16,711	0.7
1965	6,250	48,520	0.6
1966	196,013	27,086	0.7
1967	59,604	389,581	2.1
1968	25,167	25,249	1.5
1969	89,571	249,184	0.8
1970	184,269	93,203	0.7
1971	536,303	4,483,740	0.8
1972	22,908	66,045	1.1
1973	185,010	563,051	1.2

Source: *UN Year Books of Labour Statistics* and *UN Statistical Year Books.*

All this indicates that it is neither the 'citizen' nor the 'subject competence' but a new type of 'strife competence' which is gaining ground within West German industrial relations. In view of what has been discovered on the development of net wages and distributed profits in recent years (section 2f) it is no wonder that the propensity to industrial dispute has increased and that the idea of class struggle has gained popularity. It remains to be seen whether this development justified Dahrendorf's expectation that 'even in the Federal Republic the day is probably not too far off when conflict will assume the form of a "democratic class struggle", that is of clashes about particular issues and their possible solutions and not about ideologies.'[71]

Unlike the FRG, in the GDR there are no means of asking what the underdogs really feel or think. Some ninety-nine per cent of the votes cast for the united list of official candidates reminds one too much of the 'elections' of Nazi times to be taken as indicators of something other than manipulation or terror. Even if we want to dismiss the latter we can have no doubts about the magnitude of the former.

Before 13 August 1961, the East Germans had at least one channel of dissension open, namely leaving the country. From 1949 to that date, 2.6 million Germans of the GDR, i.e. 15 per cent of her population at the beginning of that period, voted with their feet in favour of the FRG. How this stream of horizontal mobility developed in individual years is shown in Table 3.18.

These figures indicate clearly that only the construction of the Berlin Wall brought the yearly stream of refugees to a trickle. They indicate also that since then the much more risky crossing was attempted almost only by adults and extremely rarely by whole families with children. On the other hand, even sentries on duty on the border sometimes ran away (2,668 soldiers escaped according to the source quoted below).

Whereas people who represent a liability for the state are more or less free to go, the young ones, who are expected to work and, if necessary, to fight, are prevented by all possible means from leaving the country. The authorities find it compatible with 'developed socialism', of which the GDR is supposed to be the embodiment, to shoot them dead at the wall rather than to allow them to go. From August 1961, when the wall was built, to mid-1974, 164 refugees were killed in such a way, while 155,147 managed to escape.[72] Only elderly people, mainly pensioners, are, as a rule, allowed to leave the GDR. Of the 208,000 who, for family reasons, were allowed to emigrate to the West from 1962 to 1967, 90 per cent were over 65. They had, however,

Table 3.18 Movement of Refugees from the GDR to the FRG

	Total number of refugees in thousands	Of which percentage of persons younger than 25	Refugees in per thousand of total population
1950	198	.	10.8
1951	166	.	9.0
1952	182	52.6	9.9
1953	331	48.7	18.3
1954	184	49.1	10.2
1955	253	52.4	14.1
1956	279	49.0	15.8
1957	262	52.2	15.0
1958	204	48.1	11.8
1959	144	48.3	8.3
1960	199	48.8	11.6
1961*	207	49.2	12.1
1962	21	38.7	1.2
1963	43	13.3	2.5
1964	42	11.1	2.5
1965	30	10.4	1.8
1966	24	9.4	1.4
1967	20	8.7	1.2
1968	16	7.6	0.9

*Mostly prior to 13 August when the wall was erected.
Source: *A bis Z. Ein Taschen- und Nachschlagebuch über den anderen Teil Deutschlands,* Deutscher Bundes-Verlag, Bonn, 1969, pp. 211, 212.

to renounce their claims for pensions and other social benefits in the GDR.[73]

Under these circumstances the only way to obtain some data on the social stratification of dissenters in the GDR is to inquire into the social background of those whose dissension was so strong that it resulted in their breaking all their ties with the country and going to the West. Unfortunately, available data reproduced in Table 3.19 show the structure of refugees by economic sectors rather than by social strata. Nevertheless judging by the comparatively small number of refugees in sensitive professions, the number of people from other than pre-socialist upper strata was considerable. As the number of workers amongst them might have been small, we have to bear in mind that these have chosen their own way of dissent, as they showed in the East Berlin riots of June 1953.

3i. Summary

As available data for Weimar Germany, the FRG and the GDR indicate,

Table 3.19 Social Structure of the Main Stream of Refugees from the GDR to the FRG (1952 to 1962)

	(thousands)
1. Economically active refugees	
from agriculture	155
from industry and handicrafts	471
from technical professions	48
from trade and transportation	268
from health and related services	114
from administration and justice	72
from cultural and religious activities	38
unspecified	234
2. Economically not self-supporting persons	
old-age and other pension recipients	132
housewives	257
pre-school and school children	466
students	15
3. Sensitive professions (1954 to 1962 only)	
Doctors	3.9
Dental surgeons and dentists	1.5
Veterinary doctors	0.3
Pharmacists	1.0
Judges and state attorneys	0.2
Other legal professions	0.7
University teaching personnel	0.8
Other teachers	18.0
Engineers and technical professions	19.1

Source: *A bis Z. Ein Taschen- und Nachschlagebuch über den anderen Teil Deutschlands,* Deutscher Bundes-Verlag, Bonn, 1969, p. 213.

a comparable, complex stratification scheme meets with conceptual and statistical difficulties. Such schemes lend themselves more easily to contradictory interpretations such as Schelsky's on the one hand and Dahrendorf's on the other. As individual elements of social status are only congruent and as there is, with respect to Germany, not enough conclusive correlation material on this topic, a multi-dimensional approach on separate lines has been adopted in this study.

Stratification by type of employment reveals in the two German states more similarities than divergencies. The percentages of blue- and white-collar workers are almost the same. The relative weight of the self-employed sector in the West equals the share of co-operative producers in the labour force in the East. Also the ratio of white- to blue-collar workers in industry is similar.

Stratification according to the type and level of education however, is somewhat different. In the GDR, there are more graduates in technical professions, whereas in the FRG, law is the most preferred subject. On the whole, the proportion of graduates in the total population seems to be almost the same in both parts of Germany. In vocational training, secondary production is more sponsored in the GDR, whereas the tertiary sector has more opportunity in the FRG.

Stratification by level of income, studied in more detail in the preceding chapter, appears to be, on the whole, steeper in the FRG than in the GDR. Level of income related to another stratification variable, such as type of employment, could be ascertained only in West Germany. There was a lot of overlapping. In a four-partite stratification by income in 1969 workers were most represented in the two middle strata; yet more than 6 per cent of them were in the upper stratum and 15 per cent in the lowest stratum. Of the self-employed outside agriculture 45 per cent were in the upper stratum and 10 per cent in the lowest one. Of the farmers, 17 per cent were at the top and 16 per cent at the bottom.

Within the category of self-employed people, the average *per capita* income from agriculture was somewhat lower than the national average but not as much as might be expected. At the beginning of the seventies, the gradual process of eliminating the less profitable farms had already advanced so far that the average income of farmers' households considerably exceeded the average income of white-collar employees' households. Yet it has to be borne in mind that a substantial contribution to the farmers' income came from other than farming activities. Nevertheless it seems that farmers as a social and vocational group ceased to be at the bottom of the earning scale.

The main lines of upward vertical mobility in both parts of Germany were education and political career. In the FRG, business career can be added as the third channel. Gradually, however, the success in the political career in the East and in the business career in the West require a higher vocational qualification. So the educational channel of upward mobility becomes linked with the other two, and in a way, their prerequisite, although this does not necessarily imply a higher income. So, in a sense the process of decomposition of social status has been reversed in both parts of Germany. As the available investigations point to a positive correlation of social prestige with education and as education becomes increasingly linked with power, there seems to be both in East and West a tendency to partial unification of social status. In view of income, however, the status incongruence persists.

A more substantial difference between the FRG and GDR is the breadth of individual channels of vertical mobility. Higher and secondary education in the GDR are more accessible to lower strata than in the FRG. In 1967 the proportion of students from workers' families was in the GDR only slightly below the percentage of workers in the population as a whole, whereas in the FRG the representation of workers' descendants in the student population was only one-seventh of the workers' proportion in the total population. Although in the GDR some groups were in an advantageous position – e.g. the sons and daughters of the intelligentsia were over-represented 2.6 times in comparison with the proportion in the population, the over-representation of the privileged in the West was much higher: the descendants of government officials were five-and-a-half times more numerous in the student population than their parents in the total population.

In comparison with 1960, workers' families representation in the student population of the GDR declined, whereas the descendants of white-collar employees, the intelligentsia and co-operative producers increased their proportion. A halt in this development might have been brought about by the change in the SED leadership in 1971, but as the East German establishment will further consolidate, the pressure for self-recruitment may be expected to continue.

The political channel of upward mobility is broader in the GDR than in the FRG. Data from different samples indicate that in the West only about 4 per cent of the élite was recruited from the category of workers; on the other hand, in the East the whole first generation of the new political élite has almost entirely been recruited from former workers. Moreover, this élite has been superimposed on other élites, i.e. the economic, administrative, military and cultural ones. The ascent through the political channel in the GDR however was dependent on joining some apparat, either that of the Party or of the state.

It is a legitimate question whether workers in power-apparats of the GDR have not become alienated from their social backgrounds. There are enough objective indications of possible conflict of interests; faster growth of productivity than of real wages is the most important one. On the other hand, workers in the GDR may be satisfied with their greater equality with white-collar employees whereas this issue seems to be still one of the reasons for dissatisfaction in the West.

It is difficult to assess workers' subjective feelings in this matter. In the West, the public opinion polls point in diverging directions. Some earlier research shows a comparatively high acceptance of authority by West German lower strata and consequently a widespread readiness to accept the *status quo*. A more recent poll however indicates a growing feeling that the class struggle is a necessary condition of modern life. Especially urban strata and young members of the intelligentsia expressed their approval with this type of strife. Also data on industrial disputes point in that direction.

For the GDR there are no comparable surveys: the only indicator of dissent was the exodus out of the country. Since the construction of the Berlin Wall in 1961, however, such a solution has become extremely risky. Apparently the much greater vertical mobility in the GDR was achieved at the expense of drastic limitations in horizontal mobility in a geographical sense.

There was also some scope for downward mobility in both parts of Germany as a result of the war. The GDR was more affected than the FRG by direct war action with dismantling and reparation, but she was able to pass over the burden connected with the absorption of expelled and refugees to the FRG. The immigrants' high propensity to work, coupled with the energetic reconstruction measures and foreign aid, gave West Germany a good start. An unprecedented increase in productivity and generous schemes for sharing the burden provided the basis for intercepting the possible downward mobility of broad strata in the West.

The GDR recovered later but then achieved a considerable rate of growth too. In the GDR, there was an additional cause of downward mobility on a large scale, namely the expropriation of private entrepreneurs and discriminatory banning of their children from higher education. On the whole, however, in both the FRG and the GDR increased educational facilities and continuous economic growth, which was only temporarily interrupted by stagnation, were more favourable for upward rather than downward mobility.

Notes

1. Helmut Schelsky, 'Die Bedeutung des Schichtungsbegriffes für die Analyse der gegenwärtigen deutschen Gesellschaft' (1953), in *Auf der Suche Nach Wirklichkeit,* Düsseldorf-Köln, 1965.
2. Ralf Dahrendorf, *Society and Democracy in Germany,* Engl. transl. London, 1968.
3. Helmut Schelsky, op. cit., pp. 331–5.
4. Morris Janowitz, 'Social Stratification and Mobility in West Germany', *American Journal of Sociology,* 1958, pp. 23–4.
5. Karl M. Bolte, *Deutsche Gesellschaft im Wandel,* Opladen, 1970, Band 2, p.332.
6. H. Moore and G. Kleining, 'Soziale Selbsteinstufung, Ein Instrument zur Messung sozialer Schichten', in *Kölner Zeitschrift für Soziologie und*

Sozialpsychologie, 19, 1968, pp. 502–52.
7. Another research in self-identification reported by E. K. Scheuch ('Sozialprestige und Soziale Schichtung', in *Kölner Zeitschrift für Soziologie und Sozialpsychologie*, XIII, 1961, p. 76) revealed the relative preference of two samples for different criteria of stratification: one was undertaken in Cologne in 1957 and the other in the whole of the FRG in 1959. The difference between the two polls was striking. In the whole of the FRG, vocational categories as indicators of strata topped the list (37.5 per cent whereas in Cologne the amount of income and living standard scored most points (35.2 per cent). Vocational categories were second in Cologne (24.6 per cent) and income and living standard were second in the whole of the FRG (7.8 per cent). (The strongly represented category of 'other models' (40.7 per cent) in the FRG is not considered because of the vagueness of the label covering very differentiated contents.)

The proportion of respondents favouring the Marxist point of view was negligible (0.9 per cent in the FRG and 3.6 per cent in Cologne). Non-antagonistic models were favoured more in both cases, but in quite different proportions (FRG 87.1 per cent, Cologne 47.6 per cent); antagonistic models scored 3.5 per cent in the FRG and 33.0 per cent in Cologne. The FRG sample was also more in favour of multi-dimensional models (FRG 60.0 per cent, Cologne 34.3 per cent), whereas a one-dimensional model was preferred in Cologne (50.9 per cent against 31.0 per cent in the whole of the FRG).
8. For explanation of this term see further below.
9. Ralf Dahrendorf, *Society and Democracy in Germany*, London, 1968, pp. 109–10.
10. Ralf Dahrendorf, op. cit., p. 107–8.
11. Janowitz, op. cit., p. 15.
12. ibid., p. 16.
13. For some more models of social stratification of West German society after 1945 see Dahrendorf, op. cit., pp. 88 and ff.
14. There was however some indication that a part of the working class, especially some of their young ones, are losing the sense of class identification and acquiring rather middle-class attitudes. (Dahrendorf quotes especially the findings of K. Bednarik and H. Kluth.) Although this might be significant, in view of our multi-dimensional approach this question might be left open.
15. Dahrendorf, op. cit., p. 92.
16. Two names especially have to be mentioned in this context: Stanislav Ossowski, *Class Structure in the Social Consciousness*, London, 1963, and W. Wesolowski, *Klasy, Warstwy i Wladza*, Warszawa, 1966.
17. *Bericht*, 1972, p. 172, translated by the author.
18. Schewe-Nordhorn, *Übersicht über die Soziale Sicherung*, Bonn, 1970, p. 135.
19. For details see Detlev Zöllner and Achim André, *Labour and Social Security*, Bonn-Bad Godesberg, 1973, pp. 17 and 23.
20. Calculated from *SJB DDR*, 1971, p. 144.
21. Data from S. Münke, *Die Mobile Gesellschaft*, Berlin-Köln-Mainz, 1967, p. 127.
22. *SJB DDR*, 1971, p. 124.
23. The GDR official statistics include in this category five-twelfths of those in the age bracket from 14–15.
24. *Zahlenspiegel*, 1973, pp. 8 and 28.
25. Institut für Demoskopie, Allensbach, April 1968, *Pressedienst Report*.
26. See the results of a comparative poll on attitudes concerning national pride undertaken in 1959 in five countries and reported in G. A. Almond and S. Verba, *The Civic Culture*, Princeton, 1963, p. 102.
27. It may be worth noting that in Communist Poland also the academic

professions were considered to be the most prestigious occupations: university professor, doctor of medicine and schoolteacher headed the list. For more details see M. Vaughan, 'A Multi-dimensional Approach to Contemporary Polish Stratification', *Survey*, No. 1, Winter 1974, p. 70. On the other hand the Czech scale of prestige put the doctor of medicine before the university professor, who did not do particularly well in either sample; in one opinion poll he scored 4th and in another, 10th place. On the whole, however, the academic or highly qualified technical professions headed the lists. It must also be added that on one scale member of government (minister) ranked first. For more details see J. Krejci, *Social Change and Stratification in Postwar Czechoslovakia*, London, 1972, pp. 99–100.

28. *SJB DDR*, 1974, p. 66.
29. *SJB BRD*, 1974, p. 94; *Bericht*, 1971, p. 414; *SJB DDR*, 1973, pp. 374–5.
30. Ralf Dahrendorf, *Society and Democracy in Germany*, pp. 232 and 233.
31. ibid., p. 235.
32. For more details see *Bericht*, 1971, pp. 188 and ff.
33. Figures in this scheme do not however do full justice to the comparative levelling of officials' income. The list of tariff salaries of government officials valid from 1 July 1972 puts the highest salary of a married official at approximately four times that of the lowest salary of a man with the same marital status. (*SJB BRD*, 1972, p. 486.)
34. Already in our inquiry on the capacity of income to produce wealth in the second section we have pointed to the high range of income differentiation among pensioners.
35. DIW Economic Bulletin 7, 1974, pp. 65–6.
36. *Bericht*, 1974, p. 496.
37. Also Czechoslovak data point in a similar direction. In the middle sixties the combined net *per capita* income (in money and in kind) of co-operative farmers' households in Czechoslovakia exceeded the combined *per capita* income of workers' households and was almost 7 per cent above the national average. (For more details see J. Krejci, *Social Change and Stratification in Postwar Czechoslovakia*, pp. 76–80.)
38. *Demoskopie Jahrbuch*, p. 354.
39. It has to be realised within this context that the party membership of parents is a relevant factor when children are to be selected for schools with a *de facto numerus clausus*. This type of differentiation might also go hand in hand with what Ludz calls 'reconsolidation of white collar strata'.
40. For a penetrating, comprehensive appraisal of the transfer of power from Ulbricht to Honecker, see Fred Oldenburg, 'Konflikt and Konfliktregelung in der Parteiführung der SED 1945–46 – 1972', in *Berichte des Bundesinstituts für Ostwissenschaftliche und internationale Studien*, Köln, 48, 1972, pp. 68 and ff.
41. *SJB DDR*, 1971, p. 487 and 1974, p. 479.
42. Hermann Marcus, *Die Macht der Mächtigen*, Düsseldorf, 1970, p. 100.
43. Data as reported in Wolfgang Zapf, *Wandlungen der Deutschen Elite*, München, 1965, p. 45.
44. Results of an investigation reported by W. Zapf, *Beiträge zur Analyse der Deutschen Oberschicht*, München, 1965, p. 27.
45. ibid.
46. *SJB DDR*, 1971, p. 487.
47. *Übersicht über die Soziale Sicherung*, Der Bundesminister für Arbeit und Sozialordnung, 1970, pp. 198, 215, 216; K.M. Bolte, *Deutsche Gesellschaft im Wandel*, Opladen, 1967, Vol. I, p. 139.
48. op. cit., p. 198.

49. op. cit., p. 216.
50. Calculated from *Bericht*, 1974, pp. 232 and 235.
51. If there is a temporary setback, for a couple of years only, the effect of the drop in income on the living standard might be negligible; as long as it can be cushioned by drawing on savings, it does not amount to social decline. Only a prolonged depression like that in the early thirties brings about irreparable downward shifts in stratification.
52. *Bericht*, 1971, p. 369, and *Bericht*, 1974, p. 235.
53. *Economic Bulletin* of DIW, supplement 1974, Vol. II.
54. *SJB DDR*, 1974, pp. 39, 41 and 42.
55. Harrland, 'Zwanzig Jahre Kampf für die Zurückdrängung der Kriminalität in der DDR', in *Neue Justiz*, 23, 1969, p. 389, quoted in *Bericht*, 1972, p. 236.
56. *Gesetzbuch der Arbeit und andere ausgewählte rechtliche Bestimmungen*, Staatsverlag der DDR, 1969, p. 31.
57. Workers in the GDR are materially responsible for any damage caused by wilful (*vorsätzlich*) or negligent (*fahrlässig*) behaviour. In the case that damage is caused by negligent behaviour, the indemnity is limited to one month's salary, if the damage is caused wilfully, the amount of indemnity is unlimited (*Das Gesetzbuch der Arbeit*, p. 49). In the FRG, indemnity can be required only in the case of wilful damage or damage committed because of gross negligence. Such cases are however, within the employment relationship, rare.
58. B. Jungmann, 'Sebehodnoceni a sebeidentifikace (self-evaluation and self-identification)', in *Československá společnost*, ed. P. Machonin, Bratislava, 1969, pp. 365 and ff.
59. J. Krejci, *Social Change and Stratification in Postwar Czechoslovakia*, pp. 122–3.
60. *SJB BRD*, 1972, p. 15.
61. Free translation from Alex Müller, *Kommentar zum Gesetz zur Förderung der Stabilität und des Wachstums der Wirtschaft*, Hannover, 1969, pp. 75 and 88.
62. For a review of the respective provisions of the Labour Code of the GDR see *Das Gesetzbuch der Arbeit der DDR*, edited by Friedrich-Ebert-Stiftung, Bonn-Bad Godesberg, 1971, pp. 10 and ff. For wording of art.24 according to the Constitution of 1974, see *Deutschland Archiv*, 1974, No. 11, pp. 1199–1200.
63. Dahrendorf, op. cit., pp. 111 and ff.
64. Almond and Verba, *Civic Culture*, 1963, pp. 217 and ff.
65. L. E. Edinger, *Politics in Germany*, Boston, 1968, pp. 100–101.
66. Almond and Verba, op. cit., pp. 225–7; reprinted by permission of Princeton University Press.
67. *Allensbacher Berichte*, 1972, No. 11, and *Demoskopie Jahrbuch*, p. 347.
68. *Demoskopie Jahrbuch*, p. 491.
69. Ibid.
70. Data from *UN Year Books of Labour Statistics*.
71. R. Dahrendorf, op. cit., p. 443.
72. Information released by the government of the FRG in August 1974.
73. *Soziale Sicherung*, p. 271.

4 POWER AND FREEDOM

4a. Conceptual considerations

Literature on the power structure in Germany is abundant, but unequal in scope and empirical documentation. There has been much more written on the West than on the East. On the whole, the main interest of scholars has been attracted to the problem of élites and here again, more to 'who they are' than to 'what they do'.

In focusing on 'who they are' and not 'what they do' (what kind of power they wield), i.e. in assessing only the social structure and not the range of decision-making, one gets only a partial insight into the different social systems, an insight which in its partiality may be misleading. The whole complex of concentration or deconcentration of power is ignored, a complex important not only for a proper under-standing of the position of élites but also, and this still more cogently, of the position of anyone subordinated to those in power.

The concern of those below is not only whether they can climb to the top and if so how, but what they can do without interference from above. Not only vertical mobility, but also the range (*Spielraum*) of self-assertion is what matters for those in subordinate positions. For them it is not only who is at the top, or who is running the business or the country that is important, but how far this running helps or interferes with their own activity and enjoyment of life. This is the dimension of power which extends beyond the concept of stratification.

Unfortunately, there is one serious complication with this particular dimension: its different evaluation and, as a consequence, conceptualisation in the two countries under comparison. Whereas in the West, individual self-assertion is understood as synonymous with individual freedom and this is considered as one of the supreme or end values, in the East the concept of freedom stands for something quite different.

In the West it has been accepted as a matter of common sense that the scope of one's own freedom is in inverse relationship to someone else's power. Max Weber fully grasped this relationship when he conceived power as the possibility of enforcing one's own will against the position of others within a social relationship. Consequently freedom is the possibility of behaving according to one's own will without the direct restraint of others or without menace by the

retaliatory action of others. The less power on one side of a social
relationship, the more freedom on the other and vice versa.

The Marxist-Leninist concept of freedom however is quite different:
a German Marxist-Leninist put it as follows:

> Freedom is the domination of men over nature and social relation-
> ships, a domination based on scientific cognition of the laws of
> nature and society. It is the capacity of men to shape their life
> conditions by means of expert decisions based on the knowledge of
> objective laws ('entsprechend der Erkenntnis der objektiven
> Gesetzmässigkeiten').[1]

Such a concept of freedom of course cannot be equated with the same
term used in a quite different sense in the West. Whereas in the West it is
primarily an individual capacity, in the East it is considered as a collective
one. It is conceived not as a freedom of *man* but as freedom of *men.* 'Not
individual activity but a social process of societal labour is the genuine
sphere of human realisation of freedom.'[2] In order not to be misled in the
consequences of the difference, one has to read the following statement
concerning the practical application of such an idea of freedom:

> Marxist-Leninists understand the freedom of men as the developing
> confrontation of men with their natural and social environment, a
> confrontation which is linked to objective social conditions and
> developed with increasing and deepening knowledge of objective laws.
> In the contemporary GDR for instance, we cannot make as a target
> that type of freedom as it will exist in the fully developed Communist
> societies. If we say that in the present, freedom means conscious
> social activity aimed towards realisation of socialism, so it is in full
> accord with objective laws of the historical process.[3]

So, freedom is not only a collective capacity but a developing capacity
changing with objective conditions of the environment and with men's
increasing knowledge of these conditions. As these conditions are
correctly understood by Marxism-Leninism ('the teaching of Marx is
almighty because it is true', said Lenin),[4] freedom is synonymous with
action aiming to achieve its forecasts. 'Free is he who acts in accordance
(*Übereinstimmung*) with, and consequently in discipline to, historical
requirements and in such a way serves towards the perfection of
human society.'[5] Consequently, in a capitalist society freedom equals
the struggle for socialist revolution, in a socialist society freedom equals

building of socialism. Whereas in the first case some spontaneity might be unavoidable, (revolutionary activity cannot be fully brought under unified command), in the second case (building of socialism) all activity has to assume planned forms. It is stressed again that the individual alone and for himself can neither be free nor become free.[6]

An additional argument for the concept of collective freedom is found in the realisation that only the society can master the objective laws of societal development.[7]

In the Marxist-Leninist view freedom is not necessarily an antithesis of power; on the contrary, freedom can under certain conditions coincide with power, namely if power is used in the direction of historical development, a development which only Marxist-Leninists are supposed to know and follow.

It is no wonder that under these circumstances the dialogue between Marxists and non-Marxists is extremely difficult. One of the basic Western values is *personal* freedom which does not find an adequate place among Marxist-Leninist values.

> Freedom is above all a class issue; as any individual belongs to a class, personal freedom is but a specific expression of the social position of this class. . . As under socialism and communism the working people for the first time have won genuine freedom so the individual has attained for the first time true freedom.[8]

Consequently it is not up to the individual to decide whether he is free or unfree; the question is settled by his class position and his class position in its turn is decided by the type of ownership of the means of production, i.e. eventually by political power.

Whereas for a non-Marxist freedom is a matter of individual cognition or rather feeling, for a Marxist-Leninist it is a matter of socio-economic formation or rather definition of it. Workers become free whether they realise it or not. If they do not agree and occasionally revolt, as in June 1953 in East Berlin, it is proof that they were misled by bourgeois propaganda. This follows logically from that definition of freedom.

In view of orthodox Marxist-Leninists, any weakening of conceptual rigidity may endanger this logic, any concession to individual evaluations may open the door to what is considered an 'ahistorical bourgeois' concept of freedom. Therefore any revision of the definition of freedom must be rejected and revisionists must be treated as enemies who have joined the hostile, by definition imperialist, camp.[9]

Although the Marxist-Leninist position in this matter is well known,
students of relationships and developments in the East are often
inclined to forget about it. Their endeavour to study reality ('pays
réel') rather than intention ('pays légal') may be justified only up to a
point. In doing so they can describe well the behaviour but hardly
understand it. For that purpose they have to know the rationale of
the political objectives and the main tenets of what everybody in a
Communist-dominated society is supposed to learn and 'internalise'.
Individuals have not only to obey the party leadership, they have to
accept it with enthusiasm, they have to identify their own wants and
value judgements with its wishes.

> Individual freedom consists in giving one's talents and energy to
> a common cause, it means spontaneous commitment. Unlike the
> bourgeois concept of personal freedom which wants to provide
> individuals with an area where he or she can, without respect to the
> interests of others, follow his or her private interests and
> propensities, Marxist personal freedom accepts the unhampered
> development of individual capacities and talents only in harmony
> with the needs of societal development.[10]

This is the most important feature of societies dominated by ideologically
strongly committed élites. In such societies individual members have to
prefer collective goals and devote their own energy to their achievement.
The individual is to be taught how he should feel about his position in
his society: he cannot conceive it spontaneously.

> Personal freedom under socialism is combined with the conscious
> acceptance (*Einfügung*) of the order and discipline for common
> action (*gemeinschaftlichen Aktionen*) whether it be vocational
> work, political struggle, etc. Otherwise it would mean individual
> licence (*Willkür*) leading to spontaneous development; then freedom
> understood as the active realisation of societal necessity would be
> undermined.[11]

Nothing can better illustrate the unbridgeable gap between Marxist-
Leninist and liberal evaluation than this juxtaposition. As long as this
dichotomy remains to constitute the pillars of value orientation in East
and West respectively, any convergence in substantial matters can
hardly be expected.

It can of course be questioned how far the Marxist-Leninist position is truly Marxist. The aforementioned question from the Communist Manifesto indicates that Marx's and Engels' way of reasoning was not so unilateral as their rather Leninist followers suppose. The 'classics' explicitly say in that passage: 'The full development of each is the condition for the full development of all.'[12] This however is of little use for our comparative analysis. We have to accept that the GDR ideology is not simply Marxist but Marxist-Leninist.

In this context one should realise that the Marxist-Leninist idea of collective rather than individual freedom falls on fertile ground in Germany. The challenge of the French Revolution and Napoleonic wars evoked in Germany a nationalistic response, with the idea of national independence or freedom as the highest value. The wars for liberation (*Befreiungskriege*) were followed by the fight for national unification, and in that form, self-assertion. The German idea of freedom became directed outwards. In Thomas Mann's words, 'It signified the right to be German and nothing else. It was a protesting idea of self-centred defence against everything that restricted and limited the national egoism, that tried to tame, control and bring it into the service of the community and humanity.'[13]

As in the contest for unification the Bismarckian alternative of 'blood and iron' won over that of 'social contract', the collective, outward-directed idea of freedom acquired the advantage of being more real, that is also in Hegel's sense more reasonable (*vernünftig*). Hegel helped, together with his apotheosis of the state, to promote respect for strength, subject competence and collective idea of freedom. This proved most helpful for all authoritarian régimes in Germany to come.

4b. Power élites, their nature and origin

Elites can be studied from two different angles: from the point of view of their personal composition and from the point of view of the content or scope of their power. Most studies of the topic have so far been mainly concerned with the former aspect. Wolfgang Zapf, the leading scholar in the study of German élites, although fully aware of this two-fold dimension,[14] has nevertheless paid more attention to 'who they are' and 'how they came to the top', than to 'what they do' and 'how far they can interfere in the life of other people'. Similarly, Peter C. Ludz, the most prominent expert on the East German élite, has so far been more devoted to its personal and ideological aspects and to the shifts in decision-making than to the content or extent of power itself.[15]

With the focus on the personal and vocational structure of the élite, Wolfgang Zapf arrives at the following basic differences between the

FRG and the GDR.

First, in the West German élite there is a majority with higher, mainly university, education, whereas in the GDR political reliability is the most important prerequisite for getting to the top.

Second, members of the West German élite have experienced as a rule a prolonged career in their respective vocations, whereas the East German élite is more often than not composed of newcomers.

Third, the recruiting ground of the West German élite is more confined to the upper strata, whereas the East German élite is more open to recruitment from the lower strata.

Fourth, according to Zapf, younger generations and women have better access to the top positions in the GDR.[16]

Although the last point requires some qualification (names and ages of the leading personalities indicate that the GDR is equally a male-dominated society with a larger representation of older rather than younger generation at the top as in the FRG),[17] Zapf's conclusions on the social origins of, and political prerequisites for, the élites are borne out by facts. In view of how the FRG and GDR were born this is an obvious truth; unfortunately features mentioned by Zapf contain only half-truths.

Dahrendorf showed deeper insight in the East/West comparison of the élites, when he said:

> The very fact that the reconstruction of society in the East of Germany begain in 1945 with the creation of a new political élite was a pointer to future developments. . . Its first steps consisted in the unification of the political class. After the enforced fusion of Communists and Social Democrats in 1946, the newly founded Socialist Unity Party turned to the suppression of the bourgeois parties. This process was supplemented by the creation of a number of satellite parties designed to mobilise hitherto undecided citizens. . . But unification of the political élite was merely the first step in a process that eventually brought about a new political class in the DDR. The second step was more difficult and more consequential; it led to the gradual fusion of élites from all sectors of society with the leadership of the party, or, where this did not succeed, to the subordination of all others to the party élite. Nationalisation of the economy and its administration by state functionaries, politicisation of the new army, reconstruction of the entire educational system, the legal system, the administration were some of the stages on this road. Only the church élites have managed to the present day to

resist to some extent the monopolistic claims of the new political class. On the whole, the second step in creating a new élite succeeded in its authors' terms surprisingly quickly.[18]

From the point of view of inter-systemic comparison this is a most relevant observation. Dahrendorf hints at the basic feature of the Communist power structure, namely the unification of political, ideological and economic domination. Without grasping the relevance of this unification, the difference between the uniform and multiple élites cannot be properly understood. In the East, there is much less scope for centrally non-supervised or non-regulated activities than in the West.

The uniformity versus multiformity of élite does not only concern the political orientation or belonging. The Communist élite is also, at least at the very top, functionally uniform. The Politburo of the Communist Party decides all issues irrespective of their specialist nature. Similarly the State Council which is the supreme legislative, executive and judiciary body of the GDR, and is composed predominantly of leading Communists, assumes competence in all fields of societal life. Local officials also supervise processes and decide issues in their areas without respect to the specialised aspects involved, but their power is not as comprehensive because some issues are reserved for the top decision of the central authority.

Otherwise middle echelons and lower echelons of the power structure are functionally and institutionally divided. This however has not much relevance because the specialised and legal decisions have to be in accordance with the political line set up from above. Moreover in each institution and association there are Communist Party groups which have to determine whether the political line is being followed.

Summing up, the difference between East and West can be outlined as follows: in the West, the main recruiting ground for new members of the élite is the ideologically and vocationally differentiated middle-class; the alternative ways of specialised advancement (political, professional or economic) lead to the top of the power hierarchy. In the East the recruiting ground for new members of the élite can be best labelled 'political class'. It consists of political activists — conformists with the party line. Only these people can get to and stay at the top not only of the political but of the specialised (economic, administrative, military, education etc.) hierarchy. Only in the first generation were they predominantly recruited from blue-collar workers. Since then the élite has become increasingly recruited from the new intelligentsia and officials. The Communist élite is uniform not only ideologically but largely also vocationally (most influential are party officials). Alternative ways of specialised advancement (in the economic, administrative and other careers) hardly reach the middle echelons of the power hierarchy. In Marxist reasoning the recruiting basis plays a more important role than the scope and intensity of power. The Marxist conventional supposition is that the élite serves the interests of that class from which it has been taken. This means the working class in the East and the bourgeoisie in the West. Neither, however, as many points analysed in this study indicate, is borne out by facts.

Dahrendorf's characterisation of the East German élite also includes one important point necessary for understanding the distinctions between East and West, namely the link with the past. Unfortunately, his concept of modernity as an analytical tool does not prove particularly helpful for that understanding. For the purpose of an intersystemic comparison, the story can perhaps be briefly retold in the following way.

The eleven years of Nazi rule in Germany eliminated from the German élite all elements not ready to co-operate with the Nazis (at least outwardly) and, with the exception of the churches, destroyed all the institutional bases of possible opposition. The collapse of Nazi rule resulted in a power vacuum which under the given conditions could be filled only with the support of occupation powers. The new power élite had a limited ground for recruitment. Its hard core in the West emerged from the debris of the pre-Nazi élite; in the East from the Communist leaders who survived either as inmates of Nazi concentration camps or as emigrants to Soviet Russia. The remnants of the pre-Nazi élite in the East were either absorbed by the Communist élites (Social Democrats willing to co-operate) or had to accept the Communist supremacy or leave for the West.

In both parts of Germany less prominent members of the Nazi élite were allowed, under certain provisions, to regain positions in the lower echelons of the power élite. Conditions were different in the FRG and GDR. In the West it was a matter of formal juridical procedure, so-called de-Nazification. Special committees of assizes (*Spruchkammer*) screened people in responsible jobs, especially in government service, and decided whether they could be considered acceptable or not for the democratic society and consequently to stay in their respective jobs or professions. As all this was undertaken in a formal way (most thoroughly in the American Occupation Zone where detailed questionnaires were used) where much depended on the presentation of the case, on testimonies and, last but not least, on the good will or connivance of the assizes, it is not surprising that many faithful Nazis were de-Nazified and consequently became 'good democrats'. There was of course a good reason for the leniency. There were just not enough non-Nazis available for staffing the apparat and the administration and, in the view of the occupation powers, economic reconstruction had priority over political considerations.[19]

In the East, the roles were reversed. Political reconstruction was of primary importance. Nevertheless the short supply of non-Nazis for administration and managerial jobs together with the political need to win mass support for the Communist régime made it necessary to undertake some conciliation with former Nazis. The usual Communist techniques were applied. Stricter retributive measures against the men at the top or with records of particular activities, and conciliatory measures of conversion for those who could be classified as merely seduced or misled elements. For their absorption into the new polity, not only spontaneously emerging bourgeois political parties were allowed to operate within the limited framework of ascribed roles but new political parties — the National Democratic Party and Democratic Farmers' Party were, within the same framework, set up. The *raison d'être* was to steer traditionally nationalist people into the Communist-dominated framework. The de-Nazification in the East was in a way more energetic than in the West. It combined more vigorous negative and positive measures; those who passed the screening became largely committed to the new régime and its ideology.

Here however one important point has to be raised: was the transition from Nazi to Communist rule and therefore the transformation from the Nazi to the Communist-orientated élite a smaller or a bigger step than the transformation of Nazi rule and élite into the liberal, parliamentary system and pluralistic multiple élite in the West? This is a question which can be answered differently according to the stress on individual elements of the respective social systems. In that sense the answer appears to be crucial for our own analysis.

Considering the content of the Nazi and Communist ideologies respectively, one finds a flagrant contradiction: the former is based on the myth of race, considering the unity, prosperity and expansion of the ethnic community as the supreme value. The latter is based on the apotheosis of the working class which, provided it has embraced the right consciousness of Marxism-Leninism, is supposed to build a truly human society in the future. Nazi parochialism and sense of ethnic strife is in deep contrast to the Communist internationalism and sense of eschatological unity of mankind.

Unlike the aims, the means are not so contradictory, and in many
respects are similar. Both Nazis and Communists were interested first of
all in the exclusive acquisition of power (*Machtergreifung*) with the help
of which they could materialise their ideals. In doing so both used
force against the non-conformists and dissidents. The Nazis were more
brutal, the Communists more sophisticated. Yet both had their political
trials, death sentences, illegal killings and concentration camps. Both
were concerned with mobilisation of the whole society to attain a
common purpose. Last but not least, both aimed at an exclusive
ideological command of all their subject citizens. Both insisted firmly
on a closed intellectual outlook, with compulsory principles of faith
which everybody had to accept.

For people of lesser intellectual capacity or inquisitiveness,
conversion from Nazism to Communism meant the substitution of one
definite view and/or security by another one. Conversion to a liberal
democratic world view, admitting alternative interpretations of reality
meant for many a jump into the void, a step into insecurity and
bewilderment from having to choose.

It is difficult to guess how many East Germans preferred the closed
security of one self-righteous world view and how many an open system
of ideological alternatives and political contradictions. We have to bear
in mind that people preferring security of closed systems exist everywhere, not only in Germany. But in Germany the authoritarian
tradition and 'subject competence' of citizens provided a particularly
favourable ground for the development and spread of such attitudes. Also
Also the particular circumstance that Marxist theory provided some
criteria for criticism of Leninist practice might have helped the
conversion of those who were not happy with the brutal reality; Nazi
myth had no such humanising antidote or consolation for the future
within its framework.

In this context the different sense of responsibility of the FRG and
GDR for Nazi atrocities has to be stressed. The West German
government considered the FRG as the true heir of pre-war Germany;
therefore it accepted moral and financial responsibility for Nazi wrongs.
The East German government considered the emergence of the GDR
as a revolutionary break with the past which it repudiated in words
beyond any doubt. Consequently, it does not feel any responsibility
for what happened under previous régimes. So there is an interesting
contrast; whereas the FRG was on the whole more lenient to former
Nazis, large amounts of compensation were paid to their victims;[20]
the GDR applied more rigorous punitive measures against the former

Nazis but did not compensate their victims.[21]

4c. Concentration and hierarchy of power in the GDR

The GDR has a hierarchical and uniform power élite which has been created and is preserved by the supremacy of the Communist Party. Technically the supremacy of the ruling party is safeguarded by what may be called a 'two-floor' junction of political hierarchy.

The top floor junction was constituted by the merger of the Communist and Social Democratic Parties on 21–22 April 1946 into the Socialist Unity Party (Sozialistische Einheitspartei Deutschlands). Formally it was a voluntary merger, but in effect, it was the first step in the process of gradual absorption and subordination of Social Democrats to the Communists. This is the more significant as both the Social Democratic Party membership and their vote were more numerous than those of the Communists. The only elections in the GDR which these two parties fought separately were those in the Soviet sector of Berlin on 20 October 1946 (in Berlin the unification materialised later than in the country as a whole). There, the Social Democrats received 43.6 per cent and Communists 29.8 per cent of the total vote.[22]

In spite of this, the posts in the Politburo and all other leading positions and functions within the Socialist Unity Party were distributed equally between the Social Democrats and Communists. Even this parity however was soon abolished. With the Soviet Army and political advisers in the country, the Socialist Unity Party (SED) was transformed into a party of a 'new type', i.e. a party based on two principles: ideological unity in Marxism-Leninism and 'democratic centralism' in its organisation. About 150,000 Social Democrats not adhering to these principles had to leave the Party.[23] Among them were many with positions in the Party apparat, and so the parity was abandoned; the recruitment of new officials took place according to the usual Communist practices.

Apart from allegiance to Marxism-Leninism there was the 'dialectical' principle of democratic centralism. The Statutes of the SED define it in the following way:

(a) All party organs from the bottom to the top are democratically elected.
(b) The elected party organs are obliged to regularly report on their activity to the organisations which elected them.
(c) All decisions of higher party organs are binding; strict discipline is required and the minority and individual have to abide in a

disciplined way by the decision of the majority.

In theory, it is an ideal combination of political input (para. a) and political output (para. c) with a certain possibility of feedback (para. b). In reality however, the provisions under (a) and (b) represent fiction whereas provision (c) stands for reality.

The democratic character of the political input is limited by further statutory provisions such as: all members are obliged to preserve the unity and purity of the Party (2a of the Party Statutes). Members are obliged not only to agree with Party decisions but to fight for them (para. 2b). They are obliged to behave towards the Party sincerely and honestly and be careful not to conceal or distort the truth from it (para. 2i). They are obliged to be vigilant (para. 2j), to defend the Party against hostile influences and elements and also against constituting factions (para. 32), and they are obliged to prevent the misuse of internal democracy in distorting the party line (para. 33).

Further on, paragraph 28 of the Statutes requires that new elections into the leading bodies have to guarantee the continuity of these bodies; for that particular purpose a certain number of their membership have to be re-elected. The renewal of the leadership takes place in a 'systematic' way which means that only a certain percentage has to be newly elected. The usual practice is that for new elections a general proposal is submitted by the retiring body or by the superior body. It is well known that there are no opposing votes.

On the other hand the output is fully centralised. Paragraph 39 of the Statutes reads: 'The Central Committee delegates the representatives of the Party into the supreme leading organs of the state and economy, and approves their candidates for the People's Chamber (Volkskammer).' The Central Committee steers the work of the elected government bodies and associations by means of the Party groups within them.

So the political élite is *superimposed* on other, possibly specialised, élites. Moreover, all institutions of the polity and society alike are supervised by the inherent cells of the Communist Party; the political élite *permeates* other élites.

Paragraph 69 of the Party Statutes states that wherever there are at least three Party members, a Party Group is to be set up. Its task is to strengthen the influence of the Party and defend its policy amongst the non-members; it is responsible for strengthening the Party and state discipline, it has to fight against bureaucratism and to control the fulfilment of the Party and government orders. The subsequent paragraph adds that the Party groups are obliged to follow strictly the lead of the superior Party organs.

This is not only in theory but also in practice; of all the Communist parties in Central Europe, the East German is considered to be the most disciplined.

The lower floor junction in the hierarchical structure of political power consists in the subordination of all other political parties to the SED. The technical means for this subordination are first, the National Front as an umbrella organisation and second, the hierarchical pattern of screening, the so-called 'Nomenklatur' system.[24]

The National Front is the Communist-led organisation of all political parties, i.e. the Socialist Unity Party and other so-called bloc parties and mass organisations. The bloc parties are: the Christian Democratic Union, the Liberal Democratic Party, the National Democratic Party and the Democratic Farmers' Party. David Childs gave them apposite characteristics when he described the East German CDU as 'Establishment Christians', the Liberal Democrats as 'Marxian Liberals', National Democrats as 'National Bolshevists' and Democratic Farmers' Party as 'Socialist Farmers'.[25]

According to the official report, the SED had, at the beginning of 1967, 1,770,000 members and candidates,[26] and all the other political parties in the GDR had about 250,000. Recently they have been encouraged by the First Secretary of the SED, Honecker, in his speech at the 13th Plenary Session of the Central Committee of the SED (12–14 December 1974), to bolster their total membership up to 350,000.[27]

The *raison d'être* of the allied (bloc) political parties is to intercept the political energy of non-Communists and to divert it from a possible opposition and channel it to the support of the Communist establishment. Two of these parties which are potentially identified with their counterparts in the West (Christian Democrats and Liberal Democrats) emerged spontaneously after the war. The other two were founded by the Communists in order to recruit support from the possibly hostile elements to the Communist régime: farmers and former military. Nationalist feelings of the latter have to be reconciled with a vision of a strong socialist fatherland which eventually may become the basis for a future reunification of Germany.[28]

The other members of the National Front are the mass organisations, i.e. trade unions (Freier Deutscher Gewerkschaftsbund), Youth Associations (Freie Deutsche Jugend), Womens Associations (Demokratischer Frauenbund Deutschlands) and the Association of Culture (Kulturbund). All the aforementioned organisations, i.e. the five political parties and the four mass organisations, send their delegates to the national and local assemblies according to an agreed representation. The proportions in the People's Chamber (Volkskammer) are as follows: SED 25.4 per cent, each of the four block parties 10.4 per cent (i.e. together 41.6 per cent) and the mass organisations have the rest, i.e. 33 per cent.[29] Although the party membership of the representatives of mass organisations is not stated, it can be expected that almost all of them are members of the SED. All leading bodies of these mass organisations are composed exclusively of Communists.[30]

The comparatively high percentage of non-Communists in the Volkskammer can be explained by the following circumstances: (a) all non-Communist representatives can get these positions only after having been screened by the Communists; (b) the People's Chamber has virtually no real power: it is a more or less rubber stamp institution. The real sovereign body in the state is the State Council. It wields the supreme legislative, executive and judiciary power. It can propose Bills to be discussed and passed by the People's Chamber (all proposals are duly passed).[31] It is competent to interpret the Constitution and other laws and has control over the activity of the supreme court. Also the highest executive body, the Council of Ministers, is subordinated to the State Council. In such a way the State Council wields supreme power both in economic and cultural matters. So it embodies the constitutional principle of the unity of powers,[32] in contrast to the separation of powers which is the basic principle of the constitution of the FRG. In January 1974, of the 25 members of the State Council, 16 were members of the SED, eight were members of the 'bloc' parties and one was without apparent political affiliation. The chairman and the five other members were simultaneously members of the Politburo of the SED.

At the beginning of 1974, of 360 leading positions in state and societal administration (members of the presidium of the People's Chamber, of the State Council, Ministers and vice-Ministers, Chairmen of government committees and agencies, Chairmen of county councils, members of presidia of mass organisations and Chairmen of professional associations), only 25 were non-Communist Party members; 302 were direct representatives of the SED and three were delegates of mass organisations in the presidium of the People's Chamber, i.e. indirect representatives of the SED.[33] Even the subordination of non-Communist Party members to the Communist Party is not considered to be a sufficient safeguard to admit these people into bodies where real decisions are taken.

In the lower echelons of power the representation of non-Communists is much higher. Of the local assemblies there was a similar percentage of representatives as in the People's Chamber but again we have to bear in mind that these are consultative rather than decision-making bodies and again their candidates have to undergo the screening of the *Nomenklatur* system.

The mere existence and thorough observance of the *Nomenklatur* system reveals more about the stratification of power in the GDR than any structural analysis of the élite.

The *Nomenklatur* system is described as the most important instrument of the cadre policy (*Kaderpolitisches Instrument*) of the Communist Party. The *Nomenklatur* is a list of leading positions in the party, state and economy, the incumbents of which depend on the approval of the respective *Nomenklatur* authority (*Nomenklatur-Stelle*). In the state and economic apparats these are the leading officials of the superior institution. The top party leadership has reserved for itself the right to decide upon the following *Nomenklatur* positions:

> government ministers,
> state secretaries,
> chiefs of the main divisions (Hauptabteilungsleiter),
> chairmen of District or Regional Councils,
> directors of the Union of Nationalised Enterprises (Vereinigung
>   Volkseigener Betriebe) and of the most important big enterprises,
> all chiefs of cadre-divisions (Hauptamtliche Kaderleute)
> all representatives abroad,
> the chief positions in the mass media,
> elected functions and membership in the People's Chamber
>   (Volkskammer),
> chief positions in the state and defence council, in district councils
>   (Bezirkstage), mass organisations and associated political parties
>   (Blockparteien).

The latter point is of particular importance. The dependence of non-Communist parties on the SED is ensured not so much constitutionally (Article 3 of GDR Constitution refers only to the National Front as the form of East German Democracy)[34] as institutionally: all important leading positions in those parties are subject to the approval of the respective cadre officials of the SED.

The most important basis for the decisions of the *Nomenklatur* authorities are the personal cadre files. These files contain not only personal and vocational data but also information relevant to the past and present political and moral attitudes and development of the persons in question. For this purpose applicants for more important jobs have to fill in extensive personal forms, one specimen of which is reproduced in translation in Appendix, Table A.15.

Nomenklatur authorities (*Nomenklaturstellen-Inhaber*) have their own apparatus — the cadre divisions, which maintain the personal files and keep them up to date. The web of cadre divisions spins round all national enterprises, government offices, education establishments, research, medical and social institutions, mass organisations such as trade unions, youth and women's organisations etc.[35] So, any movement on the stratification scale above a certain level is controlled, and the intensity of that control increases as one approaches the top.

The *Nomenklatur* and cadre-controlling system create a normative pattern of social stratification. As the old guard of the founding fathers of the GDR passes away, the actual stratification will be increasingly shaped by the cadre policy.

Whereas in the West the rigidities of the stratification barriers are given by inertia, by forces of accommodation, in the East new barriers are being built up, barriers which have nothing to do with the socio-economic status but depend exclusively on ideological conversion or at least political conformity.

Recently there has been some speculation whether or not the monolithic structure of Communist power has been weakened by more specialisation at the bottom of the pyramid.

Among others, Peter Ludz suggested that the East German élite has acquired, since approximately the middle sixties, some new features. His findings can be summarised as follows:

(a) The guiding organisational principles have been shifted and the emphasis went over from political to social and economic considerations.

(b) Operational style of problem-solving in the bureaus led to an increase in functional authority and in mobility.

(c) Central committee often functioning for years as a purely acclamatory and declamatory assembly is becoming an active and transforming body.

(d) Within the SED the older generation is being replaced by new, more highly-qualified party functionaries and there is an increase in professional mobility.

(e) There is a continuing process of professionalisation and a clear separation in functional areas of party and the state apparatuses.

(f) There is not as much interchangeability of position as was assumed previously.

On two further points Ludz's views deserve to be quoted in full:

(g) 'The increased functional separation among, and increased autonomy of, the large party and state organisations has greatly facilitated the discernment of the centers of power of the strategic clique and the institutionalised counter élite. The strategic clique continues to dominate the real decision-making bodies — i.e., the Politburo and the Central Committee Secretariat — and fills the positions of first secretary in the SED Bezirk and Kreis executives, as well as in the State Council. Centers for the aggregation of party experts are, for example, the Council of Ministers, the State Planning Commission, the Research Council, and, to some degree, the Central Committee itself.

(h) The representatives of the institutionalised counter élite . . . seek to strengthen the political and social systems of the GDR. They can therefore be regarded as major spokesmen of a new political élite. Nevertheless, their thought is still based largely on the dogmatic ideology of dialectical and historical materialism. However, it can be definitively stated that there has been a recognition of the priorities of technical and economic progress and an awareness of processes of differentiation and ongoing dynamic changes in the GDR's society, coupled with the vision of a permanent increase in productivity. These developments provide the prerequisites for further processes of rationalisation of the new élite's outlook, which could facilitate its further attunement to the needs and realities of GDR society.'[36]

On the whole these changes are characterised by Ludz as a development from a totalitarian to an authoritarian stage or, in more concrete terms, into the 'consultative authoritarian' type of society.[37]

Although all the individual changes may be correctly assessed and the partial setbacks brought about by the Honecker ascent to power may be only temporary, Ludz's theoretical evaluation seems to be an over-statement.

Any system which has been imposed by force on the nation needs a certain strategy and technique of internalisation by its subjects. Stabilisation of any such system must pass from a more military and political stage to a more civil and technical one. This requires greater stress on qualification, more stable division of labour and last but not least, wider scope for discussion on how to find the best means for attaining the programmatic goals. Also the necessity of solving unanticipated problems requires a more pragmatic orientation.

But does this mean that the system is changing so much that it might be useful to characterise it by another general label? (A Marxist would say, 'Did the quantitative changes overgrow to a qualitative change?') Can we say that East German society ceases to be totalitarian and starts to be authoritarian, and this of a particular type — consultative authoritarian?

If terms such as authoritarian and totalitarian have to be used for different types of government or social systems, the difference between the contents of these concepts should concern something more essential, something with more systemic relevance, than are changes or shifts discovered by Ludz in the East German élite.

S.M. Lipset has pointed out one essential difference which, indicating the intensity of power, might be considered as systemic. Inspired by Sigmund Neumann's distinction between parties of integration and parties of representation, Lipset suggested that in a totalitarian régime one is expected to give total loyalty to the régime, whereas in an authoritarian régime one is expected to keep out of politics.[38]

Those who have lived under different types of régime can best appreciate the relevance of this distinction. The author may be allowed to recollect his own experience:

The Nazi rule in Bohemia and Moravia during World War Two was clearly authoritarian. Unlike their German neighbours, the Czechs were not required to embrace the Nazi ideology and to fight in the war, but just to keep quiet and work for the Reich. The political opposition was suppressed but politically neutral (escapist) cultural activities were not hampered. Under the Communist régime, the Czechs were expected to embrace the state philosophy of Marxism-Leninism and actively and joyfully participate in building up socialism; not only political opposition was suppressed, but also the escapist cultural activities were discouraged and more often than not deprived of publicity.

Similarly, another relevant distinction can be mentioned with respect to the degree of concentration of power. Government grip is much more efficient if it commands not only the means of compulsion and education, but also the means of production. Marx was well aware of the three kinds of domination, but failed to imagine the full social impact of their institutional concentration.

So far, most dictatorships or authoritarian rules were satisfied with the concentration of political power only, and with the dominant influence on education; they neither required indoctrination of all citizens, nor expanded their command over the means of production.

They preferred to strengthen the economic rule of traditional owners whose allegiance they expected to gain in return. State ownership, central planning and hierarchical management of the means of production combined with concentration of political and ideological power (one political party and one state philosophy) are other possible characteristics which may define a totalitarian system.

Now to return to Ludz's systemic considerations. Has anything of the relevant variables mentioned above changed in the GDR? Are the citizens less expected to give total loyalty? Are the non-Marxist-Leninist ideologies more tolerated? Has the scope of self-determination of the satellite political parties increased? Has the government command over the means of production been really decentralised?

Nothing of this nature has happened. The scope of discussion within the ruling élite has been somewhat enlarged, and new men, better-educated, have replaced the old guard of self-made men. Moreover, the experiment of a limited economic deconcentration — or as it is often labelled in the West, liberalisation — has been abandoned. But even if it were continued, it would hardly be understood as an abandoning of the principle of one ownership.

In my opinion, only cybernetics, recommended by several Marxist theoreticians, could introduce an element of qualitative systemic change, but for that purpose it should be elaborated in practical, organisational, rather than in theoretical terms. So far, cybernetic and similar considerations seem to be, to borrow Almond's terms, a part of the exoteric (i.e. window-dressing) rather than the esoteric (i.e. operative) doctrine of the party, yet what is still more important is that the cybernetic, technocratic orientation seems to have suffered a setback with the replacing of Walter Ulbricht by Honecker as the First Secretary of the SED.

Whereas the ageing Ulbricht believed that East Germany might become a modern, powerful, more or less technocratically managed state which could eventually overtake the West and become the rallying point for reunification, the younger Honecker preferred to return to the prolonged class struggle with more stress on vertical social mobility and equalisation, and to an external policy which stressed integration within the Soviet bloc, rather than fostering expectations for all-German unity.[39]

If counter-élite is a strong label for diverging views within the East German élite, could perhaps the emergence of 'pressure groups' be considered as a more fitting characteristic of the present change within East German society? This seems to be more sensible: army, police and individual branches of heavy industry often happen to be in the position of influential competitors for resources or privileges allocated by the central leadership. The main field of such competition is the drawing up of the economic plan and preparation of the state budget. Each of these groups, including the other less influential industries, tries to get as much as possible of the national resources allocated by the plan and budget. There is no other way for these groups to compete. Even in view of the allocation of resources however, the outcome of pressurising is not automatic. The strength of the respective groups is closely connected with their respective positions within the Communist Party and their importance with regard to party policy. We have also to bear in mind that the Communist leadership is, in a state like the GDR, not absolutely free to decide the controversial issues. The general policy is decided in Moscow. There in its turn the Politburo might have to deal with similar pressure groups among which, recently, the generality seems to have acquired substantial weight.

Consequently, all the pressure groups operate within a rigid pattern of party institutions and ideology. They do not enjoy freedom of action, let alone the independence of 'platform' or institutionalisation which their counterparts enjoy in the West. In that sense Michael Waller is right when he says:

> It is difficult to conclude that anything worthy of the name of pressure-group politics is on the cards in Eastern Europe for some time to come, if ever. Far safer would it be to conclude that we are dealing with the old monopolistic party-state (or apparat state), operating now with a much improved feedback potential, in an atmosphere radically changed since Stalinist days by the effective removal of terror.[40]

Is then the improved feedback or absence of outright terror enough to justify Ludz's thesis that East Germany is changing from a totalitarian to an authoritarian consultative system? In our view a truly consultative system presupposes greater margin for deliberation than is provided by the East German establishment. There, any consultative views have to be put forward within the scope of Marxist-Leninist orthodoxy if they are to have any chance of being accepted and if the 'consultant' has to preserve its consultative function. Feedback on the other hand can consist in a realisation of limits for certain action. These limits can be brought home in a non-consultative way, as for instance was the continuous escaping of doctors and other specialists from the GDR. The government was ready to take a lesson from this phenomenon. It increased the salaries of the vital professions and sealed the border more efficiently by erecting the Berlin Wall. By doing so, however, it closed, as Dahrendorf rightly observed, one of the safety valves which enabled the GDR to get rid of malcontents. Consequently the GDR authorities have to watch the situation more carefully; they have to diffuse explosive situations by either meeting the most acute grievances or by destroying any possible focus of institutionalised dissent, a possible germ of counter-élite. For that purpose reports by the secret police might be more important than open discussion. All of this can be described as an improvement of feedback potential but hardly an improved system of consultation.

Finally the question of terror. In this respect the change in East Germany was the least conspicuous of all the Communist countries. First of all, in the GDR Stalinist terror assumed less violent forms than elsewhere. There were no executions of top Communists as in the USSR, CSSR, Hungary, Rumania, Bulgaria and Albania. There were not even as many fabricated trials as in Poland. Stalinist terror operated mainly outwards and was, in comparison with other Communist-dominated countries, milder. Consequently, there was less scope for its abolition.

Paradoxically, the same reason which apparently made terror milder in the fifties tended in the sixties to require stricter measures than elsewhere in the Eastern bloc: this was and still continues to be the proximity of a highly attractive FRG; moreover there was, until August 1961, the easy escape route through unwalled Berlin. Because of its geographical position the GDR had, from the beginning, to keep a certain balance between the ruthless reality and the pleasant window dressing of its dominant ideology. In that sense its inhabitants were luckier in the fifties and less fortunate in the sixties than other Communist-dominated nations in Europe.

4d. Structure of power and influence in the FRG

Much more abundant information is available on power relationships in West Germany than in the GDR. Much of it has also been published in English.[41] Consequently, our account can be very brief — simply a review of salient features.

It has been widely stressed that in contrast to the East, the Western élite is multiple (Dahrendorf) or polyarchic (Edinger). Multiplicity of élite is obvious in the political sphere. Five or even more political parties are competing for the allegiance of the West German voters. The ideological spectrum of these five parties is very wide, from the far right-wing, almost neo-Nazi, National Democratic Party, to the tough, almost Stalinist, Communist Party. The fact that these two extreme parties have not yet attracted enough votes to obtain their representation in the federal and state diets does not invalidate the possibility of multiple choice with genuinely wide differences. Even if the focus of observation is limited to the three parties' representation in the diets, one finds a quite considerable difference in outlook, especially between left-wing Socialists and the Christian Social Union.

Furthermore, the West German élite is multiple from the functional point of view. It is one of the most typical marks of the Western social system that both economy and culture enjoy a considerable autonomy from political interference. Economic issues are widely solved by competition (in the market relationsihp) or in a contractual way, by agreement either between enterprises or between management and labour. Both management and trade unions are only partly, probably only marginally, responsible to the government for their actions. The scope of political power is in this respect, by comparison with the East, very limited.

Only in the field of education is the government in a stronger position. Even here, however, its power is not uniform. As the FRG is a federal and not a unitary state and as education is within the competence of individual Länder (states), the educational policy, and consequently government interference, varies geographically according to the ruling party in the respective Länder. The Bavarian government keeps the educational line rather conservative whereas for example, Hessen and Bremen have allowed Marxist-Leninists to operate quite freely in their universities.

The situation is also contradictory with respect to the mass media. Although the economic élite has a good stake there, owning newspapers and popular periodicals (Springer concern etc.), a few leftist publishing houses pour forth a flood of Marxist-Leninist literature both heretic and orthodox, which is indistinguishable from the East German counterpart. Although the consumer market for the Springer Press is much wider than that for Marxist literature, the greater purposefulness of the latter and also its specific target destination (it is aimed mainly at students — the future élite) make it, in a way, a more powerful weapon than the ideologically diluted press which in order to attract its customers, has also to satisfy the lower instincts of the 'sovereign' consumer.

In television too the so-called 'Third Programme' provides the public with a critical, often leftist evaluation of current events and developments. Although it cannot be characterised as counter-systemic, it gives the counter-élite a certain scope to express their views. The boundary between élite and counter-élite is of course extremely difficult to draw because of the wide spectrum of nuances. On the whole however the main criterion can be seen in the allegiance to parliamentary rules. Consequently, the whole of the so-called extra-parliamentary opposition can be considered as counter-systemic in that sense.

Any criticism which embodies the principle that all changes have to be achieved through the constitutionally legitimate bodies, must be considered as within the system. Only those who reject parliamentary rules, and do not consider the extra-parliamentary opposition as a pressure group only (devised to put pressure on legitimate bodies), but as a means which eventually will enforce a change irrespective of the position of constitutional bodies have, in our view, to be considered as anti-systemic and, as far as they wield some power or influence, as counter-élite.

It is also extremely difficult to evaluate the respective strength of individual élites and of possible shifts in development. It is also hardly possible to assess the influence of individual focuses of power. The only assessable magnitude is the subjective evaluation in an opinion poll.

The Institute of Demoscopy asked a sample of 981 parents of children aged 2—25 the following question: 'Which institution or or group in your opinion has excessive influence on contemporary political life in the FRG?' The respondents were allowed to mention more than one group or institution. The results are reproduced in Table 4.1.

Although the sample is not a comprehensive one, it is representative for about one half of the adult population in the FRG. If answers are put together according to some more general criteria, we can draw the following conclusions: most people in the sample were concerned with the excessive power of big business (employers' organisations, big banks, the federation of industry, farmers' associations); together they scored 92 points. Second, with 59 points, were those concerned with the excessive influence of the Press (items 3, 4 and 11 of Table 4.1). Equal numbers of respondents mentioned the excessive power of the trade unions and student organisations respectively, 46 points each. Religious bodies who were considered to wield excessive power totalled 40 points and representatives of former, defeated élites, 19 points.

Table 4.1 Influential Bodies in Public Opinion — (FRG 1971)

	Total	Men	Women
1. Trade unions	46	49	44
2. Employers' organisations	29	39	20
3. The Springer Press	28	36	22
4. *Bild-Zeitung*	27	34	21
5. Big banks	26	34	19
6. Certain students' organisations	24	23	26
7. The Federation of Industry	23	30	16
8. The Catholic Church	23	28	19
9. Leftist students	22	23	22
10. Farmers' associations	14	18	10
11. *Der Spiegel*	14	15	13
12. Former Nazis	10	11	8
13. Former emigrants and the politically persecuted	9	11	7
14. The Protestant Church	8	11	5
15. The Jewish Association	6	7	5
16. The Freemasons	3	4	2
17. No opinion	21	14	27
Total	333	387	286

Source: *Demoskopie Jahrbuch,* 1968–1973, p. 217.

If these data are rearranged on more political lines, one realises that
more people were concerned with the excessive power of conservative
bodies (big business, the Springer Press including *Bild-Zeitung,* the
Catholic Church, former élites etc.) than with the bodies more or less
favouring social change (trade unions, students, *Der Spiegel*). The
respective strengths were 189 against 106 points; this is roughly the
ratio of 1.8:1.0. The rest (Protestants, Jews and Freemasons) with 17
points are considered ambivalent in this juxtaposition.

   If the sample is broken down by sex, a significant difference
emerges. Women were less prone to express their views and if they did
so, the dislike of right and left-wing power was more equally divided.
The respective scores were 127 to 105 points. On the other hand men's
greater concern about conservative power was very apparent: 219 to
110 respectively.

   However cautiously we may interpret these data, one result seems
to be beyond doubt: they do not bear witness to any uniform
manipulation of the respondents' minds. They indicate concern about
the excessive influence of different élites, possibly also about counter-
élites. They reflect the existence of a multiple élite and the subjective
evaluation of the strength of individual groups within it.

Individual opinion however is prone to being wrong; it can reflect only impressions. Therefore it seems worth while to look for some more objective, factual indicators. This might be especially useful with respect to the widely believed collusion of economic and political power. In this field there are some interesting results provided by Hermann Marcus. On the basis of data from 115 of the largest industrial enterprises in 1968[42] he found out that of the 978 top managers of these enterprises, only 23 were politically active.[43] The others apparently preferred to enjoy their economic power alone. As far as their interest in politics is concerned, this seems, according to Marcus's findings, to have been limited to keeping the other forces away from their own domain.

The 115 enterprises analysed by Marcus provided 38 per cent of industrial employment, half of the total turnover of West German industry, and two-thirds of its exports. Their real capital was evaluated at DM 73,000 million.[44] However impressive these figures may be, they indicate anything but a monopolistic situation. Nor was the ownership of the 115 industrial giants monopolistic. Marcus investigated this ownership structure according to the majority holdings; the result is reproduced in Table 4.2

Table 4.2 Dominant Influence in 115 Industrial Giants
Federal Republic of Germany 1968

Dominant Influence	All firms	With Turnover		
		over DM 4,600 million each	between DM 1,100 and DM 4,500 million each	below DM 1,000 million each
State	21	3	5	13
Families	47	2	12	33
Foreigners	22	—	15	7
Managers	16	5	6	5
Banks	5	—	1	4
Mixed forms	4	—	1	3
Total	115	10	40	65

Source: H. Marcus, *Die Macht der Mächtigen*, p. 68.

The following has to be added to the figures in the table: the state influence was mainly concentrated in the car, energy and oil industries;

foreigners had strong positions in the car and oil industries, but, suprisingly, also in the food industry; banks were directly involved mainly in the non-ferrous metal and stone and earthenware industries; the steel and chemical industries were mostly governed by managers themselves; all other branches were the domain of family enterprises.[45]

The small number of firms where the influence of banks is dominant is surprising. Marcus explained it by the fact that banks are content with participation through holding companies (*Schachtel-beteiligung*). This, since it involves slightly over 25 per cent, does not amount to a dominant position, but allows the banks enough influence on the development policy of the firm. This influence, of course, can be fully used in the case of credit requirements by the firm.[46]

Thus the economic power in the West appears to be multiple or pluralistic. However powerful the economic giants may be, their power is limited to particular sectors of the economy and even there it is oligopolistic rather than monopolistic.

Neither is the position of multi-national companies as strong as it is often assumed. The influence of foreigners appears to be dominant in about 20 per cent of the 115 biggest industrial firms in the FRG. In 1968 none of them was in the category with the highest turnover (from DM 600 m.).

According to the estimate of the Federal Bank in 1974, West German companies with foreign participation in their equity and capital accounted for some 17 per cent of the balance sheet totals, 17 per cent of turnover and 13 per cent of labour force of all West German companies in trade and industry. On the other hand, West German capital has a much greater stake abroad. Against the total nominal capital in foreign hands of DM 31,600 m. in mid-1974 there was outside the FRG capital of about DM 45,800 m. (in nominal shares plus reserves) attributable to German companies including credit institutes.[47]

According to Marcus's findings, concentration of economic power is not so much a matter of institutions as a matter of personal relation-ships. One and the same person can sit on more than one managerial or controlling board (*Aufsichtsrat*). In such a way he can exert simultaneous influence in different firms, so power can be concentrated beyond the given institutional framework. For instance in 1968 in the West German glass industry, there were five men who virtually controlled most of it.[48] Also in other industries there are a lot of personal inter-relationships.

We have, however, to bear in mind that power concentrated in such a way is limited to particular social relationships such as trading activity, price and investment policy etc. and, like the concentration of firms, is limited to only one sector. Even if the wealthy can buy influence in the Press or administration for themselves, they have to compete with other powerful claimants. Moreover, they never enjoy complete domination in the society. They have to share influence with political bosses and pundits in ideological and cultural fields.

It could of course be objected that although the economic and political bosses are different individuals, the fact that they are of the same 'class' makes this distinction irrelevant. This suggestion is supported by the tendency to recruit new members of the élite from what is usually described as the middle class. In the chapters on social mobility, an evaluation of the magnitude of this tendency has been attempted. In spite of the intricacies of a complex category such as the middle class, Dahrendorf's view that there is a reduced possibility of recruiting the élite from the category of manual workers has been corroborated. Manual workers have only two comparatively narrow channels of intragenerational advancement to the position of the élite; political parties and trade unions. In principle this is also the case with the GDR, but there the political channel of upward mobility is considerably broader; on the other hand it is the only channel for advancement to the élite.

The fact that the West German élite is recruited predominantly from what is usually described as the middle class is the main object of criticism from the left. Marxists presuppose the existence of a self-conscious bourgeois class, the members of which are primarily concerned with their class interests. This however is a theoretical rather than a practical supposition. However many common interests the 'gentlemen' may have, these do not prevent them being bitterly divided amongst opposing pressure groups and political parties. Leaders of the political parties, although often recruited from a similar social stratum (with respect to type of work, education and income), do not hesitate to canvass the support of other strata in such a way that they open the door to 'counter-bourgeois' influences. The breakthrough of the trade union élites into the power élite and the emergence of counter-élites, especially in the educational sector, is the best example of the loopholes which the supposedly self-conscious bourgeois class cannot, and, as a rule, does not even want to close.

If defection of intellectuals is the first sign of a potentially successful process of social change, as the theorists of reform and revolution have shown,[49] then this process is already under way in many countries in the West. Ironically, alienation of intellectuals is a phenomenon widespread in the Communist-dominated countries also.

Returning to the FRG, we have also to ask to what extent does the rank and file citizen in the West really influence decision-making in political and economic matters? Modern society is organised in large-scale territorial units, the membership of which runs into seven or more digits. Any individual, unless strongly motivated and qualified for an active political and/or economic career (who then becomes a member of an economic or political élite), can exert influence only infinitesimally through participation in the two frameworks of institutionalised competition: election and market.

In the elections the citizen can choose between two or more teams of claimants for power. Usually he is not in a position to decide the personal composition of these teams, nor their respective programmes or actions; but his own choice is real and tangible. Another question is how far it is tangible for the society as a whole. An effective alternation of the governing teams requires a change of mind of a considerable number of the electorate; it cannot be otherwise: the individual's decision in itself is infinitesimal. In contrast to the East, the choice is a genuine one and there is no system where the percentage representation of individual parties is arranged by the leadership of one particular party. Although election results in the West can be predicted, they cannot be prearranged. There is always scope for the unexpected.

However weighty the tradition may be, and however individual voters may imitate their kin or fellows, or follow the advice of the Press or other mass media, the scope for influencing voters by concentrating on influential groups or groups likely to produce decisive shifts in almost equal forces, can hardly be compared with the manipulation of elections practised in the East.

The situation is more complicated in the case of the market mechanism. Its objective impersonal function can be more easily circumvented by agreements limiting its equilibrating role. Although 'horizontal' agreements limiting competition (cartels) are forbidden by law (*Das Gesetz gegen Wettbewerbsbeschränkungen*) in the FRG, in practice it is hardly possible to forestall agreements with similar consequences, such as agreements on common sellers' organisations, or on prices within the holding companies. Nor does similar prohibition of agreements limiting competition contained in the Treaty on European Economic Co-operation increase the efficiency of West German laws in this respect.[50]

Nevertheless the existence of these laws bears witness to the fact that the opinion of responsible politicians is in favour of free competition. In this respect the opinions of political and economic élites diverge; it is up to the tribunals to decide individual cases. Here 'manipulation' appears to be a more appropriate characteristic. It stands for contractual limitation of economic freedom, i.e. freedom to run a business according to the rules of perfect competition. Yet the economists know all too well that perfect competition is something of a theoretical supposition. The real questions are how many would-be entrepreneurs are excluded and at what level prices are maintained by cartel and similar agreements. Assessment of these questions however is beyond the means of economic statistics. The mathematics of theoretical models is of little help in a factual analysis.

In this context we must also mention the power of well-organised and disciplined pressure groups, the professional and interest associations. There has been some criticism of this particular kind of power which is described as the domination of associations (*Verbandherrschaft*). Firstly, the power of professional associations has been considered excessive from the constitutional point of view. In the constitution it is only political parties that are conceived as mediators and synthesists of the political will of the people; they are the exclusive legitimate vehicles for transforming political inputs into political outputs according to the constitutionally accepted rules of representation. One of these rules is the principle of proportional representation in legislative assemblies with their power to confirm governments. The power of the associations however is neither anchored in the constitution nor is their influence proportional to the number of their members or supporters. The power of these associations is rather based on the supply of and demand for services which their members provide, or as is the case with the churches, on their ideological influence.

The other critique is from the political point of view. As the representatives of the associations are predominantly recruited from the 'upper class', the mere existence of these power focuses strengthen the already disproportionate prevalence of the upper class in the constitutionally legitimate power channels. This objection however is partly offset by the opposite one. The trade unions also belong to the association whose influence on West German economic policy is increasing.

The West German trade unions have not yet attained the strength to challenge parliamentary power and upset the government as the British trade unions have done. Nevertheless there seems to be no institutional

obstacle to a similar development in the FRG. Any possible defiance of
parliamentary rule depends on the following factors: (a) on the
willingness of the trade union leadership to take such action; (b) on the
support or obedience of the trade union membership and (c) on the
acquiescence of the non-organised labour force. So far, it seems that only
the first condition is lacking, the other two are more commonly found.
The trend towards an increasing use of the strike as a lever in industrial
disputes in the FRG has already been mentioned in section 3h.

The third objection is that the associations actually exert and sometimes even legally possess an authority over their members which
according to the constitution is reserved to the state and its bodies or
agencies. This is understood to be particularly the case with farmers'
associations and trade unions. Exclusion from membership of these
associations may have grave consequences for the person concerned. As
Eschenburg put it, 'The Constitution protects the individual from the
power of the state but not from the power of the group.'[51]

A pressure group is particularly influential if it can gain support in
the judiciary procedure. As a classical example of this we can cite the
recent rejection of the Abortion Law by the Federal Constitutional
Court. Although the Law legalising abortions was duly passed by the
Bundestag, the political will of national representatives was thwarted by
judges who, influenced by Christian or rather Roman Catholic doctrine,
came to the conclusion that abortion is against the constitution which
forbids 'action designed to destroy life'.

On the other hand it is being maintained that the existence of strong
non-political associations strengthens the pluralistic character of the
FRG. Independent professional associations such as trade unions,
employers' organisations, farmers' unions etc., and ideological
associations such as churches, clubs etc. provide a more ample framework for individual satisfaction or 'self-realisation' than the closely
supervised pattern of dependent bodies subordinated to one political
party which is found in the GDR. A wide range of human needs and
interests is being met and a differentiated pattern of self-sustaining
institutions and mobility channels gives a greater number of people
opportunity for personal self-assertion.

Also, a richer institutional framework of non-political bodies
provides better opportunities for the regulation of conflicts. As
Dahrendorf has pointed out, liberal democracy can work only in the
context of a society whose institutions are characterised throughout by
the recognition and rational canalising of conflicts.[52] Recently,
however, Dahrendorf placed the main emphasis on the need for

regulation of conflict.[53]

This, however, is easier said than done. Not everybody is prepared to face a conflict. Even a regulated conflict offers better opportunities to the strong. This is especially the case when groups' interests clash and when, in addition, such groups do not share common end-values. Unless there is an impersonal or neutral referee (market, election, tribunals, arbitration committees etc.) vested with strong powers for arbitration, the outcome of a conflict may be merely a trial of strength, a trial beyond any framework of regulation. In West Germany, there is so far a widespread respect for the law and most people are ready to accept the decision based on legal position, whether this is taken by administrative or judiciary branches. It remains to be seen, however, how far this attitude might be changed by the increasing 'strife competence' in view of industrial relations and above all by the growth of the anti-system counter-élite. Both these tendencies would expand the pluralistic features of West German society, the latter, perhaps, beyond the bounds of cohesion.

In using the term pluralistic as a possible characteristic of the West German power structure, we have to bear in mind the criticism which Marxists and often also Western liberals make on this point. Recently, Kurt Sontheimer has summed up such a criticism in the following points:

(1) the established pluralism is a firmly established, relatively rigid power system which strongly opposes social change;

(2) the social interests of the large, powerful social groups have different chances of being carried out (for example, the interest of employers in this society has much more momentum than that of employees);

(3) the forming of political will within the pressure groups themselves is by no means always effected democratically and their members often have little or no opportunity to participate in this process;

(4) there are some important general interests as, for example, the interest in public health, which are not really taken into account because there is no powerful representation of this interest;

(5) finally, thanks to the overall power of the pressure groups, public interest often takes second place to the many powerful private interests.[54]

This criticism indicates that it is not the pluralism as such but its underdeveloped or unbalanced structure and functioning which cause concern among liberals. (Those who because of these and similar short-comings reject pluralism outright are hardly interested in any kind of pluralism or polyarchy; they prefer unlimited power to their own liking.)

There is also terminological misunderstanding. In my opinion, meaningful concepts cannot be used in such a broad sense as to cover more than one parameter of societal structure (cf. our discussion on totalitarianism in the previous chapter). If pluralism has to have any precise meaning, it can describe only the fact that power is divided among different bodies whose respective policies may differ within an accepted framework for regulation of possible conflict. In such a sense pluralism does not mean that everybody has access to power or that this access is spread evenly over all social strata or that all power focuses are equal. These are other issues which have to be viewed separately and, if possible, quantified by other indicators. This I am trying to do in this study.

4e. Power and self-assertion in employment

The dependence of one man on another may assume a variety of forms. If we exclude all the types of family relationships which constitute a highly complex network of mutual dependencies, we can perceive two main areas of human dependence on a certain established power (authority) relationship: political and economic.

Whereas political power is usually embodied in the state and performed by its specialised and/or regional agencies, economic power is institutionalised mainly by three more or less contractual relationships; hired employment, rented premises, and loaned or invested capital.

Hired employment is undoubtedly the most frequently experienced type of economic dependence; credit and tenancy were more socially relevant in the pre-industrial societies, but since the nineteenth century hired labour has become one of the main socio-political issues in Germany. The history of the labour movement is the history of advancement of those hired. Germany was a country where this endeavour scored its first successes and where it eventually attained its height. The milestones in this development are well known: accident and health insurance, pension scheme, 48-hour week, paid holidays, right to strike, right to associate, collective bargaining, unemployment insurance, and most recently co-determination (*Mitbestimmung*) in at least some branches of industry.

Both parts of Germany inherited the already well-established system of social insurance and trade union representation. Yet according to the socialist postulates this was not enough. And here the ways of the GDR and the FRG depart most conspicuously. In the GDR the main stress has been on the change of ownership and in the FRG on the reform of management.

Almost all the big enterprises in the FRG are joint stock companies. In mining 90 per cent and in manufacturing 25 per cent of the labour force was employed in this type of enterprise in 1970.[55]

According to the laws valid in 1975 joint stock companies have three bodies with specialised competence in decision making. These are:

(a) The general meeting of the shareholders, responsible for matters such as change in capital stock, liquidation of the company, election of the members of the supervisory board, distribution of the annual net profit and dismissal of the board of directors and supervisory board.

(b) The supervisory board which has to appoint the board of directors and supervise the conduct of business; it may under certain circumstances make business acts dependent on its consent. The supervisory board is as a rule elected by the general meeting.

In the coal and steel industries the supervisory board consists of three groups of members; as a rule there are 11 members altogether: five representatives of the shareholders, five representatives of the workers and one neutral person.

The workers' representatives are from three sectors. Two are elected by the workers in the plant, two sent by the trade unions represented in that enterprise, one is the representative of the public interest; he must not be employed in any organisation of either the employers or the workers.[56] Usually he is a civil servant, a scientist or a member of a fiduciary profession.

In the holding societies the supervisory boards have fifteen members. Four workers' representatives are elected by the electoral college and three delegated by the trade unions.[57]

In industries other than coal and steel, workers' representation is less impressive. In enterprises with more than 500 employees, only one-third of the supervisory board is composed of workers' representatives; all are directly elected by the workers of the plant.

(c) The executive board (board of management) which runs the business and controls the administrative apparatus. It is appointed by the supervisory board. In the coal and steel industries one member of the executive board, the labour director, is the representative of the workers. He is responsible for matters concerning the staff, such as salary and wage policy, employment, annual holidays, dismissals and giving of notice, old-age pensions, factory hygiene, factory canteens, factory-owned flats and houses, factory-owned kindergartens, matters of rationalisation and prevention of accidents.

Apart from the leading bodies there is in each joint stock company a 'works council' (*Betriebsrat*). According to the Factory Constitution

Act (*Betriebsverfassung*) of 1952, amended in 1971, this should exist
in all enterprises with at least five full-time employees. Its members
are elected by all workers, but by manual and clerical workers
separately. Works councils' power is limited to co-determination in the
social field only; in economic matters legislation has granted them
merely the right to be informed.

The policy of West Germany trade unions has been to extend the
type of co-determination which had been introduced in the coal and
steel industries to other areas of production. The one-third workers'
representation has been found inadequate for the following reason:

> Workers are not represented in the board of management, and in the
> supervisory board the representatives of the shareholders are in the
> majority and hardly dependent on the consent of the workers'
> representatives. The representatives of the shareholders often take
> their decisions before the meeting of the supervisory board and thus
> try to keep all important decisions away from the board meeting. As
> a consequence, the supervisory board changes from a supervisory
> and controlling body into a source of information where the
> workers' representatives cannot really co-determine but where they
> can only get certain information which the management would
> otherwise deny them. This graduation in the co-determination rights
> of the works council always causes the workers' representatives to
> fear that they will be neglected; a general atmosphere of distrust
> against management is created, and this prejudices responsible
> co-operation.[58]

The coalition government of Social Democrats and Free Democrats
attempted to expand the sytem of workers' co-determination
(*Mitbestimmung*) valid in the coal and steel industries to all major
companies with two out of the three following criteria: with more than
2,000 employees, with annual turnover of DM 150 million, or with a
balance sheet of DM 75 million. According to these criteria about 650
enterprises with a labour force of about 6 million would be affected.
The supervisory board had to be composed of 10 shareholders and 10
employees' representatives. Of the 10 workers' delegates one would be
a middle-rank manager and 3 trade union officials from outside the
firm. All 10 workers' representatives on the supervisory board,
including the three from outside, would be chosen by an electoral
college which in its turn would be elected by the entire labour force in
a secret ballot. Unlike the supervisory boards in the coal and steel

industries where the two sides select an independent chairman from outside, the chairman and his deputy would be chosen from the board members, both of them originating from different sides.[59]

The Christian Democratic majority in the second chamber (Council of the Länder — Bundesrat) rejected this proposal on the grounds that the electoral college deprives workers of direct voting rights and minorities of any representation at all, that there is no means of resolving a situation where the opinion is equally divided, that the leading employees are not sufficiently represented and that the proposal does not take into consideration the position of the FRG in the European Economic Community and in international competition.[60] Yet the government hopes that with some small amendments, the Bill will be acceptable to both chambers before the end of 1975.[61]

An opinion poll in the summer of 1972 revealed that skilled workers were the most interested in greater co-determination (*Mitbestimmung*) in enterprises. Sixty-six per cent considered the present co-determination unsatisfactory, whereas 31 per cent were satisfied, and 3 per cent considered the present co-determination excessive. Among the unskilled workers 56 per cent were dissatisfied, 39 per cent satisfied, and 5 per cent found too much co-determination. In the category of lower-level white-collar employees the proportions were similar. Fifty-three per cent thought there was 'too little', 41 per cent 'enough' and 6 per cent 'too much' co-determination. Management staff's opinion was more equally divided: 49 per cent 'too little', 42 per cent 'enough', and 10 per cent 'too much' co-determination.[62]

In the GDR, economic power is a specialised agency of political power. State ownership of the means of production provides the legal and factual basis for government nomination of management, for detailed information on enterprises' conditions and activities (there are no business secrets *vis-à-vis* the state) and for central planning of production, prices and wages (limitation of market forces). Consequently the economic power, i.e. the possibility to impose one's own will directly on others within producers' and consumers' relationships, is much wider in the GDR than in the FRG.

As in the political sphere, economic decision-making is concentrated at the top level of the power hierarchy; fulfilment of planned targets is the main concern of directors of individual enterprises. Formally there is a lot of collective decision-making. In each large enterprise there is a production committee, a consultative and controlling body, formally elected by employees, but virtually (*de jure* and *de facto*) led by the Communist Party group in that enterprise.

Moreover in large enterprises there are the so-called *Aktive*; i.e. consultative assemblies of activists. In all enterprises employees are frequently summoned to production meetings and to plenary sessions where not only technical and economic, but also political questions are discussed.

As both directors and the different consultative and/or controlling assemblies have the same main task, i.e. fulfilment of the plan, their decision-making is virtually limited to finding the best means to do it. Their juxtaposition has only one practical aim: mutual control and supervision. Here again a particular feature of the Communist power structure is exemplified: uniformity of command (uniform élite) at the top, multiformity of execution and of mutual control (multiple élite) at the bottom.

In the GDR, workers' co-operation with management is formally arranged through trade unions, through the factory branch of the Communist Party, through the mass organisations (for Youth, Women etc.) or through the so-called workers' and peasants' inspectorate. As all these organisations depend, through the National Front and the *Nomenklatur* system, on the unavoidable leadership of the Communist Party, they represent in effect merely different forms, different operators of the same societal factor.

Officially, there is quite extensive co-operation from the trade unions; they have to take part in decisions on hiring and firing, and on matters of rationalisation (concerning groups of employees). Trade unions are entitled to make suggestions about the economic plans which the management is then obliged to discuss with the members of the trade unions. The trade unions are especially entitled to collective bargaining, which in its turn however has to keep within the limits of the economic plan. They have even the right to control and supervise the fulfilment of the collective contracts and also to supervise the conditions of health and environment. The main concern of the collective agreement however should be higher efficiency and rationalisation of production rather than concern for increasing earnings.

According to the principles put forward by the council of ministers and presidium of the trade unions (Freier Deutscher Gewerkschaftsbund – FDGB), for the planning period 1971–75, collective agreements have to help harmonise personal interests with the interests of the enterprises and with the requirements of the whole socialist society. For that purpose the trade unions pledge themselves to ensure the fulfilment of the planned production targets.

Directives for bargaining between management and labour require explicit agreements on the following points:

(a) co-operation of employees with the management;

(b) material incentives (wages and premiums);

(c) planned development of cultural life in the enterprise, especially care of women and young persons;

(d) realisation of the right of the working people to protect their capacity to work;

(e) working time and holidays;

(f) social care in the factory;

(g) ending or change of employment.

Unlike in the West, East German trade unions are not supposed to concentrate their activity on the struggle for higher wages; their concern with wages has to be harmonised with the requirements of the plan. Higher earnings are legitimate only as a means, as an incentive to higher achievement or to higher productivity.

Nor is the so-called Workers' and Peasants' Inspectorate an agency defending workers' or peasants' interests. This is in effect a bureaucratic body, possibly manned by former workers. Only the best innovators and qualified people, experienced apparatchiks and political workers can become officials in this body. Its main task is to control implementation of government and party decisions in the enterprises; it has to discover shortcomings in the production process and look for improvements.

On the whole, the basic role of workers' co-operation in the GDR is to make the 'political output' acceptable to them; they can co-operate in the 'political input' only in so far as they accept the basic directives of the plan, i.e. among other things, a faster growth of productivity than wages. This is a principle which no free trade union (in the Western sense of freedom) would accept. Therefore the Eastern workers have to accept another concept of freedom. They have to be ideologically convinced that the development of the society according to the requirements of the Communist leadership is more important than their own proportionate share of the labour value.

4f. Family and women's predicament

Both political and economic powers are unequally divided not only among individual social strata or status groups, but also among the two sexes. In an intersystemic comparison, the pivotal question is which role is assigned by the respective systems to women, especially with respect to the division of labour within the family.

Both German states recognise equality of sexes before law and put the family under the protection of their respective laws. Both recognise the rights of men and women to form families as an association for life (*Lebensgemeinschaft*) and reserve for the family a certain right of privacy.

According to the GDR law however, the legal and economic inferiority of women should be abolished and economic considerations, supposedly so often decisive in bourgeois marriages, should cease to play a substantial part. The GDR legislature is also more explicit with respect to the aim of marriage from which, according to the law, a family has to arise. This family however should be of a new type — a socialist family. According to paragraph 3 of the family law, children have to be educated to become active builders (*Erbaurer*) of socialism. Consequently the state reserves the right to interfere in family matters on behalf of state ideology. It is explicitly stipulated that marriage involves not only mutual obligation of man and wife but also obligations towards the state.

The equality of the sexes before the law is in the GDR manifested by the provision that the newly married couple can adopt either the man's or the woman's name. In West Germany, the newly married couple has the choice between the man's or the composite name. According to the new law in preparation, however, adopting the woman's name should also be possible.[63] In practice however, newly married couples choose the man's name, both in the FRG and GDR.

Another equalising provision of the East German family law, yet this time the other way round, is the minimum age for marriage, which is 18 years for both sexes. In the FRG the limit is 21 years for men and 16 for women; according to the new law in preparation the age limit for men should be reduced to 18,[64] which since 1975 is also the age at which one has the right to vote.

A more important question is the division of labour between the two sexes. The West German law presupposes that the wife will as a rule take over the care of children and household, whereas the husband will earn the livelihood (*Hausfrauenehe*). It is however up to both partners to decide any division of labour. Both are equally entitled to be employed. The East German law presupposes employment of both the man and the woman, (*Berufstätigenehe*).

Yet the stress on the employment of women and especially the tendency to allow women to work in any industry (often irrespective of their physiological capacity for it) clashes with another objective, namely to stop the declining birth rate. The gravity of this problem can be seen from the following figures. Whereas in 1938 and 1939 there were over 18 live births per 1,000 population on what is now the GDR territory, in 1947 and 1948 there were only 13 births per 1,000 population. In the early sixties the birth rate went up to over 17 but since 1965 it has again declined and in 1973 it dropped below 11 live births per 1,000 population, which is less than the death rate (about 14 per thousand in the early seventies).[65] In spite of the Berlin Wall and in spite of the considerable reduction of infant mortality (from 23 per thousand in 1949 to 9 per thousand in 1973), the East German population is declining. In mid-1974 it sank to 16,924,700, the lowest level since the war.

Under such conditions there is a tendency to provide working women with those facilities which might establish a more harmonious link between employment and child-bearing and child-rearing activities. The three-phase system prevailing in the West (vocational training and employment until the birth of the first child — interruption for as long as children grow up — re-employment) is rejected in the GDR. There is a fear that a long interruption of women's employment might lead to their declining vocational capacity; therefore part-time employmentt is preferred to retirement from work for family reasons. Consequently the percentage of working women is continuously increasing.

Considering only women of working age (between 15 and 60) the percentage of women employed increased from 60 per cent in 1960 to over 77 per cent in 1973.[66] In the same period the percentage of children below 3 years put into nurseries (*Kinderkrippen* and *Dauerheime*) increased from 13 to 35 per cent. Of children aged from 3 years to school age, 46 per cent were in playgroups (*Kindergärten* and *Wochenheime*) in 1960 and 77 per cent in 1973.[67] In the FRG in 1972 only 45 per cent of women between 15 and 60 were employed[68] and only 2.3 per cent of children between the age of 3 and 6 attended kindergarten.[69]

The differences are striking. They reflect not only women's rights but also women's duties. Lower male earnings in the GDR than in the FRG make the wife's contribution to the family budget necessary. On top of that, lower supply of household services and shopping facilities make the household work in the GDR more tedious than in the FRG.

A special inquiry on time spent on different activities in the GDR has shown that because of shortcomings in supplies of goods and services, women are increasingly engaged in home needlework, food conserving etc. Women over 18 spent a fifth more time on the household than they spent on all their employment.[70]

It has been widely observed that women in the Communist-dominated countries envy their Western counterparts their shopping facilities, supply of services for easing their housework, and the variety of available goods.

In the West 59 per cent of women (against 57 per cent of men) said in an opinion poll in May 1972 that they were satisfied with the general conditions in the FRG. Twenty-eight per cent of women (and 33 per cent of men) said that they would like a good deal of change.[71]

The only comparable data with the GDR are those on the firmness or fragility of the family. East German marriages are less permanent than West German ones. The divorce rate in the GDR is considerably higher than in the FRG. In the late sixties there were on average 10.5 divorces per 10,000 population per annum in the FRG, but 15.7 in the GDR.[72]

In comparing these data it has to be borne in mind that with respect to the upbringing of children, marriage is more relevant in the FRG than in the GDR. Although there are legal provisions for children born out of wedlock in the FRG, these children enjoy less equality with legitimate children than their counterparts in the GDR. According to the newly prepared civil code in the GDR any difference between children born in and out of wedlock should be completely abolished.

As the statistics indicate, this problem is more grave in the GDR than in the FRG. Of the children born between 1965 and 1969, 10.9 per cent were born out of wedlock in the GDR whereas only 4.7 per cent were born out of wedlock in the FRG.[73]

It remains to be investigated whether the unfavourable household position of the East German woman is at least compensated by a better position in their jobs. According to an East German study for 1963, female workers in East German industry were more represented in the upper wage brackets than female workers in West German industry. Whereas in the GDR 15.5 per cent of female industrial workers were in the top wage groups and 20.7 per cent in the bottom wage group, in the FRG the respective percentages were 6.2 in the top and 47.9 in the bottom group.[74]

On the other hand, comparison of wage rates assigned to male and female production workers in East German industry with the income distribution of the total of gainfully employed men and women in the FRG points rather in the other direction, namely to a higher percentage of women in the top income brackets in the FRG than in the GDR.

Unfortunately there are no comparable data on East German female income distribution. Neither are the women's earnings reported separately. There is also no research which might indicate how the East German women themselves consider their position within the GDR.

In the absence of East German data, comparison with another neighbouring Communist country may be useful. In Czechoslovakia, for instance, women's average earnings from employment were 66 per cent of men's average earnings during the late sixties. In the FRG female workers' earnings were 70 per cent and female salaried staff's earnings 64 per cent of the equivalent earnings for men.[75] The difference does not appear to be significant.

More data are available for the comparison of women's share in the position of power. These data are especially revealing if compared with data on women's participation in employment and higher education.

Table 4.3 Women's Share in Employment and Position of Power

Women in per cent of		FRG	GDR
1. Total population	(1973)	52.2	53.7
2. Working population	(1973)	36.6	49.1
3. Wage and salary earners	(1973)	34.6	50.4
4. Student population (university level)	(1972)	32.7	41.2
5. Regional deputies	(1971)	7.5[1]	36.0[4]
6. Members of parliament	(1971)	6.4[2]	31.8[5]
7. Leadership of political parties	(1974)	n.a.	4.2
8. Government and top civil service	(1974)	5.5[3]	3.2

1. Landtage; 2. Bundestag; 3. 1971; 4. Bezirkstage; 5. Volkskammer.
Sources: *SJB BRD*, 1974; *SJB DDR*, 1974; *Facts about Germany*, Bonn, 1973; *Der Staats und Parteiapparat der DDR*, Bonn, 1974.

Although in both German states slightly more than half of the population are women, only in the GDR is the labour force reported as being composed by half of women. Even if we take into account that the labour force in the army, police and uranium mines is not included in the GDR data, it can be accepted that in the East, the women's share of the labour force is larger than in the West. East German women are also more strongly represented in the student population. However the ratio of students to the working female population is higher in the FRG.

Concerning the women's share in power, the situation seems to be ambiguous. In parliament and in regional assemblies there are, in terms of proportional representation, five times as many women in the East than in the West. One has however to bear in mind that these assemblies in the GDR exist more for window-dressing than for decision-making. In the bodies where the effective power rests (and this more effectively in the East than in the West), i.e. in government and the top civil service, women's participation is negligible in both German states; but in the East it is even lower than in the West. Nor are women represented in significantly larger numbers in the leading councils of the political bodies in the GDR.

If we compare the position in the top decision-making bodies, i.e. the state and party bosses in the GDR and government and Bundestag in the FRG, we find that women are better represented in the West than in the East. This is shown more clearly in the comparison with the percentage of working women: Although this gap is considerable, it does not indicate a substantial participation by women in power in either parts of Germany. Male supremacy in both German states appears to be firmly established.

Now a sensible question of course emerges: how far are women really interested in obtaining positions of power in society? So far all opinion polls have indicated that women are less interested in politics and less interested in permanent jobs. This is not the place to decide whether this is due to their education or their nature. Comparing two different socio-economic systems we have to take into consideration that a situation where women hold few positions of power does not necessarily mean that they are less satisfied, and therefore more alienated. On the other hand women's dissatisfaction with smaller earnings and, if employed, with the double burden of job and household can be taken for granted.

There is yet another question which has to be mentioned in this context, namely that of the social role of the family. Of families in five countries compared by Almond and Verba, the German family was the second most authoritarian. Germany was only slightly ahead of Italy in terms of the percentage of those who remembered having, at the age of about 16, had some influence in family decisions, but this was far behind the percentage in the US and the UK. Of almost 1,000 people questioned the percentages were as follows: USA 73, UK 69, Mexico 57, Germany 54, and Italy 48.[76] Of those who did not remember having had any influence Germans responded in a similar way to Italians and Mexicans. The percentages were as follows: US 22, UK 26, Italy 37, Germany 37 and Mexico 40. It is however extremely difficult to evaluate how much this characteristic applies to the individual German states. The only guess which can be made in this respect may be based on the correlation between religious affiliation and family discipline. It has already been found on several occasions that Catholic families tend to be more authoritarian than Protestant families. As Catholics represent less than 20 per cent of the population in the GDR whilst in the FRG they are almost equally represented, it may be inferred that for this particular reason the family in the East would be less authoritarian than that in the West. It can be expected that Communist education has helped also towards this situation. In the GDR it is supposed that the family influence on the children is rather conservative and therefore children must have been more influenced from other quarters, by the school and Communist-led or -inspired associations. The perhaps less authoritarian family in the East does not however make for a less authoritarian structure in general. On the contrary family authority is replaced by the authority of the state and the leading political party, which in their turn are more heavy-handed than the circumscribed and, for the individual, temporary rule of the family.

4g. Education for citizenship

By contrast to the FRG, the GDR's laws require definite ideological education. As was said earlier, the family law required that children be educated to become active builders of socialism. Other laws make this requirement more explicit with the stipulation that children have to acquire socialist attitudes to learning and working, to learn to esteem working men, and to uphold the rules of socialist communal life (*Zusammenleben*), i.e. solidarity, socialist patriotism and internationalism.[77]

A special Law on Youth (*Jugendgesetz*) puts it as follows:

1. The pre-eminent task in the shaping of the developed socialist society is the education of all young people to become state-citizens who are devoted to the ideas of socialism, who think and act as patriots and internationalists, who strengthen socialism and can be relied upon to defend it against all enemies. Young people themselves bear a high responsibility for the formation of their characters according to socialist principles.

2. It is the task of every young citizen to work, learn and live according to socialist principles, to be selflessly and steadfastly active in furthering the good of his socialist fatherland — the German Democratic Republic — to strengthen the bond of friend-

ship with the Soviet Union and the other socialist brother-countries and to promote the general co-operation of the socialist community of states. It is the honourable task of young people to esteem and defend the revolutionary traditions of the working class and the achievements of socialism, to further the cause of peace and friendship between peoples and to promote anti-imperialist solidarity. All young people ought to distinguish themselves by a socialist attitude to work, by well-founded knowledge and skill, should live according to high moral and cultural values and should take an active part in social and political life and in the running of the state's and society's affairs. Their efforts to assimilate Marxism-Leninism, the scientific *Weltanschauung* of the working class, and to undertake their own offensive against imperialist ideology are encouraged from all quarters.[78]

There may arise a question of how to reconcile socialist patriotism with internationalism. These terms are not supposed to be contradictory. The antitheses of these are, in the Marxist-Leninist view, 'bourgeois nationalism' and 'cosmopolitanism' respectively. Bourgeois nationalism is rejected because it does not recognise solidarity of socialist countries, which is the necessary prerequisite of 'socialist patriotism'. Moreover, within the socialist camp, socialist patriotism acknowledges the leading role of Soviet patriotism. This is believed to be one of the essential marks of internationalism.

Of course Communists also have to be internationalist towards members of non-Communist-led nations especially in so far as they are working people, but even here certain care has to be taken. Initiative has to be left to the Communist leaders, who decide who has to be contacted for display of internationalist feelings and under what conditions.

By contrast to internationalism, cosmopolitanism is understood as a label for a complete lack of national belonging. It stands for an undemarcated and undifferentiated human consciousness which does not realise the dividing line between Communist- and capitalist-led nations.

Cosmopolitanism is supposed to be more contagious among the upper than amongst the lower strata. Soviet historiography abounds with world-wide examples of national betrayal by the power élite in contrast to the self-sacrificing patriotism of the common folk.[79]

Yet this idea is not as absurd as the standard cliché of Marxist-Leninist historiographers makes it sound. Because lower strata, unless

ethnically mixed, rarely speak foreign languages and have less opportunity to travel abroad, they are more nation-bound and display
patriotic characteristics. Consequently they are more inclined to let
themselves be represented for international contacts rather than
contact other nationals themselves. This observation has also been
corroborated by Almond and Verba's findings on the role of education
in the structure of political culture. They found 'that those with less
education share less of a common cross-cultural experience with one
another and are more affected by the particular history and culture of
their own national systems'.[80] No wonder that they can become
'inter-nationalist' rather than 'cosmopolitan' in their world view and
feelings.

What happens, however, with the Marxist-Leninists' intelligentsia?
Experience from Communist-dominated countries outside the USSR is
not quite conclusive in this respect. Nationalism in these countries
increasingly acquires anti-Soviet features and these are also displayed
by lower rather than upper strata. Yet this difference seems to be
more a matter of tighter discipline and greater existential fear among
those 'above' than among those 'below'. Moreover, Soviet patriotism
as a pillar of socialist internationalism does not appear to be appealing
for genuine internationalist, let alone cosmopolitan feelings. So the
educators in Communist-dominated countries attempt the difficult
task of squaring the circle. To educate the young generation to socialist,
Soviet-led, patriotism — internationalism.

In the West there is an increasing tendency to consider higher
education as an inalienable right and it becomes widely accepted that
the subject of education has to be chosen as far as possible according to
the wishes of the students. This is often supposed to be one of the
characteristics of the socialist society. Therefore, it might be particularly
useful to quote the view of the GDR government which claims to be,
and is also widely considered to be, a socialist one.

Paragraph 22 of the Law on Youth states:

(1) Study at a university, institution of higher learning or specialist
school is a mark of high social recognition and involves a personal
obligation, binding on every student, towards the working class and
the socialist state.
(2) Admission to a course of study follows only as a result of the
attainment of the requisite standards in the fields of employment
and social commitment; this takes account of the needs of socialist
society and has regard to the social structure of the population. The

executive committees of the Free German Youth are entitled to a say in the admission of young people to university courses.

Paragraph 23 requires the students to 'acquire a thorough basic grounding in Marxism-Leninism and in their specialist field'; 'particular attention is to be given to students' energetic attempts to keep abreast of the most modern developments, in particular in the fields of Soviet learning.'[81]

These however are not only pious declarations. More than in any other Communist-dominated country these requirements are put into practice. It is difficult to say with how much success. There are no legal means to express opposition and deviant views within the party line are sooner or later suppressed. Nevertheless, it is possible, from contacts with East German youth or from scattered evidence of escapist tendencies, to infer some dissatisfaction. There is especially a certain sense of boredom which the steered and supervised social relationships produce. Not only the choice of goods and services but also scope for learning and entertainment are limited. In spite of the sealed boundary, East Germans have the possibility of comparing their fate with that of their Western counterparts. Radio broadcasts and television cannot be completely jammed throughout the whole country. However critical East Germans might be of many aspects of Western life, they seem to appreciate some basic features of it. As people with contacts in East Germany have realised, people there seem to feel a certain envy for the possibility of greater choice in the West, a choice of goods and services and choice of political and cultural orientation.

It is however sometimes objected that the possibility of choice in the West is an illusion; that people are more often than not manipulated into their decision, either by the necessities of their respective situations (Germans have for this a special term — *Sachzwang,* i.e. pressure of things) or by skilful propaganda. Necessities of particular situations operate everywhere; the question is how stringent they are. As will be shown further below, the FRG despite all her shortcomings provides the individual with greater scope for satisfaction within the given pressures of situations (*Sachzwange*) than the GDR. Also, however skilful commercial advertising in the West might be, it can hardly induce people to alter their basic patterns of demand. There is always the scope for decision not to keep up with the Joneses, as anti-consumerist demonstrations by West German students indicate.

What is more, education in the FRG does not espouse one particular world view. Although tradition may weigh heavily over the vast majority of the West German population, there are some alternatives to it, such as Catholicism, Protestantism, secular liberalism and democratic socialism. Moreover, a certain emancipation from all of these traditions seems to be gaining ground. Some establishments of higher education are becoming the focal point of alignments other than those supposed to be the pillars of the Western establishment and/or tradition.

In the two parts of Germany certain contradictory situations emerge. In the West there is a stress on non-political education; and political values conveyed by the schools are general and rather vague; yet anti-systemic opposition is explicit and consciously political. In the East, education is highly politicised; opposition takes the form of an escapist, politically neutral activity. The contradiction may be labelled as that between *homo civilis* and *homo politicus*.

Quantitative proportions of these two types of attitude can be gauged only in the FRG. In an opinion poll involving about 500 students in the establishments of higher education in July 1967, 73 per cent responded that they did not belong to any organised student group. Only 7 per cent said that they belonged to a political group and 6 per cent to a religious group. To the question of which political party was nearest to their opinion, 42 per cent answered in favour of Social Democrats, 34 per cent in favour of Christian Democrats and 18 per cent in favour of Free Democrats; 2 per cent favoured the right wing National Democratic Party and 4 per cent the leftist Peace Union (Deutsche Friedensunion).[82]

When, however, the question was more specific, and students were asked their opinion of individual concrete groups, 37 per cent of the sample said that none of them corresponded to their own opinion; 32 per cent identified themselves with the Sozialdemokratischer Hochschulbund (SHB), loosely related to the Social Democratic Party — but in practice more to the left of it; 17 per cent identified themselves with a Christian Democratic group — Ring Christlich Demokratischer Studenten (RCDS); 10 per cent with the moderates in the Sozialistische Deutsche Studentenbund (SDS),[83] i.e. with Marxists but not exclusively of revolutionary brand; and 4 per cent with the radical, revolutionary, Marxists among SDS.

When asked which group they considered most influential, 30 per cent answered the revolutionary Marxists, 27 per cent the radical socialists (SHB), 17 per cent the moderate Marxists and only 5 per cent the Christian Democrats (RCDS); 2 per cent of respondents considered as the most influential the Maoist group, the opinion of which however did not find any support among the pollsters.[84]

The difference between subjective identification and evaluation of influence is striking. The power of the opposition groups appears to be far beyond their numerical strength. If the percentages of evaluated influence are compared with percentages of identification, the following influence intensity ratios, indicating how many times the influence is stronger than numerical representation, are obtained. Revolutionary Marxists 7.50, moderate Marxists 1.70, radical socialists 0.84 and Christian Democrats 0.29. It is clear that the intensity of conviction and political fervour is strongest amongst the anti-systemic opposition. The results of elections to the students' representative bodies corroborate this contention.

In the absence of comparable data from the GDR, we have to attempt to draw some conclusions from indirect evidence.

East German research is confined to a few limited fields such as utilisation of leisure, employment of women, popular professions and personalities among young people etc. Some of the results point to a certain value orientation. For instance Günter Fischer found that of 1758 names of exemplary personalities reported by a sample of young people, only 16 per cent were politicians. Surprisingly the percentage was somewhat higher among the girls (17 per cent) than among the boys (15 per cent). In another research (Werner Henning), positive ideas were compared with negative ones. Here, politicians scored the highest negative values especially among the boys. The girls were apparently more conformist than the boys.[85] In both sex groups however, *homo civilis* was put more often as an example than *homo politicus*.

It seems that this is the preference in both parts of Germany. The social significance of this similarity however, is different. In the West, the official tradition is more often than not in favour of *homo civilis*. To be non-political is the conformist attitude. In the East, the official position is definitely in favour of *homo politicus,* without however a choice of political orientation. Conformist attitude has to be political in the sense required by the Communist Party. The only legal possibility of dissent is to be non-political.

The question might arise whether and how far conformism in the above-mentioned matters coincides with the subject competence stated by Almond and Verba on West German society. In the absence of comparable data (both with respect to the two German states and with respect to different periods) we can only suggest that a positive correlation might be expected between the subject competence and conformist attitudes.

On the strength of West German opinion polls, however, it seems that, as in labour relationships (see pp. 114–16), the subject/conformist attitude is being gradually substituted by a more political consciousness. In November 1970, 31 per cent of a population sample expressed their support for student demonstrations, but in the age cohort 16–29 the proportion was 50 per cent.[86] According to another poll repeated at different intervals within the time span of 21 years, the percentage of those interested in politics increased from 27 in 1952 to 49 in 1973; the proportion of those completely disinterested declined from 32 to 11 per cent of the sample, whereas the percentage of only slightly ('not particularly') interested remained rather stable (41 and 40 per cent in 1952 and 1973 respectively).[87]

Increasing political interest and increasing propensity to strife does not however exclude the acceptance of the framework within which the strife takes place. In an opinion poll in February 1973, the Institute for Demoscopy found 72 per cent of respondents satisfied with the present political system of the FRG, 15 per cent favoured a change and 13 per cent were undecided or did not know.[88]

As long as no similar poll under similar guarantees of discretion for the respondents can be undertaken in the GDR, any expectation of convergency in political matters will remain a matter of mere conjecture.

One cannot of course deny a certain logic or consequentiality in the Marxist-Leninist juxtaposition. The accordance of individual actions with historical requirements of the time presupposes individual cognisance of these requirements. As they are not a matter of direct perception but of historical interpretation they have to be taught and propagated. For the individual to be a convinced, believing subject, this interpretation has to be accepted as the only correct one. Hence converting to Marxism-Leninism is similar to a religious conversion. To become a fully conscientious member of the Communist Party is different from becoming a member of any other party. To borrow Sigmund Neumann's terminology, it is a 'party of integration', not 'representation'.

In view of this, the discussion resulting from the Third Conference of the SED revealed that 'the development of socialist consciousness is a practical problem of the first order in the planned building of socialism. Socialism acquires in such a consciousness a societal propelling force which in essence establishes its superiority over the capitalist system.'[89]

This is a most penetrating observation. It indicates the nature of the competition between East and West. It also shows how much more than their liberal opponents are the Marxist-Leninists aware, for practical purposes, of the crucial role of individual conviction, of individual value judgement.

Again, a paradoxical situation emerges: despite the stress laid on the economic basis, Marxist-Leninists understand (like Max Weber) that man reacts to any external challenge according to his own image of the situation and according to his hierarchy of values. This is why Marxists are so concerned with moulding the social consciousness of their followers, and, if they win the domination of a country, of other subjects also.

This is something which their liberal opponents can and never will do because it is against their own principles. And yet, paradoxically, the same liberals who in theory are much more ready to agree with Max Weber, are in practice inclined to operate and influence others through material incentives and formal legal institutional arrangements rather than through indoctrination. The liberals rely more on tradition and on the almost automatic interplay of the forces of the establishment without realising that in a complex, fast-changing world any new generation's support has to be won anew, i.e. by methods which are not dissimilar to a new individual conversion. Only in such a way can the potentially non-conformist elements, elements which more often than not are the most active and most energetic, be held within the fold. On the other hand, the majority easily becomes an amorphous, inert mass whose main motivation to social conformity is imitation rather than conviction.

World history is rich in examples of strifes and conflicts when small numbers of convinced, indoctrinated and enthusiastic fighters beat and routed big and sophisticated but not fully involved armies, when consequently the leaders of the former imposed their rule upon the communities of the latter. (Vietnam can be mentioned as the most outstanding contemporary example.) So far it seems that this fact has been fully appreciated by historians rather than social scientists.

In this respect Marxist-Leninists prove to be more pragmatic than in other directions where their doctrine is too specific. Especially in economics they continue to be constrained by their doctrine. On the other hand in social psychology, which was only occasionally mentioned by their 'classics', they feel more free to proceed empirically.

So Marxist-Leninists try to achieve something which is eventually more important to the ongoing struggle than mere economic and/or technical achievements. Although the latter are not underestimated, Marxist-Leninists are realising that in economics and technology, 'capitalism' is a hard foe. Communist-dominated countries have not yet succeeded in catching up, let alone overtaking, the developed capitalist countries. The struggle for consciousness, i.e. the struggle for souls, seems to be more promising, especially when the Westerners themselves are so conspicuously negligent in that direction.

Divided Germany is an excellent example of this difference. In the East ideological education is put forward as a widely publicised aim; it is pursued in an offensive way and with pride. In the West the liberal ideology or ideology of the social market economy and the welfare state, which can between them be considered as rationalisation of parliamentary democracy, are advocated defensively. Within the atmosphere of scepticism there is not too much pride in these values and they are defended rather than pushed forward, defended against residues of authoritarian conservatism on the one side and Marxist-Leninist aspirations on the other.

The defensive character of the Western ideological argument can be best illustrated by the attempts to oust from or not to admit to jobs in government service those who belong to groups which work for or propagate aims contradictory to the Federal Constitution (so called *Berufsverbot*). The possibility of taking such action is based on a law of 1957, revised in 1965.

The implementation of this law is a matter for individual Länder and only a few of them (mainly those led by Christian Democrats such as Bavaria or Rhineland-Palatinate) make full use of it.[90] Both socialists and liberals are, with a few exceptions, such as Hamburg, rather hesitant to apply it. To deny somebody employment in the civil service because of his political activities seems to them incompatible with democracy and freedom. They do not consider democracy as a mere framework of procedure which can function only as long as all participants want to abide by its rules; they consider it as a matter of principle which has to be preserved at all costs. So liberals in the West are hampered by their very principles from defending their system. Only the memory of the tragic collapse of the Weimar Republic makes them feel that they have to do something to prevent a similar development in the Federal Republic. Because of their principles however, they are ashamed to defend it vigorously. If they think they have to do something, they do it half-heartedly, on behalf of the Constitution in a legal, formal way rather than in a politically active, polemical way.[91]

This has particularly characterised the whole question of making the Communist Party illegal in West Germany. The main argument for doing so in 1956 was that its programme and activity were against the Constitutional Law.[92] Officially this ban has never been defended as a retaliatory action against the subordination of non-Communist parties

to the SED in the GDR. Again the contradiction in method is striking:
positive acts of manipulation in the East (National Front and
Nomenklatur system), negative acts of prohibition (outlawing of a
political party) in the West.

When the situation changed and some kind of *modus vivendi* with
the GDR was sought, it was enough that the Communists slightly
changed their label (Communist Party of Germany to German
Communist Party) and the Communist Party was allowed to be
reactivated legally in the FRG.

One has of course to bear in mind that prohibiting a Communist
Party in a liberal democratic régime by no means implies that it will be
wiped out of existence. Based on a hard core of enthusiastic and fully
dedicated fighters it can survive and even build up its political potential
in conditions less favourable than those in the FRG. Negative measures
unless accompanied by consequent ruthless suppression, often have
rather the opposite effect. They appear to be the right challenge to stir
the minds, to nourish the fighting spirit and to give those discriminated
against a halo of martyrdom. This is well understood in the East. As a
rule opposition there is nipped in the bud. If this is not the case and if
something similar happens as in 1956 Hungary or 1968 Czechoslovakia
then an intervention of the 'true sovereign' in the bloc takes place.

Western Marxists seem to have been more aware of the necessity of
an ideological and political struggle with Stalinism than the official
representatives of the FRG who relied rather on juridical means with
all the intricacies of their interpretation and compliance with the
written constitution. Wolfgang Abendroth expressed this criticism as
follows:

> Nobody would maintain that the typical forms of the Stalinist
> régime which for so long moulded the life of the German Communist
> Party can be harmonised with a free democratic system. The
> Federal Supreme (Constitutional) Court has however hardly dealt
> with the special contents of this typical form of Stalinism and its
> realisation in the contemporary KPD and consequently necessarily
> missed its own task.[93]

The juridical, formal handling of the Defence of the Constitution Act
could not prevent, in a federation with different ruling political parties
in its individual member states (Lander), the establishment of a genuine
counter-élite, especially in the educational sector. One of the means of
achieving an institutional basis for this has been the principle of

'tripartite' parity (*Drittelparität*) giving, in governing bodies of universities, equal representation to higher academic staff (professors and the so-called 'Dozenten'), lower academic staff (assistants, lecturers, etc.) and students. In practice the concrete form and range of competence of such a comprehensive representation, wherever introduced, varies from one German Land to another and even from university to university. It is therefore difficult to evaluate how many of the West German universities have fully applied the tripartite principle in their structure.

Concerning the political orientation of students themselves, some additional information can be given on the basis of data compiled for the Conference of West German Rectors in 1975.[94] According to these data students' participation in the elections to the student assemblies (parliaments, conventions, etc.) in 1974 and 1975 varied, in individual cases, between 21 and 54 per cent of the electorate (respective student body). On 31 July 1975 the position was as follows: of the 49 elected student assemblies in the universities and technical universities (Technische Hochschulen or Gesamthochschulen) 32 had one form or other of left-wing majority. This included different bodies not always with explicit labels but, in about 20 cases, with a strong participation of explicitly Communist groupings. (It is difficult to say how many of the non-Communist left-wing groups can be considered as more or less 'system immanent' and how many of them stand for the thorough transformation of the whole social system and, in order to achieve this, are ready to resort to non-constitutional methods). On the other hand, 13 student representations have had a majority of Christian Democratic and Liberal student groups and 4 had a majority of indeterminately profiled groupings. Of the 27 colleges of education (Pädagogische Hochschulen) 22 had a broadly left-wing and only 2 a centre-right majority. In the remaining 3, the reported representation had no clear political profile. On the strength of the same data there were no spectacular shifts in the political composition of students' representation between 1974 and 1975.

4h. Self-assertion as a citizen

Previous chapters have already indicated how far the citizen's self-assertion might be affected by different structures   and constellations of power in the FRG and GDR. In this chapter an attempt will be made to complete and summarise the picture from below, from the position of an individual citizen. First of all we have to assess which of an individual's activities are subject to the influence of the government or any other regulation from above. Then individual freedoms (liberties) have to be considered in terms of individual needs, interests and real possibilities. There is no point in having freedom if one has neither the means nor sufficient interest to make use of that freedom. Therefore the spectrum of individual liberties has to be juxtaposed with the spectrum of individual possibilities, and, last but not least, with individual interests. Although quantification might not always be easy, at least an approximate juxtaposition is worthwhile attempting.

In both parts of divided Germany people have a free choice of employment. In the East they have the right and also the duty to work in accordance with the society's needs. In the West, there is no constitutional right to work but work is not considered as a duty. As stated above, the state has merely a constitutional duty to ensure full employment and economic prosperity. This duty was seriously tested in 1975 for the first time in West German history.

In the FRG, people can also be self-employed, although in some cases (handicraft, retail trade) they need a government licence; otherwise availability of funds and a receptive market are the main prerequisites. In the GDR, the right to self-employment is subject to increasing restrictions and new openings are reserved for maintenance and repair businesses.

In both countries the citizens are free to buy what is offered for sale on the market provided they have enough purchasing power to do so. In both these respects the average West German is better off than his Eastern counterpart. As stated above, the average real income is about a third higher in the West than in the East and the assortment of consumer goods and services is much wider and richer.

West and East Germans are also equally free to travel within the country. Unlimited travel abroad, however, is available only to the West Germans. East Germans can now travel freely (i.e. without a special exit visa) to some but not all Communist-ruled countries. Travelling to the West is reserved mainly for people whose remaining abroad would not harm the interests of the GDR, i.e. for pensioners; (the rule is to give them exit visas for four weeks if they want to see their relatives in the West).

The above-mentioned limitations, however, do not affect every citizen. Not everyone wants to travel abroad. In the absence of a better indicator which would express how many people in the GDR would like to go abroad we can be helped only by analogy with the FRG. For instance, comparing the number of persons from the West travelling abroad for their holidays (195 per 1,000 population in 1966) and applying a similar ratio to East Germany (where in 1966 only 53 per 1,000 spent holidays abroad) we find that approximately 14 per cent of the population might have suffered by being restrained from travelling abroad.[95] Of course this figure does not reflect the nature of the exit permits (duration of stay, amount of currency and choice of the country); it is only a quantitative indicator.

That this assessment by analogy is not entirely an arbitrary undertaking can be seen from figures on holiday travel within the home country. In 1966, the respective ratios per thousand population were 390 in the FRG and 350 in the GDR. Nor does the social stratification of travellers appreciably differ. In both parts of Germany holiday travelling was enjoyed mainly by the intellectual professions. In 1966, in the GDR, 65 per cent of the intelligentsia and 50 per cent of white-collar employees travelled during their holidays. In the FRG the proportion in the comparable category of all salaried employees (private and government officials) was 67 per cent. Self-employed had better opportunities in the West (48 per cent) than in the East (38 per cent), but the handicraft co-operatives' members in the East (with 51 per cent of holiday travellers) restored the balance. A higher percentage of holiday travellers were the students, 41 per cent in the East. Unfortunately data in the FRG lump students together with pensioners and persons without a profession; of this broad category 49 per cent were holiday travellers. In the GDR, pensioners travelled only a little (18 per cent). Surprising is the high percentage of holiday travellers among the workers: 33 per cent in the FRG; in the category of skilled workers the percentage was somewhat higher (37 per cent). For the GDR the data are differentiated: there were 38 per cent of holiday travellers among the skilled, 34 per cent among the semi-skilled and 30 per cent among unskilled workers. Also housewives travelled a lot: 40 per cent in the West, 31 per cent in the East. Those who did the least holiday travelling were the peasants: 18 per cent of co-operative members in the East and only 8 per cent of people working in agriculture in the West.[96] So our estimate of the number of people dissatisfied with the limitations on travelling abroad in the GDR might not be far off the mark.

In a similar way, the number of people prevented from becoming self-employed in the East can be evaluated by comparison with the West. In 1971, 10 per cent of the West German working population were self-employed whereas in the GDR only about 2 per cent (family members helping in the business are not included) were in this category. Judging from the analogy with the West, limitations on free enterprise in the GDR appear to be less onerous than limitations on

travel abroad. It may however happen that many of those who resent
limitations on travel are also those who would like to become entrepreneurs if they could. So the two estimates cannot be cumulated.

Also limitations on political and ideological differentiation may
concern largely the same people as above. Leaving out those who
remain politically indifferent, i.e. people ready to accommodate to any
established ideology, we can again make some inference from
comparison with the Western situation. According to the opinion polls,
the interest in politics is constantly increasing in the FRG. As stated
earlier, from 1952 to 1973 the proportion of respondents actively
interested in politics increased from 27 to 49 per cent. Meanwhile the
proportion of those explicitly disinterested declined from 32 to 11
per cent.[97]

An opinion poll by another Institute in 1972 found in a voters'
sample 32 per cent strongly interested, and 40 per cent with moderate
interest in politics. Further details revealed by these polls were as
follows: interest in politics was higher among the male respondents,
among those with higher education and among those with more
prestigious occupations. But there was no appreciable difference with
respect to age and political orientation.

Self-identification with a political position was, according to a poll
in 1970, as follows: 3 per cent far left, 18 per cent moderate left, 34
per cent centre, 16 per cent moderate conservative, 3 per cent strongly
conservative, 26 per cent no information. This shows quite a
symmetric distribution of orientation. In the breakdown by sex, age
and educational level, the symmetry was slightly different: skewed to
the left in the case of men, in the younger age group and in the higher
levels of education: to the right in the case of women, older age group
and lower levels of education. Respondents from villages tended to be
more conservative   in orientation, but in the urban brackets with
respect to the size of the population, there were no significant deviations
from the average.[98]

If the West German pattern represents the normal, i.e. spontaneous
distribution of political orientation among the German population, then
the East German exclusion of the conservatives would affect about 20
per cent of GDR citizens. Here, however, the analogy cannot be pushed
too far. East Germany represents a particular brand of socialism which
many Marxists, in West and East alike, find wanting. On the other hand,
the GDR's authoritarian and élitist fabric may find approval among
some right-wingers, i.e. people on the conservative end of the West
German scale. It would be arbitrary, however, to assume that the

respective magnitudes of these qualifications cancel each other out.

Moreover, the differences in the importance and the 'existential' role of politics in the two German states have to be taken into account. In the GDR, a political career is the only way of getting to the top of the power pyramid. Membership of the Communist Party is also an insurance for better jobs and also offers easier access to higher education for one's children, especially for the children of those parents who are not manual workers. In the GDR as in other Communist-dominated countries, membership of the Communist Party is an important element of social status. In the West, membership of political parties is neither vital for individual self-assertion nor an element of status. Consequently it is much less desirable. In this respect the difference between the FRG and the GDR is striking. Whereas in the West total membership of political parties is slightly more than 3 per cent of the adult population, in the East the SED membership alone is above 15 per cent.[99] After adding the membership of the so-called block political parties the proportion may reach 17 per cent.

In the FRG, the 3 per cent of political party membership in the adult population is virtually the same as the percentage of those who in the opinion poll in 1970 considered themselves to be actively participating in politics. Interest in politics without active participation was shared by 37 per cent of the respondents. 43 per cent said that they are no more interested in politics than in other matters and 16 per cent expressed their complete disinterest in politics. Only 1 per cent of the poll gave no answer.[100]

This seems to contradict a comparatively high turnout for the West German elections (between 86 to 91 per cent in federal elections, between 81 to 89 per cent in the Land elections).[101] However, as Almond and Verba have already found on the basis of an earlier public opinion poll, this apparent contradiction reflects a particular attitude of the majority of West German citizens towards politics. They were not enthusiastic about it but they accepted it as a necessary condition of their lives; they were comparatively well informed and they performed their political duties, voting being the most important one.[102] Thirty-one per cent of German respondents in Almond's and Verba's investigation in 1959 reported in that way. As Verba further reports, many respondents explicitly stated that their obligation to participate in politics was exhausted by the fulfilment of their voting obligation.[103]

Bearing all this in mind, it is only with extreme caution that we can use the analogy as a means for quantification of the possible number of

people concerned with the limited assortment of political and/or
ideological choice in the East. The tendency towards left/right symmetry
in the West and the tendency to join the SED for security reasons sets
two possible limits for our estimate. The upper limit for those who
would like to join a political party in straightforward opposition to the
Communists may equal the percentage of the SED membership, i.e. 15
per cent of the adult population. The lower limit might be that of
those actively involved in politics in the West, i.e. 3 per cent of the adult
population.

So the basic limitations of personal liberties, liberties in the sense of
taking part in some manifest activity (foreign travel, private enterprise,
outspoken political opposition) may concern only a minority of the
population. What then about the majority? Here some less manifest
activities or attitudes have to be considered. Three basic points have to
be envisaged: firstly, one should not forget that human consciousness
is not always apparent in behaviour. Conformism is often due to
'existential' reasons, it is often a matter of opportunism. Secondly,
legal or administrative limitations often enhance the desire for
forbidden fruits and produce greater tension than if the enjoyment of
these fruits depends only on personal taste and the size of one's purse.
Thirdly, limitations in the economic sphere, especially in essential
consumer goods and services are particularly irritating and, if compared
with better-off neighbours or reference groups, may produce widespread dissatisfaction.

West Germany is for East Germany an exciting and alluring reference
group. This is not only the case with material goods such as food,
clothes, footwear, consumer durables, household services etc., but also
in the field of culture and entertainment. Here a Westerner has a
wide variety of choice ranging from offerings of a high cultural and
moral value to those which completely lack such standards. In enjoying
them the individual can evade all social commitments and responsibilities.
In the East the escapist alternatives to the political patronage of social
life are limited: music, folklore and sport are the main legitimate
channels. In literature, drama and the arts, socialist realism has to be
accepted as the right style.

Against all these limitations of choice, one has however to
acknowledge that the East German citizen is being protected from that
type of consumption which results from the combined impact of
unchecked personal freedom and market-value orientation in the West.
As freedom is indivisible in the West, freedom to criticise and freedom
to publish dissident views also means freedom to publish and sell

rubbish. As the consumer market is getting especially keen on sex and violence, publishing freedom becomes easily diverted to these channels. It is commercialisation and not manipulation, lack of positive orientation and not of individual freedom which constitute the seamy side of Western culture.

Recently, the difference between East and West in this respect has been emphasised by a Western visitor to East and West Berlin in the following vivid report:

There was a general air of purposive domesticity pervading daily life in the Eastern sector of the city. People seemed busy, sober and self-respecting. Nobody loitered on the clean and somewhat puritanically ordered and designed streets.

There was no 'night-life' in our Western metropolitan sense: no night-clubs, naughty shows, strident solicitation of the idle senses by neon-lights, posters, advertising etc.

Everywhere one was struck by a kind of ostentatious decency, if I may so speak. Public prostitution, if it existed at all, was certainly not in evidence. Pornography, one quickly ralised, was simply unthinkable.

The police were courteous, attentive to public need and mixed freely with the people in cafés and shops. Of course, I saw only the surface of things as a visitor.

There was an over-seriousness about 'culture', in the sense of 'high' culture; yet books, other than technical works, were hard to come by.

The 'Western' sectors were — I do not wish to dramatise, but I cannot avoid the phrases — an epic in ostentatious vulgarity. Yet they somehow failed to establish an impression of *character,* other than that curiously a-specific character of megalopolitan international featurelessness that makes tourist Cairo almost identical with tourist Rotterdam.

Everything struck the visitor's superficial glance as essentially cosmetic glamour — free, vulgar and designed to strike upon the senses below the level of intelligence. This must inevitably seem unfair and harsh. Indeed it is. I am morally certain that the great mass of men and women, in both East and West, lead quite ordinary decent lives. But these, after all, are the *two ways in which the two systems have chosen to present themselves.* It was impossible not to be impressed by the quality of the choice each has made.

Almost every West Berliner to whom we spoke was quick to point

out that *they* had a freedom of choice. I do not intend to be
cynical or smart when I say that the apparent choice actually made
by West Berlin in its public *persona* was the exercise in freedom to
be infantile and, in appearance, frivolous.[104]

The resulting image, the respective visiting cards of the way of life in the
FRG and GDR are far from being a question of black and white.
Although self-assertion of the individual is incontestably wider and
deeper in the West than in the East, the fruits of this self-assertion are
not necessarily nicer. As the observer above has rightly pointed out
however, the surface of things may not be representative. Whereas
sexual entertainment and prostitution used to be advertised for
commercial reasons in public, intellectual prostitution, occasional in
pluralistic societies but widespread in societies with an ideological
monopoly is, for 'existential' reasons, rather concealed.

It is also significant that the official West is not ashamed of its base
face. It shows itself in all its beauty and ugliness indiscriminately. As
shown on p.109, reported criminality is higher there than in the East
and is gradually increasing. Newspapers and mass media are most
pleased when they can disclose any dirty event. Is it for ethical reasons?
Or rather for the sake of commercial effect? Moreover strict legality
prevents the government and judiciary from interfering in matters
which are not clearly established as illegal activities. Although
occasionally the police or the administration overstep the mark, there
remains a wide legal scope for activities which may endanger the
freedom and security of other individuals. Political anti-systemic
opposition is also able to operate within the legal system.

All this seems to have contributed to a desire for tougher policing in
the FRG. In a 1971 opinion poll 69 per cent of respondents said that
the police should do more (for security and order) whereas only 22 per
cent were satisfied with their performance. To the question whether
the size of the police force in the FRG was satisfactory, 62 per cent
answered that there were not enough police and only 8 per cent that
there were too many policemen. In 1972 the percentages were 64 per
cent and 4 per cent respectively.[105] Results of other polls indicate that
more police were required for defence against criminal rather than
political anti-systemic activities; political opposition was conceived
quite liberally. In 1968 only 44 per cent of a poll approved the
emergency law, giving the government special powers to limit personal
freedom in case of war.[106] In another poll, only 18 per cent of the
respondents considered the Baader-Meinhof people (an anarchist group

which became known for its terrorist activity) as a criminal gang, whereas 51 per cent considered them as a political group; 13 per cent were
undecided and 18 per cent had never heard of these people.[107] In 1975
however, the terrorist acts of this gang became so daring and widely
publicised that its image might have changed considerably.

Unfortunately there are no counterparts to these investigations from
the GDR. Questioning people who have left the East would be of little
use because this highly conscious anti-systemic category would
certainly not provide a representative sample. The views of average
West Germans appear to be more revealing for an East/West comparison.
In the summer of 1972, the Institute for Infratest Social Research in
Munich asked a sample of voters in the whole of the FRG, including
West Berlin, a series of questions which are of particular relevance for
our intersystemic comparison.

Firstly, there were questions concerning the subjective evaluation
of political self-assertion: 46 per cent of the whole sample considered
the political co-determination of West German citizens satisfactory; 47
per cent unsatisfactory; 3 per cent found it excessive and 4 per cent
gave no answer. Similarly distributed were views on co-determination in
enterprises: 45 per cent 'sufficient', 46 per cent 'too little', 5 per cent
'too much' and 4 per cent 'no answer'.[108]

From these figures it may be concluded that almost a half of the
West German voters did not consider the West German democracy
democratic enough. On the other hand the Institute of Demoscopy
found, also in 1972 (May), that only 19 per cent of the poll expressed
their wish to abolish capitalism, 53 per cent were in favour of keeping
it and 28 per cent were undecided. In February 1973, 31 per cent of
respondents agreed with the suggestion that political equality is not
possible if there is economic inequality, 20 per cent did not agree and
49 per cent were undecided.[109]

In the same sample of voters questioned in the summer of 1972, 21
per cent were decidedly in favour of the *status quo,* 53 per cent found
it satisfactory, 21 per cent considered reform necessary and only 3 per
cent favoured a revolutionary restructuring.[110]

One may conclude from all these results that the majority of West
Germans view their socio-economic system favourably on the whole,
but that a large number of them find it wanting, from the point of view
of the degree to which it is democratic.

The second type of question in the Infratest poll concerned a
comparison with the GDR. This was assessed by means of 18 characteristics. The West German respondents had to answer whether these

characteristics were better fitted to the FRG or the GDR. The respondents had also to evaluate how intensively a particular characteristic applied to the East or West. For that purpose, the respondents had to use a six-grade scale (from 0 to 5). The published results, abbreviated by amalgamating two scales, are reproduced in Table 4.4.

Our previous analysis makes it possible to examine how far these answers reflect real differences. In most cases West German opinion corresponds to the findings in this study. There can be little doubt that there is greater personal freedom (in the Western sense), more citizens' co-determination and higher economic efficiency in the West than in the East. The big differences in scale values indicate that the systemic differences on these points are widely acknowledged. Also government interference in private lives and greater equality of wealth (smaller gap between rich and poor) in the East has been correctly assessed.

Surprisingly, distributive justice (fair income distribution) has been found equally wanting in both German states (the scale values were virtually identical). Exploitation was considered higher in the GDR than in the FRG. In terms of analysis in the first section of this study there seems to be only a slight, if any, anti-Eastern bias in the answers concerning income distribution and exploitation. Similarly, on the issue of job security the respondents considered the situation in both German states equal. In reality, higher security with respect to economic fluctuation in the East may be matched by lower security against political disqualification (in more responsible jobs).

Of the other values, the East is considered to be better off in view of lower rents, wider educational opportunities, more comprehensive health services, greater concern with youth and sport, lower criminality and lower divorce rates. With the exception of the last point where the opposite is true (see section 4f, p. 165), the subjective evaluations appear to be borne out by facts. The evaluation of the promotion of science and technology is not quite conclusive; the respondents' verdict was slightly in favour of the GDR but this seems to reflect the relatively greater weight attached to science and technology in the life of the GDR in comparison with the West. On the other hand the respondents considered that the FRG as a country was doing more for peace and lowering of international tensions than the GDR. With regard to West German politics since 1969 there can be little doubt on this count.

Although all these questions are not directly concerned with citizens' self-assertion, they are nevertheless worth reporting in this context, because they reveal subjective views on the respective quality

Table 4.4 West German Evaluation of some Systemic Qualities in the
FRG and GDR

Quality		Scale values			
		not the case %	to a limited extent %	exten- sive %	Arithmetic mean
Personal freedom	FRG	1	9	85	4.5
	GDR	54	36	6	1.4
Influence of the state	FRG	41	42	12	1.9
on private lives	GDR	6	18	70	4.0
Policy of peace and	FRG	3	33	59	3.8
easing of tension	GDR	28	54	12	2.2
Co-determination of citizens	FRG	4	34	58	3.7
in political matters	GDR	46	38	10	1.6
Co-determination of	FRG	6	49	40	3.3
employees in enterprises	GDR	30	44	18	2.2
Economic efficiency	FRG	2	20	75	4.1
	GDR	9	56	29	3.0
Fair income distribution	FRG	13	61	22	2.7
	GDR	13	59	22	2.7
Job security	FRG	5	44	47	3.4
	GDR	3	43	46	3.5
Exploitation of labour	FRG	21	55	19	2.5
	GDR	8	44	42	3.3
Big difference between	FRG	5	41	49	3.6
rich and poor	GDR	13	57	24	2.7
Low rents	FRG	48	37	10	1.6
	GDR	6	20	68	4.0
Equal educational	FRG	4	48	43	3.4
opportunities for all	GDR	4	31	58	3.7
Furtherance of science	FRG	1	45	50	3.9
and technology	GDR	1	23	70	4.0
Good health service	FRG	3	48	44	3.4
	GDR	2	27	64	3.9
Extensive support for	FRG	7	60	28	3.0
youth	GDR	1	14	78	4.2
Furtherance of sport	FRG	5	59	31	3.1
	GDR	1	11	83	4.4
High criminality	FRG	2	30	63	3.9
	GDR	22	60	10	2.6
Excessive divorce rate	FRG	3	48	43	3.4
	GDR	12	60	19	2.7

Source: *Bericht,* 1974, p. 100.

of the compared systems. Unfortunately only Western opinion has been scrutinised and the results made available. Easterners have never been asked similar questions.

Already this very difference is significant enough. However dissatisfied the West Germans may be with the quality of their democracy, they are allowed to express their views on it. The East Germans are supposed to be happy and agree with what their leadership does on their behalf. If they are not, it depends on the nature of their grievances. If these concern only inadequate supply and quality of individual goods or services, or minor shortcomings in administration, they may be considered as legitimate and if presented in the proper way, i.e. through the political party or mass organisation, they may be used as a welcome feedback. But if the grievances are of a more general nature, if they aim at the system of a centrally planned and managed economy, or still worse, if they contain critical hints on the politics of the society, they are rejected as hostile or, at best, as expressions of a 'false consciousness'. There can be nothing basically wrong witht the system in the East; only with individuals living in it.

4i. Nation, unity and alienation

So far in the preceding analysis it has been implicitly supposed that citizens alone are interested in some type of individual self-assertion. As social psychologists well know, self-assertion may also be achieved through identification with a particular group or even with a wider community, such as a nation.

Self-assertion by means of group identification appears in all societies. In Germany however this type of self-assertion has been particularly virulent. Perhaps because of a long-lasting fragmentation German national unity acquired priority in societal values from the mid-nineteenth century. It was largely considered as the ultimate value. Individuals were often ready to sacrifice other values, even their lives, for its achievement and/or promotion. The military became an indication of national strength, a symbol of unity and object of pride.

Self-assertion through service in the armed forces, or through active participation in war cannot simply be explained by residues of primitive masculinity. Aggressive instincts were sanctified by service to the nation which in its all-embracing and perennial nature, provided a powerful objective for self-assertion through group identification. For its full satisfaction, political unity of the whole ethnic community was required. German unity became a collective value which in a way gave meaning to individual lives and endeavours. In that sense it acquired almost religious features.

During the last hundred years the concept of German unity under-
went considerable mutations. First the main stress was only on a
common political framework for the whole ethnic community. Then, in
addition to that, an ideological unity was required. Eventually after the
collapse of the Nazi two-fold (ethnico-geographical and ideological)
unity, both the ethnic and political unity seems to have been gradually
abandoned as an imminent objective. In the Eastern part of Germany,
a more thorough unity of the whole society has been attempted.

German political tradition has symbolic expressions for the different
types of unity; 'One God, one Empire, one Emperor' (*ein Gott, ein
Reich, ein Kaiser*) for the Wilhelmian (Second) Empire and 'one
Nation, one Empire, one Leader' (*ein Volk, ein Reich, ein Führer*) for
the Nazi (Third) Empire.

Significantly, the second Empire's slogan did not talk of the unity
of the Church but of God. Consequently, ideological unity was not
required. For this purpose, unity of Church would have been a better
prerequisite. Yet in the past, when unity of the Church had still been
preserved, there had been virtually no unity of the empire. At least the
first (medieval) empire had not constituted one political or ethnic unit
in the modern sense. The second, Nazi, slogan, in proclaiming the unity
of ethnic Germans as the supreme value, reimposed an ideological
monopoly on the nation and, on top of that, added to the unity of the
empire the unity of an exclusive leadership.

The Communist régime drops the unity of the ethnic community as
the supreme value and postulates a more intense unity of the societal
structure, based on the exclusive supremacy of one political party, one
philosophy and a centrally planned and managed economy. In terms of
slogans, the Communist principle might be expressed as follows: 'one
Party, one Doctrine, one Employer'.

The particular unity of the GDR was also boosted by the abolition
of the federalist structure (Länder) and by the revival of the prestige of
the armed forces.

In contrast to the FRG the GDR is a unitary state. Traditional
Lands (Saxony, Thuringia, Mecklenburg etc.) were abolished and the
country redivided into 15 districts (including East Berlin; only West
Berlin is considered as a separate entity by the Easterners). Similarly,
autonomous Länder were substituted by administrative regions (Gaue)
for several societal purposes during the Nazi rule.

Also in the GDR greater stress has been laid on one particular
institutional prerequisite of national sovereignty, namely the armed

forces. The army was one of the main agents of the reunification of Germany between 1848 and 1871. German nationalists explained the defeat of Germany in World War One not because it was the army's fault but because of the betrayal by politicians' 'stabbing in the back'. Also for the defeat in World War Two the Nazi leadership rather than the army might be blamed. So the army remained, in a way, an infallible symbol of German nationalism. At the same time the officer corps was the stronghold of authoritarian conservatism in the society. Authoritarian attitudes contributed, among other forces, to the weakening of the Weimar Republic. Therefore the responsible leaders of the FRG were careful not to give the newly constituted armed forces the status of the imperial army and made provisions to keep it under political and judicial control. Moreover the West German law (*Soldatengesetz*) gives soldiers the right not to carry out an order which would offend human dignity or which would result in crime.

In view of the position and social role of the armed forces, the structure in the FRG seems to differ considerably from that before the war. The army lost a good deal of its national charisma. Several opinion polls (in 1964, 1969 and 1971) have shown that only slightly above a third of respondents had a good image of the West German army (Bundeswehr); about a quarter hold a negative view. The explicit question whether young men who had served in the army enjoy a higher esteem amongst the other population was in 1968 answered in the negative by 59 per cent of the respondents. Only 22 per cent, and among them more women than men, considered former draftees with more appreciation than those who had not been soldiers at all.[111]

Recently however this trend seems to have been reversed. Whereas in May 1973 only 50 per cent of respondents considered the Bundeswehr important, in 1974 58 per cent and in 1975 78 per cent held this view. The percentage of those who thought that military service was unimportant dropped from 14 to 4 per cent.[112]

On the basis of a sample investigation it has been observed that temporary service in the army does not promote authoritarian attitudes or respect for authority. On the contrary, deprivation resulting from the military style of life increases the draftees' sensibility to values such as respect and tolerance for other citizens.[113]

In contrast to the West, in the GDR the army's tradition has been re-established. Since its constitution (or rather amalgamation of different paramilitary units) on 18 January 1956, the National People's Army (Nationale Volksarmee) has enjoyed particular attention from the political leadership who have tried to give it a good image and as much prestige as possible. It is not insignificant that the Volksarmee was constituted on the anniversary of the creation of the Prussian kingdom in 1701 and the German Empire in 1871. The East Germany Army is also under the political control of civilians but this, in different circumstances, gives it more prestige than is the case in West Germany. The East German Army is one of the pillars of the Marxist-Leninist establishment also in the sense that it is an additional means of ideological education. It is a political army whose conscripts have to be trained not only in the military art but also in the doctrine of the state. Although in that sense the Nationale Volksarmee differs from the Prussian Army, it follows its tradition with respect to discipline. Unlike the West, the East German conscripts are supposed to give their superiors unconditional obedience.[114] In outward appearance, in public display of military strength and virtues such as parades with goose-step etc., the East German Army preserves more of the German military tradition than the army in the West.

The extent and cost of the military is higher in the East than in the West. Active military service in the East is 18 months whereas it is only 15 months in the West. The regular armed forces in the GDR absorb 3.5 per cent of the male population of working age (between 15 and 65), whereas in the FRG it is only 2.2 per cent. The workers' militia which comprises about 7 per cent of the male population of working age has to be added to the regular armed forces in the East. The trained military reserve contains, in the East, about 20 per cent of the male population of working age, whereas in the West it is only 8 per cent.[115] As stated earlier (p. 37) the percentage of national income on military expenditure is   higher in the East than in the West.

The new type of unity in the East could be achieved only at the price of geographical disunity and reduced popular appeal. The majority of the German population is beyond   its pale. Also, judging by the population movements since the partition and by the Eastern ban on westward movement, the more differentiated pattern of the West still appears to be preferred among Germans.

Moreover there are some pointers to the effect that the Germans have renounced their collective quest for self-assertion in the traditional sense. Opinion polls in the FRG indicate a growing accommodation of the West Germans to divided Germany. In the summer of 1962, 61 per cent of respondents found the existing partition intolerable; 28 per cent said that they grew gradually accustomed to it. At the end of 1967 the answers were: 31 per cent intolerable and 54 per cent gradually accustomed. The rest in both cases were undecided.[116]

According to another poll the proportion of Germans ready to accept the *status quo*, i.e. the existence of the two German states and renunciation of the territories beyond the Oder-Neisse line, increased from 36 per cent in 1967 to 50 per cent in 1969. Meanwhile the proportion of those preferring to wait for reunification, even at the price of international tension, dropped from 34 per cent to 24 per cent.[117] In 1971, 60 per cent of a West German poll considered the existence of one German state as the best possible solution; among the youngest age cohort (16–29) however this opinion was held by only 48 per cent of the respondents.[118] The preference for unity was strongest among Christian Democrats (69 per cent) and weakest among Liberals (45 per cent). Social Democrats were, with 54 per cent, in between.[119]

In view of other circumstances this development seems to be a sign of resignation rather than of programmatic orientation. There are good reasons to believe that under changed circumstances this type of opinion might be reversed.

By contrast to the FRG, in the East only the official position can be ascertained. From the founding of the GDR until the early seventies, East German leaders did not consider the GDR as a separate nation. Opinion voiced by some West German philosophers such as Jaspers, that two separate German nations are in the making, was rejected as a reactionary Utopia. Article I of the GDR Constitution of 1968 proclaimed the GDR as a Socialist state of the German nation.

After the fall of Ulbricht a new tendency started to develop. At the theoretical conference of the district officials of the SED in Berlin, a Politburo member, Hermann Axen, put forward a new theoretical evaluation of this issue.[120] He re-emphasised Lenin's stress on the economic connotation of nationality and virtually resuscitated Stalin's definition of nationality according to which a different socio-economic system is, among others, a constitutive element of separate nationality.

The relevant passage of the GDR Constitution of 1974 omitted any reference to the 'nation'. This gives the impression that it either accepted the changed view, or by-passed this issue. In the new Constitution, Article I reads: 'The GDR is a Socialist state of workers and farmers.'

On the strength of more recent evidence however, it seems that the second explanation is more plausible. At the 13th Plenary Session of the Central Committee of the SED (in December 1974), the top man in the party and state hierarchy, Honecker, struck a balance between the two views. Bearing in mind the difficulties of some GDR citizens who, being receptive to the stress on the double German nationality, were at a loss as to how to complete the item 'Nationality' on their personal questionnaires, Honecker declared: 'The answer to this question is straightforward and clear without any ambiguity: Statehood — GDR, Nationality — German, such is the matter.'[121]

Whereas before the end of November 1974 the commentaries in the East German Press gave the impression that the concept of two German nations was an article of official doctrine, from December of the same year the situation was seen in a more 'dialectical' way. There are two states and societies but one nation. The new position might be better understood in juxtaposition with the expectation that possibly also the West may eventually be won for Marxist-Leninist socialism. Honecker hinted at this objective in a diplomatic way: 'Otherwise we are of the opinion as we always were that socialism will not avoid the FRG.' ('. . . *dass der Sozialismus auch um die Bundesrepublik Deutschland keinen Bogen machen wird'*.)[122]

Whereas officialdom and public opinion in the FRG are gradually abandoning the policy of reunification, the official representatives of the GDR reinstate the unification of Germany on their terms as a viable proposition. By contrast to the fifties, when the reunification fromn the West and on Western terms seemed to be the only alternative, in the mid-seventies there is quite a different situation. Although the possibility of uniting Germany from the East in a Bismarck-like way still appears to be remote, the purposefulness and perseverence of East German leaders seems to be a more efficient prerequisite to this aim than anything that is being undertaken in the opposite direction from the West. Though values such as personal freedom and affluence may be more desired than other values by the majority of the German population, there is no proselytising spirit amongst those who stand for these values. The Western élite does not even envisage the possibility that their world view might acquire that particular dimension.

The turn of fortune can best be illustrated by the development of the 'Free University of Berlin' initiated by refugee students from East Berlin and founded with the co-operation of all major political parties in the West (Social Democrats, Christian Democrats and Liberals). The new university in West Berlin was designed as a model of a genuinely democratic establishment of higher education. Students were represented in all bodies and decision-making with the only exception of disciplinary matters of teaching staff. During the first ten years of its existence, the Free University of Berlin basically supported the policy of the West German government. In 1951 the university expressed its solidarity with the Adenauer government policy of reunification. In 1954 discussions with representatives of universities in the GDR were rejected and in 1957 two students were banned from the representation because of their participation in the Moscow Youth Festival.

In 1958 however the situation changed. Growing student concern with and criticism of the situation in the West clashed with attempts by the university administration to re-establish more authority. Since then a chain reaction has set in. Confronted with the reluctance of authorities to accept their criticism of the West as well as their criticism of the East, the politically involved students became stimulated to concentrate their criticism in the direction where it met strongest opposition within the university. In spite of the Berlin Wall with which the East emphasised, in a manifest way, its anti-liberal attitude, student opposition to the Marxist-Leninist establishment, which had been the main cause of the University's birth, gradually became a non-issue. Students' concern increased both in geographical scope (Vietnam, Portuguese colonies,etc.) and in intensity of dissent (demonstrations against foreign official visits such as that of the Shah of Iran in 1967).

In 1967, the Polish students' opposition to creeping re-Stalinisation in Poland and the students' demonstration in Prague reminded West German students of the fate of freedom in the East. In 1968 some tokens of solidarity were shown to the students involved in the Reform Movement in Czechoslovakia. Yet, as the discussion between radical student leaders from West Germany and the students in Prague indicated, there was not a great deal of mutual understanding. After the reformist Communists in Czechoslovakia had been crushed by Soviet military intervention, an intervention in which the GDR had taken an active part, quite a few West German radical leftists (in contrast to their Italian, French and British counterparts), were ready to accept and rationalise the official position of the USSR and GDR on this question.

It is amazing that the Communist Party in the FRG has a strong pro-Soviet orientation and that among the West German leftist students the Communist faction is strongest in West Berlin. Can this be dismissed as insignificant because Communists in the FRG, including West Berlin, are numerically a tiny minority? Or is it significant because it reveals the appeal of force and discipline on German radicals? Or does it in connection with the still more radical, anarchist and terrorist groups indicate a broader scope for political polarisation in Germany than in other West European countries?

The amount and intensity of anti-systemic features in the opposition can be considered as the degree of alienation of the respective group from the political régime (polity) or perhaps also the society. The West German students' opposition appears to be alienated from their society and polity alike. Any opposition in a Communist-dominated country is alienated from their respective régimes. In the West, the students criticise the whole way of life and the public reaction to their attitudes is either indifferent or more or less hostile. There is little understanding, if any. In the East, the policy is superimposed on the society, which has no independent life of its own. All its activities are either directed or at least supervised by political bodies. So the alienation from society can take place only if the society is identified with the polity. This however cannot be assumed. There is a lot of apathy and disguised dissatisfaction. Judging by the taboos of East German censorship and by the stream and direction of refugees, East German polity seems to be more alienated from the society than is the case in the West.

To sum up, in the West there is no general alienation of the society from the polity which in its turn is less weighty than in the East. There is however an intensive alienation of a numerically small segment of the population, composed mainly of students, from both the polity and society. Their aim is a complete change of both. In the East the society is not in a position to express itself against the polity and any opposition is directed against the pressures created by the polity.

In static terms the total amount of alienation appears greater in the East than in the West. On the other hand, in the West the alienation can afford to be more vociferous and above all has succeeded in organising its own institutional focuses, among those who prepare themselves both professionally and ideologically to become the power élite in the future. The potential for spreading alienation by ideological education cannot be underestimated. With the growing student population and with an increasing percentage of alienated students among them, the weight of the counter-élite and anti-systemic opposition may be expected to grow. Even if some young 'radicals' turn to 'moderates' with age and even if the 'Berufsverbot' excludes the most militant radicals from the civil service, the present trend shows a gradual increase of those who are 'in the society but not of the society' in the West.

Only the fact that the radicals have been unable to exploit a major economic depression makes their protest somewhat hollow. Their main criticism aims at alleged bourgeois acquiescence with good material standards and supposedly benevolent rulers (precisely those qualities which in the East European countries would be most welcomed by the Communist governments). Radical leftists do not like the citizens to become satisfied subjects. As they want to change not only the polity but the society, they do not want any compromise. In their own words, 'the students don't want any arrangement; they will carry on their protests and provocation because they want a basically more human society'.[123]

As the radicals' representatives do not want compromise, the government is in an awkward position. It wants neither to yield to, nor to suppress the counter-élite. It tries rather hard to play down the whole issue and vacillates between small concessions and small retributions. In doing so it stimulates rather than weakens the opposition. The door remains open, to borrow Dutschke's term, for the radical leftists' 'march through institutions'.

On the other hand neither is the door closed for a possible right-wing backlash. Students' opposition to the whole, widely accepted way of life and not only to the economico-political system, makes it more likely. If the combined effects of continuous irritation from the left and genuine economic grievances succeed in awakening the sleeping ghost of middle-class radicalism, those who maintain that 'the enemy is always on the right in Germany'[124] may eventually be found correct.

Whether left or right, more authoritarianism rather than democracy might easily be the outcome of the radical democrats' campaign on the left. This may limit the amount of visible alienation in the West and, indirectly, help to alleviate the latent alienation in the East.

Unfortunately, as the people with personal experience in the East know, latent alienation is something which only moral and literary giants such as Solzhenitsyn can reveal to the outside world. Otherwise sociologists and political scientists alike increasingly tend to apply to it the time-honoured principle of the Canonic Law: *Quod non est in actis non est in mundo.*

4j. Summary

Power, as a possibility to enforce one's own will against the opposition of others within a social relationship, whether based on authority or influence, can be identified by its range (scope of coverage) and its level (grade of hierarchy). Both the dimensions are relevant not only to those who wield the power but also to those who are subject to it.

Freedom, as the reverse corollary of power, has analogous but opposite dimensions. Comparison which does not consider power in juxtaposition with freedom cannot do justice to systemic differences. So neither Wolfgang Zapf's nor Peter C. Ludz's conclusions on the development of the German élite could be considered as an adequate basis for an inter-systemic comparison. Dahrendorf's characterisation based on concepts of uniformity and multiformity of the élite proves more helpful. Yet, this dichotomy has to be further developed.

There may not only be differences between political and other élites but also between higher and lower echelons of the élite. In the GDR the power élite at the top is uniform, whereas the lower strata of power are multiform. Uniformity at the top is not only institutional but also functional. Decisions on all societal questions, especially those concerning economy and culture are taken by the same supreme body. Moreover, its range of power is much wider than that of all the multiform élites in the West put together.

This is a corollary of a different concept of freedom in East and West. In the Western sense any increase of the scope of power necessarily decreases the freedom of the subject. In the East freedom does not mean individual self-assertion (self-determination) but the collective self-determination of the organised society as a whole, a purposeful self-determination towards a goal, a protective self-determination both against forces of nature and against retrograde forces within the society itself. As Ludz puts it, Hegel's thesis that history is the progressive realisation of freedom is interpreted to mean a constant expansion of areas for controlled or regulated action.

So, in the Marxist-Leninist sense, power and freedom are in a way synonymous, rather than contradictory concepts. This may be well appreciated by those at the top who, in having acquired more power, have also got more freedom for their purposeful action. Those below, however, whether in the West or in the East, understand freedom as a quality of their personal position, as scope for decision-making, with which other persons do not interfere. From that perspective, those below are not so much interested in who the élites are but what they do, what is the range of their power, and how effective are the means of compulsion they command.

The heavier the pressure from above, the more the desire to evade it. There are two alternatives: to run away, or to climb up. In the GDR only the latter is legally available. Enhanced vertical mobility enables the active individuals to acquire more power, but not necessarily more freedom. For that, they have to climb right to the top, and even there they discover the limits set on their sovereignty by leaders of another country. Yet even without commensurate freedom, a greater command over the others may be appreciated, often as compensation for previous hardships and/or inferiority.

The main differences in the pattern of decision-making between East and West can be summarised as follows: in the West, in any field of action, whether political, economic, administrative or cultural, the scope of decisions on behalf of those below is more limited than in the East. On the other hand, Western holders of power have, as a rule, decisions less limited by those above them. Moreover individual fields of the exercise of power (especially economy and culture) are in the West usually separated from each other. Also, for some trials of strength, there are in the West two objective referees: the market in the economic and elections in the political field.

In the East, decisions which in the West are taken by elections, are usually taken by the Politburo, or rarely, by the Central Committee of the Communist Party. Also, decisions made on the market are to a considerable extent taken over by authorities subject to those political bodies. In the East there is, as a matter of principle, a mistrust of spontaneity. Purposeful steering of the society cannot be made dependent on the vacillation of uncontrolled forces.

Western observers are often keen to discover fundamental changes in the economico-political structure of the Communist states. In doing so, they tend to exaggerate structural details at the expense of basic issues. These, in the author's view, are the degree of concentration of power at the top, and the degree of loyalty required by the subjects. Should concepts such as authoritarian and totalitarian rule be used to describe any reality, then these two issues have to be considered as a possible demarcation. With respect to the first issue (that of constellation of power), a totalitarian régime is that régime where not only political and cultural but also economic power is concentrated in one body. With respect to the second issue (that of loyalty of subjects) a totalitarian régime is that régime which, as Lipset has put it, requires full loyalty of its subjects, loyalty manifested in everyday action; it is not satisfied with mere passive obedience of subjects as an authoritarian régime is.

With respect to these two issues, nothing has changed in the GDR during the last decade. In the GDR both the constellation of power and the required loyalty of subjects remains totalitarian. The political élite continues to be superimposed on the other élites. On the other hand, the pluralistic character of the FRG has become more apparent. The great coalition, i.e. a coalition of the two big rival political parties which in some quarters was considered to be a menace to a pluralistic system has gone; the increasing influence of a vociferous counter-élite has become a salient feature of the changing political culture.

In individual areas of self-assertion, such as family life, employment and citizenship, West Germany has provided better opportunities than East Germany. In the GDR, married women are supposed to be employed, to send their children to nurseries, kindergartens etc.; parental education has to conform with the state's ideology. A thorough ideological education of the young generation is one of the primary targets of East Germany policy; the citizen has to be a *homo politicus* in the East whereas in the West the preference in education is still for *homo civilis*. Churches also have different roles; whereas in the West they are unhampered in their activities and often operate as strong pressure groups, in the East there is a concentrated effort to make them another transmission belt of party and government policy.

Co-determination in employment is formally more developed in the East, however its virtual effects are minimised by the dependence of trade unions on the party decisions and supervisory role of the Communist Party groups in individual enterprises. In the FRG the workers co-determination is formally more modest but actually more efficient, at least in two industries (coal and iron) where it has been fairly established. Elsewhere it is an unresolved political issue between Social Democrats on one side and Christian Democrats on the other.

Citizens' self-assertion is not only a matter of political co-determination or of so-called political input; it can be understood as a wide spéctrum of activities which the state reserves for the discretion of individuals. Consequently not only elections and membership in political parties, but also free choice of, and participation in, professional, ideological and interest associations, private undertakings and free geographical mobility (foreign travel) are relevant indicators of personal liberties. West Germans have, at least legally, a wide variety of choice and opportunities. In fact, however, there is a considerable number of those who either cannot (for lack of personal contacts, education or money) or do not want to (for lack of interest) use some of these choices.

The discrepancy between legal and factual opportunities is the main concern of socialists of all brands. As criticism of this discrepancy is often related to Marxist ideology, it is sometimes not quite clear whether the critics really want more genuine freedom for individuals or whether they are more or less ready to accept the Eastern alternative.

In the GDR the situation is quite different. The East German citizen cannot match his Western counterpart in affluence and personal freedom; his orientation is being turned to collective and future achievements. The Marxist-Leninist objective is to convince men that in behaving as they are required to they are fulfilling their historical role and in so doing they enjoy 'freedom'.

Notes

1. G. Redlow, 'Die Marxistisch-Leninistische Auffassung von der Freiheit', in *Freiheit und Gesellschaft*, Frankfurt a/M, 1973, p. 89. Translation of this and subsequent quotations in this chapter are the author's.
2. H. Steininger, 'Die Grundlagen der Freiheit der sozialistischen Gesellschaft', in *Freiheit und Gesellschaft*, p. 162.
3. Redlow, ibid.
4. Redlow, op. cit., p. 101.
5. J.R. Becher, 'Erziehung zur Freiheit', in J. R. Becher, *Auswahl*, Vol. 5, pp. 45–6.
6. W. Sauberlich, 'Freiheit als bewusste und planmässige Gestaltung der gesellschaftlichen Lebensbedingungen', in *Freiheit und Gesellschaft*, p. 193. Here reference is made to a rather contradictory passage of the Communist Manifesto which reads: 'In place of the old bourgeois society, with its classes and class antagonisms, we shall have an association in which the free development of each is the condition for the free development of all.' (Quoted from the English translation published by George Allen and Unwin, London, 1967, p. 146.) In Marx's and Engels' formulation the relationship is the other way round: Individual freedom is the condition for the collective freedom.
7. Sauberlich, ibid., p. 195.
8. G. Stiehler, 'Die Dialektik von gesellschaftlicher und persönlicher Freiheit', in *Freiheit und Gesellschaft*, p. 228.
9. cf. Redlow, op. cit., pp. 98–100, and Stiehler, op. cit., p. 264.
10. Stiehler, op. cit., p. 235.
11. Stiehler, ibid., p. 242.
12. Also the often quoted passage from the 3rd volume of Capital on Freedom does not seem to square with the general interpretation drawn by the Marxist-Leninist orthodoxy. Marx said:
    'The realm of freedom does not commence until the point is passed where labour under the compulsion of necessity and of external utility is required. In the very nature of things it lies beyond the sphere of material production in the strict meaning of the term. Just as the savage must wrestle with nature in order to satisfy his wants, in order to maintain life and reproduce it, so civilised man has to do it, and he must do it in all forms of society and under all possible modes of production. With his development the realm of natural necessity expands, because his wants increase; but at the same time the forces of production increase, by which these wants are satisfied. The freedom in this field cannot consist of anything else but of the fact that socialised man, the associated producers, regulate their interchange with nature rationally, bring it under their common control, instead of being ruled by it as by some blind power; that they accomplish their task with the least expenditure of energy and under conditions most adequate to their human nature and most worthy of it. But it always remains a realm of necessity. Beyond it begins that development of human power, which is its own end, the true realm of freedom, which, however, can flourish only upon that realm of necessity as

its basis. The shortening of the working day is its fundamental premise.'
(Quoted from Frederick Engels' edition, Chicago, 1909, pp. 954–5.)

13. Thomas Mann, 'Deutschland und die Deutschen', quoted in Kurt Sontheimer, *The Government and Politics of West Germany*, London, 1972, p. 67. In quoting this passage Sontheimer says that the German idea of freedom was always directed outwards. This however seems to be a literary hyperbole rather than a serious statement.

14. Wolfgang Zapf, *Wandlungen der deutschen Elite*, München, 1965, p. 204.

15. Peter C. Ludz, *The Changing Party Elite in East Germany*, Cambridge, Mass. and London, 1972.

16. Wolfgang Zapf, *Beiträge zur Analyse der Deutschen Oberschicht*, pp. 27 and 29.

17. There are no comprehensive data on the age structure of the leadership in the GDR but the data on the age structure of the People's Chamber in 1967 and 1971 indicate a decline in the representation of the youngest age cohorts. The proportion of those above the age of 40 increased from 54.6 to 67.5 per cent (*Bericht*, 1972, p. 41). Regarding the women's share in work and power see section 4e.

18. R. Dahrendorf, *Society and Democracy in Germany*, pp. 426–7.

19. According to Edinger's findings, the results of de-Nazification in West Germany could be assessed in 1956 as follows: of an élite sample (529 individuals of political, administrative, interest and communications groups) about 24 per cent might have been considered former supporters of the Nazi régime, 57 per cent ambivalent or 'oscillating' and 19 per cent more or less consistently opposed. (Lewis J. Edinger, 'Post-Totalitarian Leadership; Elites in the German Federal Republic', in *American Political Science Review*, Vol. LIV, 1960, pp. 58–82.)

20. According to the information in *The Economist* from 1–7 March 1975 West Germany has paid out compensation worth 23 billion dollars and is expected to provide another 11 billion dollars by the time the whole restitution process is completed.

21. In 1975, however, the East German government seems to be ready to reconsider its position because of the American government's unwillingness to send an Ambassador to East Berlin unless the GDR compensates Jewish victims of Nazi persecution now living in the USA. (Information from the same source as above.)

22. *Parteien in beiden Deutschen Staaten*, ed. Friedrich-Ebert-Stiftung, Bonn-Bad Godesberg, 1972, p. 21.

23. ibid., p. 24.

24. Also, the Communist character of the nominally Socialist Party (Socialist Unity Party) has been more openly stressed in recent times: in official speeches and documents of the GDR there is an increasing tendency to refer to the SED as the party of Communists. (F. Oldenburg, in *Deutschland Archiv*, 1975, No. 1.)

25. David Childs, *East Germany*, London, 1969, pp. 104–23.

26. Eckhart Förtsch, *Die SED*, Stuttgart, 1969, p. 66.

27. F. Oldenburg, 'Blick zurück nach vorn', *Deutschland Archiv*, 1975, No. 1, p.7.

28. For more detail on the historical origin, political role and social structure of these parties, see D. Childs, op. cit.

29. *SJB DDR*, 1974, p. 479.

30. 'Staats-und Parteiapparat der DDR, Personelle Besetzung, Stand: 18', Januar 1974, Gesamtdeutsches Institut, Bonn, 1974.

31. The other body with legislation initiative is the Council of Ministers. Of the 107 Laws passed between 1961 and 1970 by the People's Chamber, 62 were

proposed by the Council of Ministers, 45 by the State Council, none by the People's Chamber itself. (*Sozialistische Demokratie,* 1961–1971, and *DDR Gesetzblatt,* 1961–1971 quoted in *Bericht,* 1972, p. 63.)

32. Sontheimer und Bleek, *Die DDR,* Hamburg, 1973, p. 105.
33. Calculations from the list of the members of state and party apparats of the GDR on 18 January 1974 quoted above.
34. This passage has been only slightly altered by the New Constitution of 7 October 1974. For comparison with the former text of the Constitution of 9 April 1968, see *Deutschland Archiv,* 1974, No. 11, p. 1190.
35. For more details see *Bericht,* 1972, p. 47, *Deutschland Archiv,* 1972, No. 2.
36. Peter C. Ludz, *The Changing Party Elite in East Germany,* pp. 408–12.
37. Ludz, ibid., p. 408.
38. S. M. Lipset, *Political Man,* London, reprint 1973, p. 174.
39. cf. Fred Oldenburg, op. cit., p. 80 and ff.
40. Michael Waller, 'Socialism and the Market Place', *Government and Opposition,* Vol. 9, No. 4, p. 522.
41. Apart from the English translation of Dahrendorf's *Society and Democracy in Germany,* already mentioned several times, the following studies deserve special attention: Almond and Verba, *The Civic Culture,* Princeton, 1963; Lewis J. Edinger, *Germany,* Boston, 1968; G. K. Roberts, *West German Politics,* London, 1972; Kurt Sontheimer, *The Government and Politics of West Germany,* London, 1972.
42. Including the 115 industrial giants, there were in 1970 2,200 joint stock companies, and over 88,000 corporations with limited liability; further, about 65,000 private unincorporated enterprises with proceeds of over DM 100,000 and 19,000 farms with over 50 hectares of holdings. The owners and managers of these undertakings may be considered the lower echelons of the economic élite. (Data from *SJB BRD,* 1972.)
43. H. Marcus, *Die Macht der Mächtigen,* Düsseldorf, 1970, p. 226.
44. ibid., p. 18.
45. H. Marcus, op. cit., p. 71.
46. A list of the main banks' industrial participation is reproduced in Appendix, Table A.16 (H. Marcus, pp. 88–89).
47. Bundesbank Monthly Report, November 1974, quoted from the *Financial Times,* 19 November 1974.
48. Marcus, op. cit., p. 523.
49. See especially L. Edwards, *Natural History of Revolution,* re-edited Chicago, 1965; Crane Brinton, *Anatomy of Revolution,* London, 1939.
50. For more details see *Bericht,* 1972, pp. 154–7.
51. Theodor Eschenburg, *Herrschaft der Verbände,* Stuttgart, 1963, p. 63.
52. Dahrendorf, op. cit., pp. 144–5.
53. Ralf Dahrendorf, *Conflict and Contract: industrial relations and the political community in times of crisis,* The Second Leverhulme Memorial Lecture, Liverpool UP, 1975.
54. Kurt Sontheimer, *The Government and Politics of West Germany,* London, 1972, p. 108.
55. *SBJ BRD,* 1974, pp. 188–9.
56. *Bericht,* 1972, p. 214.
57. *Bericht,* 1972, p. 214.
58. Guenther Esters, *Workers Co-determination in Germany,* Friedrich Ebert-Stiftung, Bonn-Bad Godesberg, 1972, pp. 37–8.
59. 'Latest from Germany', issued by the Embassy of the FRG in London, 29 January 1974, No. 5, p. 3.
60. *Basler Nachrichten,* 6 April 1974.

61. 'Latest from Germany', 6 March 1975, No. 6.
62. *Bericht*, 1974, p. 96.
63. *Bericht*, 1972, p. 112.
64. ibid.
65. *SJB DDR*, 1974, p. 442.
66. Calculated from data in *SJB DDR*, 1974, pp. 58 and 420.
67. *SJB DDR*, 1974, pp. 34 and 35.
68. It is interesting that in 1973 a higher percentage of married women (53 per cent) declared their preference for employment in a survey of the Institute for Demoscopy. In 1961 the corresponding percentage was only 22. (*Demoskopie Jahrbuch*, p. 91.)
69. Calculated from the *SJB BRD*, 1974, pp. 44, 83 and 136.
70. G. Lipold *et al.*, *Das Zeitbudget der Bevölkerung*, Berlin (East), 1971, p. 113.
71. *Demoskopie Jahrbuch*, p. 351.
72. *Bericht*, 1972, p. 117.
73. *Bericht*, 1972, p. 120.
74. Herbert Thur, ed., 'Was willst Du Werden', *Neues Leben*, Berlin (Ost), 1967, p. 27.
75. Czechoslovak data from J. Krejci, *Social Change and Stratification in Postwar Czechoslovakia*, p. 65. West German data from Information 13, Bundesrepublik Deutschland, *Die Frau*, Bonn.
76. Almond and Verba, *Civic Culture*, p. 275.
77. For the juxtaposition of different laws, see *Bericht*, 1972, p. 119.
78. Translated from the Third Law on Youth, in *Deutschland Archiv*, 1974, No. 3.
79. This plot reappears many times especially in each volume of the *Soviet Official World History* (*(Istoriya mira)*, Moscow, 1952–60).
80. Almond and Verba, *Civic Culture*, p. 320.
81. For the original text see *Deutschland Archiv*, 1974, No. 3.
82. *Demoskopie Jahrbuch*, p. 456–7.
83. This organisation belonged to the Social Democratic Party but was excluded in 1961 because of its radicalism.
84. ibid., p. 462.
85. For details, see P.C. Ludz, *Studien und Materialien zur Soziologie der DDR,ʼR*, Köln and Opladen, 1964, pp. 392–3.
86. *Demoskopie Jahrbuch*, p. 464.
87. ibid., p. 213.
88. ibid., p. 225.
89. My translation, from *Freiheit und Gesellschaft*, p. 319.
90. One important point of implementation is with whom the onus of proof lies: whether with the employer or with the applicant. The coalition government of Social Democrats and Liberal Democrats has prepared a Bill in favour of the latter. It was assumed that members of antisystemic but legally operating political parties cannot be *ipso facto* considered as anti-constitutional. Yet the draft did not pass in the Second Chamber (Bundesrat) where the Christian Democratic opposition had the majority. Moreover, on 25 July 1975, the Federal Constitutional Court delivered the judgement according to which membership of a party regarded as hostile to the constitution could in itself represent an insuperable obstacle to a post in the public services. Loyalty to the state, so far as its servants are concerned, has priority over party allegiance.
91. For an account of legal provisions, combined with a pro-left criticism of the West German practice of occupational disqualification see Kenneth H.F. Dyson, 'Anti-Communism in the Federal Republic of Germany: the case of the "Berufsverbot" ', in *Parliamentary Affairs*, 1974–75, No. 1.
92. Similarly, in 1952 a right-wing party, the Sozialistische Reichspartei, was

banned for Constitutional reasons.
93. Wolfgang Abendroth, *Antagonistische Gesellschaft und Politische Demokratie*, Darmstadt, 1972, p. 169.
94. Supplied by the courtesy of Professor Konrad Repgen of the University of Bonn.
95. Calculated from data in *Bericht*, 1971, pp. 60, 147 and 256.
96. *Bericht*, 1971, p. 147.
97. *Demoskopie Jahrbuch*, p. 213–14.
98. *Bericht*, 1974, p. 98; *Demoskopie Jahrbuch*, p. 216.
99. West Germany: G. K. Roberts, *West German Politics*, London, 1972, p. 122; East Germany: Eckart Förtsch, *Die SED*, Stuttgart, 1969, p. 66.
100. *Demoskopie Jahrbuch*, p. 214.
101. *Zahlenspiegel*, Bonn, 1974, p. 6, and 'Latest from Germany', London Embassy, 14 May 1975.
102. Almond and Verba, *Civic Culture*, p. 428.
103. Sidney Verba, 'Germany: The Remaking of Political Culture', in *Political Culture and Political Development*, ed. L. W. Pye and S. Verba, Princeton, 1965, p. 148.
104. Communication of a friend.
105. *Demoskopie Jahrbuch*, p. 240.
106. ibid., p. 229.
107. ibid., p. 237.
108. *Bericht*, 1974, p. 96.
109. *Demoskopie Jahrbuch*, p. 228.
110. *Bericht*, 1974, p. 93.
111. *Demoskopie Jahrbuch*, pp. 497–8.
112. Public Opinion Poll of the Institute for Demoscopy as reported by the daily press.
113. For more details see Klaus Roghmann, 'The Impact of Military Service on Authoritarian Attitudes: Evidence from West Germany', *American Journal of Sociology*, Vol. 78, 1972, pp. 418–33.
114. Since 1962, when, because of the lack of recruits, the Volksarmee ceased to be a volunteers' army and became manned by universal conscription, an Oath of Allegiance was introduced binding the soldiers to unconditional obedience to the government and, moreover, to unconditional support of the Soviet Army and armies of socialist allies . (For more details see T. Forster, *The East German Army*, London, 1967, p. 30.)
115. Calculated from *Zahlenspiegel*, Bonn, 1973, p. 8.
116. *Demoskopie Jahrbuch*, p. 506.
117. ibid.
118. ibid., p. 510.
119. ibid.
120. Hermann Axen, 'Zur Nationalen Frage', reprinted in *Deutschland Archiv*, 1974, No. 2, pp. 192–212.
121. Quoted from Fred Oldenburg, 'Blick zurück nach vorn', *Deutschland Archiv*, 1975, No. 1, p. 3.
122. ibid., p. 2.
123. Mager and Spinnarke, *Was wollen die Studenten?*, Frankfurt, 1967, pp. 63–5.
124. Slogan put forward by Professor Reinhard Kuhnl at the Düsseldorf Colloquium against the *Berufsverbot* in May 1974, quoted from K.H.F. Dyson, 'Anti-Communism in the Federal Republic of Germany: the case of the *Berufsverbot*', *Parliamentary Affairs*, XXVIII, Winter 1974–5, p. 51.

5 CONCLUSIONS

5a. Practical conclusions and evaluations

Any serious comparison of two societies cannot result in a simple
black and white conclusion. It is bad enough if one society displays
more negative features than the other. Yet the evaluation of the
merits and shortcomings of a society is in itself a subjective process,
and any judgement depends on the end-values acknowledged (internalised) by the observer. Even if a factual comparison can be firmly
established — that, for instance, West Germans have a wider variety
of choice in most spheres of societal life than East Germans — the
result need not necessarily be accepted as advantageous for the FRG.
Neither higher material standards nor greater equality are values
which everyone would consider equally relevant for the evaluation of
a social system.

In an intersystemic comparison, evaluation can be undertaken from
as many angles as there are 'systemic philosophies'. Each German
society can be judged either according to its own (intrinsic) or to the
other (extrinsic) objectives or ideals. The first procedure seems to be
more pertinent.

From the intrinsic point of view the West has to be judged in
relation to the ideal of a liberal, pluralistic, welfare society; the East
has to be seen as a society which aims to shape its future according to
a specific plan and gives greater opportunity to manual workers and
their descendants. When we examine the two parts of Germany from
this perspective, we have to acknowledge that both have gone far along
the separate paths they have chosen.

The FRG is a fairly liberal, pluralistic society with guaranteed civil
rights, including the right to private property, and an institutionally
independent judiciary. Its citizens have an ample choice of material
and cultural goods and, up to a point, also of political and ideological
orientation. Changes in supply of goods and services are in principle
governed by the almost impersonal forces of the market; changes in
the representation and power of political parties are governed by
periodical elections; changes in income and wealth distribution are
governed by a combination of market forces, the bargaining power of
vocational associations (employers' and trade unions) and tax policy,
which to a certain extent depends on election results. Employees are

represented in the management of the coal and steel industries and an expansion of this kind of 'co-determination' is a current political issue. A considerable proportion of national resources is devoted to social welfare. So far the FRG has been a prosperous, highly productive and affluent society with a comparatively low percentage of the population below the subsistence level.

The GDR is a country where power is monopolised by one centrally-ruled political party. The means of production have been almost completely nationalised; state ownership prevails over co-operative ownership. Changes in allocation of resources and in income distribution are governed by the economic plans. Production and distribution are centrally planned and managed. Productivity and incomes are on average lower than in the FRG but the earnings, the social status and the conditions of blue- and white-collar workers are more equal. There is a uniform basic (comprehensive) and ideological education. Trade unions, youth organisations and other mass organisations mobilise their members for fulfilment of economic and political targets. The power élite is freely accessible to the descendants of manual workers provided they fulfil the requirements of political reliability and involvement.

According to her Constitution (Article 20), the FRG is a democratic, social and federated state. Article 1 of the Constitution of the GDR gives the following self-definition: 'the socialist state of workers and farmers . . . under the leadership of the working class and its Marxist-Leninist party.' Official sources in the GDR also use labels such as 'dictatorship of the proletariat' or 'socialist democracy' as synonyms. These terms are supposed to be identical in a dialectical way. They indicate that democracy is understood differently in East and West.

Democracy in the West means government with the consent of elected representatives of the population which presupposes two or more political parties and free elections under conditions of universal and equal suffrage. In the East, democracy means, in practical terms, a higher social status for the 'working class' which provides a larger proportion of members of the power élite. In neither case is it a true 'government by the people'.

Socialism, too, is viewed differently in East and West. Social Democrats in the FRG are mainly concerned with workers' co-determination, the bargaining power of trade unions, social benefits and welfare policy, whereas Communists in the GDR consider the state ownership of the means of production, the centrally planned economy and the leading position of their party as the essential characteristics of socialism.

In the Eastern and, to a great extent, also in the Western view, the FRG is considered, by contrast to the GDR, a capitalist society. On the other hand Westerners pay more attention to differences in the political sphere, calling the Western system pluralistic and the Eastern system totalitarian.[1]

Simple labels however may be confusing especially if they are derived from incomplete observation. Even so, reality often contradicts theoretical claims or suppositions. If abolition of exploitation and alienation is the aim of socialism and if the means of achieving this is collective ownership, why then, within the GDR where ownership has been collectivised, is there an increasing amount of surplus product and why is it not utilised according to the socialists' expectations? Why are workers not trusted to defend their interests without an elaborate system of guidance and supervision from the centrally ruled political party? If the FRG should still be considered as a capitalist country, why is there so much concern with welfare which is more comprehensive than that of its supposedly socialist counterpart? Why is greater confidence placed in workers who not only have their independent trade unions but can also press for co-determination in management which they have virtually achieved in the coal and steel industries? How can it be that in the FRG real wages in the long term keep pace with productivity, whereas in the GDR productivity has to increase faster than real wages? Finally, why does the FRG permit criticism and opposition to its establishment from both liberal Marxists and authoritarian Marxist-Leninists, whereas in the GDR only a Marxist-Leninist orthodoxy is allowed? Realising all these inconsistencies, one has to accept that Eastern socialism is less socialist and Western capitalism less capitalist then respective concepts suggest. In view of the concern with profits (private or state) in both countries and in view of the use of surplus, 'welfare capitalism' for the FRG and 'state capitalism' for the GDR might be more appropriate labels.

Yet even with these qualifications the traditional labels do not do justice to the complex reality of the different systems. In ignoring the political and cultural spheres they offer only incomplete characteristics. A more comprehensive characteristic can be obtained by reviewing the points which became real issues, objects of criticism either from within or from without the system in the respective countries.

As the previous analysis has shown, the main intrinsic grievance in the West is that there is not enough genuine democracy. In spite of a considerable 'decomposition' of social status, access to power and wealth is difficult for those whose parents did not belong to upper or, at least, middle strata; the educational system in particular does not provide equal opportunities for all. There is still some discrimination between the white- and blue-collar workers, and workers' representatives have achieved co-determination only in the coal and steel industries. Pressure groups within the élite exert influence far beyond their constitutional position or the numerical strength of those whom they represent. Further, there are menacing signs that the welfare state cannot maintain sustained economic growth or even stability. No completely effective counterbalance for the economic cycle has been found. In some quarters there is a growing feeling that the permissive society has gone too far and that the common man should be given more protection. Criminality is on the increase; a terrorist gang of anarchists attempts to disrupt the legal order.

On the whole, judging from the opinion polls, about two-thirds of the West German population are happy with their socio-economic system and about half of them are happy with the quality of their democracy. Of the others only one-fifth favour substantial changes and only 3 per cent are in favour of a revolutionary restructuring.

It is not quite clear how many of the malcontents criticise and require changes in West German society from the instrinsic point of view, i.e. from the theoretical principles on which the FRG is built, how many are under the spell of Eastern political philosophy, and how many are led by principles opposing both German establishments. The line of demarcation between them is difficult. Dissatisfaction with too little democracy in the West may be based either on 'bourgeois' liberal or 'liberal' Marxist reasoning. Many Marxists, especially in Western Europe, reject the Leninist interpretation and the Soviet and East European practice of Marxism as an élitist and authoritarian one and want to develop Marxism on more liberal, radical democratic, lines. They agree more with Marx's intentions than with his practical recommendations which have thus far led to an excessive concentration and abuse of power.

The East German establishment can, in its turn, be criticised either from its own Marxist-Leninist, or the 'liberal' Marxist, or from the 'bourgeois' liberal position. Marxist-Leninist orthodoxy does not see any significant difference between the latter two which are both considered reactionary. Robert Havemann and other East German Marxists who tended to express more liberal attitudes can carry on their criticism of West and East alike in public only by occasionally publishing in the FRG. In contrast to the West, in the GDR there are no opinion polls of citizens' satisfaction or dissatisfaction with the system. Possible grievances have to be listed on the evidence collected in our investigation.

The main grievance from the Marxist, as it seems more 'liberal' than Leninist, point of view, is that state socialism in the GDR has not abandoned 'exploitation' of the 'toiling masses'. The ratio of surplus is approximately the same as in the FRG but it is used neither for greater consumer satisfaction nor for greater domestic investment. Productivity in the West is much higher and workers there can obtain many more consumer goods for their hourly earnings than workers can in the East. As the GDR accepted, like other Communist countries, the principle that productivity has to grow faster than wages, the effort/reward relationship for the labour force is deteriorating. As trade unions have become simply transmitters for the party directives and the Communist cells supervise all societal activities, workers do not have adequate bargaining power with which to alter this development. Although individual workers or their children can more easily advance on the scale of power, income and prestige than those in the West, the working class as a whole does not participate as conspicuously in this improvement. On the whole, the enhanced vertical mobility has been thwarted by limited geographical mobility. Income levelling in the GDR has also not affected all groups of the population. Pensioners in particular lag far behind and family allowances are inadequate. This, coupled with a high rate of employment for women and an inadequate supply of housing has produced a drop in the birth rate below the death rate. Even if the exodus of malcontents has been stopped by sealing off the frontier throughout Berlin, East German society is one whose numbers are constantly decreasing. Last but not least, due to the thorough system of political screening, the East German citizen has lost a great deal of his human privacy. Nonconformism became a risky attitude.

All these grievances may have a certain effect on what Marx conceived as alienation. Much depends however on whether such shortcomings are considered intrinsic to the Marxist-Leninist system or whether they are considered as only accidental, whether it is believed that they can be abolished without changing the system or, to put it more cautiously, without abandoning Marxist principles. In the latter case there is a contradiction between Marxist objectives and Marxist-Leninist establishment. This contradiction provides the ideological basis for a comprehensive reform movement in Communist-dominated countries. In contrast to Poland, Hungary and Czechoslovakia, the reformist potential within the GDR proved to be weak.

This difference can be best understood with respect to the role of Marxism in the Leninist interpretation in post-war Germany. During the Nazi period, if only for a limited time, most Germans asserted themselves through identification with a militaristic, nationalistic and, in a way, totalitarian movement. Even for many non-Nazis it was difficult not to be affected by the extraordinary military successes during the first half of World War Two. After the war, other bases for self-assertion through identification with a collective had to be found. The defeat of Nazi Germany produced a certain socio-psychological vacuum in the German community.

The FRG substituted for the ideal of the German Reich the pluralistic, parliamentary democracy coupled with a free market economy and generous welfare measures (*Sozialstaat*). This brought unpredicted affluence to her citizens and also freedom of a certain kind; these blessings however were not distributed with sufficient fairness and, above all, were not adequately matched by a sufficiently vigorous positive, collective ideal. Only the religious tradition, as far as it persists, fulfils this role. Neither secular liberalism nor legalistic constitutionalism provide an adequate basis for a genuine spiritual integration of the society. Socialists in their turn have not found enough courage to redefine, in an impressive way, their social philosophy.

The GDR was able to satisfy her subjects neither with affluence nor with personal freedom (in the Western sense of this word) but she gave them a collective purpose, an almost eschatological idea of building an ideal society in the future. Working for this aim requires discipline and even austerity. Strict discipline and sobriety are well in line with the Prussian tradition. Marxism in its turn, with its Hegelian roots, is firmly embedded in the philosophical tradition of Germany as a whole. Both can be viewed as embodiments of German virtues, virtues which eventually will re-establish German prestige and, provided the population does not decrease too fast, also influence in the world.

As soon as 'ageing capitalism' exhausts its potential for growth and adaptation, radiation of a thriving, highly developed socialist society is expected to provide a rallying point for the West Germans as well. In view of the unfilled spiritual void and widely de-concentrated power structure, the West is susceptible to a more vigorous reaction to material shortcomings than the East. If the economic growth in the FRG is reversed and the affluence disappears, her frustrated subjects might be open to any spiritual conversion which could heal the wounds of defeat, partition and loss of prestige.

5b. Theoretical suggestions

Some theoretical suggestions were already touched upon in the previous chapter. At the very end of the whole study an attempt will be made to present these suggestions in a more comprehensive and coherent way.

Comparison of only two countries might not be considered a broad enough basis for general conclusions; but the countries under scrutiny are exemplary forms of two fairly successful systems, and this may be a sufficient reason for such an attempt.

On the strength of this particular comparison it seems to me that the traditional dichotomy, socialism versus capitalism, is not an adequate formula to describe the systemic differences between the European West and East. Variables which define these two concepts are less socially relevant than other variables which are not necessarily related to these concepts.

Distributive justice or exploitation (whatever term one may prefer for ideological reasons) depend less on ownership than on the distribution of power in general. Private ownership of the means of production confronted with strong, i.e. unified, disciplined and militant trade unions or with a government influenced by them, provides less scope for the growth of profits than a system of state ownership where the trade unions become an extension of the ruling political party which prefers to use any increase in national production in ways that do not benefit the consumer.

So, the degree of concentration of power in general appears to be a more socially relevant variable than ownership. It can be viewed from different angles with reference to individual aspects or dimensions of power. Some are more relevant for citizens' self-assertion, some for appropriation of the products of labour. There are always two variables to be considered: (a) the number of decision-making bodies or persons (holders of power) and (b) the field of their decision-making (range of power). Within these two variables there is a wide scope for combinations of institutional and functional division (specialisation) of power.

Usually power is assumed by the state but the scope of the issues it claims to determine (its range of power) varies considerably. Outside the state there are enterprises, political parties and other associations in which some power relationships also develop. Political parties are supposed to express the differentiated national will. They are considered the main channels of 'political input'. Together with the state and its ramified organisation they can be described as the 'polity'.

The basic issues are as follows: firstly, how much scope for power relationship is left outside 'polity'; secondly, how far the power within polity is concentrated in the hands of a limited number of people. Outside the polity, power is vested mainly in the owners and/or managers of enterprises, representatives of vocational associations (including trade unions) and ideological establishments such as churches. So it is mainly the spheres of the economy and culture which, as the case may be, remain to a greater or lesser degree outside the polity.

In view of this, it appears sensible to divide all possible power relationships into three categories: political, economic and ideological. Marx, too, distinguished these three kinds of 'domination'. Yet he was more concerned with their social background (the recruitment of those in power from particular classes) than with the structure of power itself. Experience with Marxist-Leninist rule in Eastern Europe has shown that, even if the power élite is recruited mainly from the 'working class' or their descendants, a tight concentration of power within the polity and an extension of the polity's power at the expense of other focuses of power within the society has resulted in a new kind of what Marx called 'exploitation' and 'alienation'.

For the citizens' self-assertion and for the appropriation of the products of labour, the type and degree of the concentration of power are the most relevant. With respect to the institutional and functional subdivisions within the society in general and within the polity in particular, the whole complex of alternatives and nuances can be described as the constellation of power.

Individual alternatives to the constellation of power can be conceived as a scale between two poles. One extreme position is where power in all the three fields is dispersed; when the range of the state power is limited by law, the state's authority is functionally and constitutionally divided (legislation and judiciary are independent of the executive power); and when there is a genuine competition of at least two political parties. This pattern can be described, to borrow a widely used term, as a 'pluralistic' constellation of power.

The other extreme is where all the three kinds of domination are wielded by one body. This is the case when one political party dominates the state and the power of the polity (the state and the dominant party) is extended over all the other focuses of power within the society. This may best be called a 'unitary' constellation of power.

It may be tempting to use the term 'totalitarian' instead. However, as we have seen earlier, this term can be employed in another context as well to refer to the requirement for complete loyalty from the subjects of a particular country. Shapiro has shown that there are some more ambiguities which have emerged in the course of the historical development of the term.[2] Therefore to avoid confusion and emotional overtones, a neutral and more semantically acceptable term has been suggested.

Another relevant question is the distinction between authority (an institutionalised power exerting itself as a rule through sanctions of a penal nature) and influence (where the possible sanctions consist in various forms of socio-psychic pressures). State power belongs essentially to the first category (authority). In the economic sphere, possible sanctions can be applied only on the basis of what are essentially contractual obligations. Yet the uneven market position (supply versus demand) may lead to what are virtually relationships of authority in this field also. Whenever work becomes a political duty, state authority supersedes the contractual relationship.

Political parties and the other associations exert authority in so far as their 'will' has been embodied in the state's acts. This is the case with the ruling party. Otherwise parties and other associations exert influence rather than authority; vocational associations can also enjoy some authority. This is also often the case with the churches, but their power is increasingly one of influence rather than authority. Experience from East-Central Europe shows that the churches are able to exert their influence even where they are deprived of all independent authority. When this happens, unitary constellation of power means virtually none other than unitary constellation of authority.

In Europe, and, it seems to me, in the world as a whole, extreme cases of constellation of power were infrequent. More often than not there were combinations and nuances within the scales between the two extremes. Whenever a pluralistic constellation of power was operating as, for instance, in Ancient Greek cities and the Roman Republic, its potentialities were always confined to a limited number of 'citizens', leaving large sectors of the population beyond the pale, especially as slaves under the highly concentrated authority of their owners. On the other hand, most typical cases of so-called oriental despotism did not achieve the unitary constellation of power. More often than not one pillar of this particular constellation was missing, and economic or ideological power was shared with one or more independent holders of power. Private property or the virtual economic independence of great feudatories on the one hand and the more or less independent religious institutions on the other hampered the full development of a unitary constellation of power.

It may be surprising that both these contradictory constellations of power appeared in their purest form in the present century and that both proved to be compatible with modern industrial society. Yet it was precisely industrial technology with its mass communication and education media which made possible the full development of these contradictions.

Nowhere do the pluralistic and unitary constellations of power confront each other in such a manifest fashion as in divided Germany. The German experience indicates that these constellations of power are not functions of the productive forces; they are independent variables.

Nor is the concentration of power in itself the ultimate cause of the systemic differences. A particular constellation of power is a means of achieving something beyond it, a means of achieving a certain ideological postulate or implementing a certain hierarchy of values. Ideological postulates are not necessarily connected with a certain technological level.

As is well known, Marxist-Leninists do not merely want industrialisation and economic growth to catch up and overtake the developed capitalist countries. Nor is a complete restructuring of society their final aim. The final goal is a change of man's attitudes and behaviour, a change of an anthropological dimension. Man will become better and happier. Present generations are required to make some sacrifices in order that their descendants eventually achieve an ideal which the pre-Marxist ideologies like to locate, in the Marxist view erroneously or deceitfully, in another world. Without this eschatological element in Marxist thought which, in secular terms, offers hope to the 'wretched of the earth', it would be difficult to ensure the spontaneous support for the unitary constellation of power from its followers. As present generations can hardly expect to enjoy the coming change, the ideal acquires for them a certain transcendental dimension.

Whenever there was a unitary constellation of power or something near to it in the past, it was always sanctified by transcendental, religious ideals. In an age when scientific theories have largely replaced religious beliefs, it is natural that the concept of transcendence has also had to adapt itself; it has to pass from the realm of religion to that of philosophy. The road from religion to philosophy in this sense is symbolised by two names, Hegel and Marx. Significantly, both were Germans. Their thoughts represent the main stages in the transfer of transcendence from the dimension of space to time. With Marx, eschatology has been pinned down to the earth without however losing its metaphysical substance.

Viewing Marxism-Leninism from this perspective, we realise that its socio-cultural features are not less, but more important than its socio-economic ones. In my view Talcott Parsons is right when he puts at the top of the hierarchy of social structure the 'hierarchy of cybernetic control' and when he believes that within the social system the 'normative elements are more important for social change than the material interests of constitutive units.'[3]

Of course normative principles do not emerge in an arbitrary fashion, they have somehow to be linked with the other elements of the societal structure or embedded in the tradition of the society. Therefore, for instance, Marxism-Leninism could more easily win ground in countries with a tradition of greater concentrations of power than in countries where the constellation of power always tended to be more or less pluralistic.

Germany is a country where both these tendencies are endemic. During the spiritual domination of the Roman Catholic Church, ideological unity was checked by economic and political pluralism. Political and economic powers coalesced only in comparatively small areas. Germany as a whole was a conglomeration of principalities and city states, with different constitutions and power relationships. After a prolonged period of complete disintegration lasting from about the mid-thirteenth to the mid-nineteenth century, aggravated from the sixteenth century by a religious split, unification became an ideal, a means of collective self-assertion. It materialised in two successive rallies with different types of power constellation. The Second Empire was content with a pluralistic, albeit strongly authoritarian structure. In the so-called Third Reich, the unification was more intense, but the constellation of power was totalitarian only with respect to the enforced loyalty of its subjects. Despite progressive concentration, ownership and management (economic domination) remained largely dispersed.

After 1945, the two contradictory tendencies in Germany acquired their own territorial bases where they were able to develop unchecked: a pluralistic constellation of power in the West, a unitary constellation of power in the East. This, of course, happened because these two different areas were incorporated into two different societal frameworks on a broader, geographical scale.

The respective cornerstones of these frameworks are the end-values expressly acknowledged by the respective power elites and accepted (internalised) by sufficient numbers of their subjects. Understandably, a pluralistic constellation of power requires a greater number of sympathetic subjects than the unitary one.

Viewed as a whole and with due regard to priorities laid down or acknowledged by the respective power élites, the social systems investigated in the two German states can be more accurately described with respect to their end-values rather than in terms of the individual institutions which emerge from them.

The end-value in the West is individual self-assertion. However inadequately utilised, however deficient it may be, a few important general rules are nonetheless observed. Possible conflicts between individuals and groups respectively are regulated by a legal order, with a wide scope for contractual agreement, by precise rules for an orderly change of government, by limitations on state interference in individual life and by functional-cum-institutional division of state power.

The end-value in the East is the collective striving towards a societal ideal which has to be gradually accomplished. The possibility of internal conflicts is minimised by subordination of all societal activities to one common goal through uniform ideological education and through a taut structure of organisational discipline.

All other systemic features are a logical consequence of these end-values. Individual self-assertion requires a pluralistic constellation of power. In a liberal system however, the stronger can always assert themselves more effectively than the weak, the weak can be protected only against excesses. The outcome is a system of greater or lesser power focuses dispersed over the political, ideological and economic fields. In other terms, the pattern of power is oligopolistic. On the other hand, concerted action towards a common goal requires, especially if anthropological changes are envisaged, a unitary constellation of power. Consequently the pattern of power in the East is monopolistic.

Economic oligopoly in the West is linked with private ownership and the market mechanism; economic monopoly in the East requires nationalised means of production, central planning and management and only limited scope for the market mechanism. The corollary of private ownership is independent trade unions. The market position and bargaining power of capital and labour respectively decide between them the relative amount of profits and wages. Comprehensive state ownership requires dependent trade unions operating on behalf of the whole community (state) rather than on behalf of their membership. Consequently the ratio of profits and wages is decided unilaterally by the planning authorities.

In my opinion, by looking at the whole structure in terms of end-values we can obtain a more coherent and sensible picture than by looking at it from beneath, from the perspective of one particular relationship such as, for instance, the ownership of the means of production. Relationships resulting from the constellation of power are much more relevant, they determine a wider range of variables of significance for an inter-systemic analysis. It is however impossible to understand them (and here I am following Max Weber's path) without reference to the normative, or as a Czech economist-philosopher, Karel Engliš put it, 'teleological' principle. This principle provides the rationale of the system, a rationale both in terms of social usefulness (*Zweckrationalität*) and in terms of human virtues (*Wertrationalität*).

Although with the help of a unitary constellation of power coercion can be taken further than in a pluralistic system, there must always be a nucleus of committed men both in positions of command and manning key posts, who also exert some influence on those whose main motivation to loyalty is imitative impulses. A pluralistic society can tolerate greater laxity, provided it is held together by a more or less spontaneous observance of some traditional normative or teleological principle. If it is not the case, if two or more normative principles begin to compete, conflicts arising from contradictory end-values can hardly be brought within a framework of regulation.

There have been much greater social contradictions and hardships in the past than there are now but they did not destroy the coherence of the society. Only confrontation of two contradictory normative principles brought about a substantial, systemic change into the societal structure. Although individual elements of this change might have attracted greater attention, (industrialisation, abolition of feudal rights, collectivisation etc.) their emergence was ultimately due to a tangible shift of human aims and values.

Here, in my opinion, is the main field in which the contemporary struggle of different systems, not only in Germany and Europe but in the world as a whole, will be fought out and eventually decided.

Notes

1. Recently there has been a growing tendency in the West to drop the latter label because it had acquired a pejorative meaning which was more suited to the conditions of the Cold War. But abandoning of the term capitalism which is also largely used in a pejorative sense, is not required as a *quid pro quo*. Is

it the result of a greater sense of fairness in the West or of more readiness to move towards ideological demobilisation?

2. L. Shapiro, *Totalitarianism,* London, 1972.
3. T. Parsons, *Societies: Evolutionary and Comparative Perspectives,* New Jersey, 1966, p. 113.

APPENDIX

Main problems of quantification of labour value

The main problems of quantification of labour value are (a) the definition of value-producing activities and (b) the use of current prices and wages as indicators of labour values in individual sectors of production or categories of employment within the economy.

As has been said in the text, the Communist countries adopted the Soviet statistical practice which, following Marx's concept of 'objectification of labour', does not consider all gainful activities as value-producing; only in embodying labour into things, in transforming natural resources into useful objects (subjective use values) does man create exchange (objective) labour values. Moreover, the value-producing activity is defined not according to the character of the respective work, but according to the economic branch in which it is performed. The following branches are considered as value-originating, i.e. in this sense, 'productive':

production of goods	—	agriculture, fishing, forestry, mining, manufacturing, construction.
and material services	—	public utilities, catering, repairs, trade, cleaning activities, freight transport, and communication serving the other material branches of economy.

Consequently, an accountant in an industrial enterprise is productive (value-producing) whereas in a hospital he is not. On the other hand, a manual repair worker is 'productive' if he is employed either in a factory or in a repair shop but not if he is employed in an insurance company, hospital, etc. Thus productive work can be defined as work which somehow contributes to the production and distribution of goods which can be stored, i.e. related to the 'stock account'. The costs of distributing material goods until their final stage of use are included; consequently, goods sold to private households are calculated inclusive of the retail trade margin.

On the other hand the 'classical' concept of 'productive' work applied by Western national accounting is broader and also more expedient both for analytical and practical (planning) purposes. Aggregates calculated on this basis can be directly related to the labour force balance sheet, because all activities undertaken against compensation, whether material or non-material, are productive, i.e. produce economic values. The only arbitrary assumption is that some income in kind from material production (especially from agriculture) and from owner-occupied dwellings, is imputed to the total, whereas own household services (performed mainly by married women) are not. The rationale, however, is that the latter are as a rule not paid for, whereas the former goods and services are predominantly exchanged under market conditions.

Fortunately for our comparison, the East Germans deviated from the Soviet concept of national income and, unlike some other Communist countries, also incorporated passenger transport and communications serving private households. Thus the East German statisticians have saved themselves the painstaking job of assessing the material and non-material quotas in transport and communications and eased comparison with the West into the bargain.

A far more serious problem arises from the price/value relationship with respect to individual sections and groups within the economy. The theoretically attractive alternative of establishing a firm price/value relationship by using the labour cost of gold as the basis of national currencies, proved, for obvious reasons, to be a blind alley. Another less simple assumption has to be accepted, namely that prices of individual commodities fluctuate around the labour values according to the supply and demand. This amounts to saying that labour values can best be established under perfect market conditions. This, however, can be a viable supposition only for a fully competitive capitalist society. In a socialist society this kind of market does not exist. Consequently, there was some uncertainty as to whether the labour theory of value could be applied to the socialist economy at all. Originally Communist economists tended not to use the concept of labour value for practical purposes. Yet from the middle sixties almost all Communist countries embarked on a campaign for a 'rational price formula' which in reality was an attempt to bring prices closer to values.[1] Some of them started to publish data on the primary division of national income which in fact is another label for variable capital and surplus product.

Unfortunately, the East Germans participated only in the first drive but not in the second. Therefore, for our purpose, some figures had to be obtained with the help of calculations from other figures such as indices or *per capita* averages; further, scattered data had to be fitted into aggregates and some missing data assessed as residual items.

Notes

1. For more detail on the origins of this development, see for instance Harry G. Shaffer (ed.), *The Soviet Economy*, London, 1964, pp. 340–421.

Table A.1 Surplus Value in the Federal Republic of Germany (A) Net Material Product

SJB BRD, 1972, pp. 515—6, 1975
pp. 510—11, col. 5.

	1960	1965	1967	1970	1971	1972[1]	1973[1]
1. Agriculture, fishing and forestry	15,470	16,740	17,540	17,460	17,770	19,920	21,960
2. Energy and mining	13,340	14,870	14,620	20,460	21,580	22,920	25,250
3. Manufacturing	118,180	176,950	180,690	263,350	282,490	301,980	336,140
4. Construction	20,250	34,470	34,500	52,400	60,400	67,450	70,790
5. Commerce	38,920	59,840	63,470	81,840	89,760	96,520	108,210
6. Transport and communication	15,690	21,000	23,020	30,370	33,240	37,680	42,300
7. Sub total	221,850	323,870	333,840	465,880	505,240	546,470	604,650
8. Half of banking and insurance[2]	3,210	5,185	6,210	8,720	10,485	12,290	14,630
9. One-third of other services[3]	6,433	10,540	12,017	17,123	20,313	23,010	26,247
10. Total (lines 7+8+9)	231,493	339,595	352,067	491,723	536,038	581,770	645,527

(B) Net Labour Income in Material Production

SJB BRD, 1972, pp. 515—6, 1975,
pp. 510—11, col. 8.

Gross labour income in	1960	1965	1967	1970	1971	1972[1]	1973[1]
11. Agriculture, fishing and forestry	2,670	3,000	2,970	3,520	3,810	3,930	4,230
12. Energy and mining	6,620	8,280	7,720	9,450	10,470	—	—
13. Manufacturing	61,670	98,720	102,660	154,720	171,010	—	—
14. Construction	12,750	22,780	22,210	31,640	36,000	—	—
15. Commerce	12,740	22,080	25,110	33,850	38,400	—	—
16. Transport and communication	10,780	16,190	17,750	23,320	27,120	—	—

continued

Table A.1 *continued*

SJB BRD, 1972, pp. 515–6, 1975, pp. 510–11, col. 8.	1960	1965	1967	1970	1971	1972[1]	1973[1]
17. Sub total (gross income including employers' contribution to employees' social insurance)	107,230	171,050	178,420	256,500	286,810	312,668[4]	354,000[4]
18. of which gross wages and salaries (calculated from *SJB BRD*, p. 508) in per cent	87.2	88.3	87.9	86.7	86.2	85.7	85.0
19. Gross wages and salaries in million DM (line 17 x line 18 : 100)	93,504	151,037	156,831	222,385	247,230	274,302	293,250
20. of which tax in per cent *Bestandsaufnahme*, 1974, p. 408	6.4	7.8	8.8	11.9	13.4	13.0	12.6[5]
21. of which tax in DM (line 19 x line 20 : 100)	5,891	11,781	13,801	26,463	33,129	35,659	36,950
22. Labour income net of taxes (line 17 – line 21)	101,339	159,269	164,619	230,037	253,681	284,413	317,050
23. Number of self-employed (*SJB BRD*, 1972, p. 122, 1974, p. 137)	5,916	5,129	4,896	4,422	4,311	4,220	4,148
24. per cent ratio of self-employed to employed population (i.e. to wage and salary earners)	29.1	23.6	23.3	19.9	19.2	18.8	18.4
25. Labour income from self-employment net of taxes (line 22 x line 24 : 100)	29,490	40,136	38,356	45,777	48,707	53,470	58,337
26. Total labour income (line 22 + line 25)	130,829	199,405	202,975	275,814	302,388	337,883	375,387

continued

Table A.1 continued

SJB BRD, 1972, pp. 515–6, 1975, pp. 510–11, col. 8	1960	1965	1967	1970	1971	1972[1]	1973[1]
27. Surplus value (line 10 – line 26)	100,664	140,190	149,092	215,909	233,650	243,887	270,140
28. Surplus ratio (line 27 : line 26)	0.77	0.70	0.73	0.78	0.77	0.72	0.72

1. Provisional figures.
2. Of the total credit operation in 1971, 35 per cent were on account of the savings banks and 13 per cent on account of mortgage banks; of these 70 per cent of mortgages were on behalf of dwelling houses. Insurance business was mainly concerned with life, health and accident insurance (data from *SJB BRD*, 1972, pp. 356–7).
3. Of the other services over the period 1960–1970 almost a half was specified as culture, health and accommodation, of these only a small part is supposed to be performed on account of business. The other half which is not specified is considered to be half of household and half on account of business. Data from *SJB BRD*, 1972, pp. 515–17).
4. Estimate according to the proportion of the respective item to the gross labour income in the whole economy (including non-material branches).
5. Extrapolated.

Additional note to Table A.1

Herbert Wilkens recalculated the West German GNP to national income produced according to the Eastern method from 1960 to 1972. (Herbert Wilkens, 'Sozialproduktrechnung in Ost und West', in *Vierteljahrshefte zur Wirtschaftsforschung*, Heft 4, 1973.) His figures on national income produced are 0.7 to 3.3 per cent higher than mine.

Even if Wilkens' figures may be more accurate than mine, they are broken down only by industrial origin and not also by distributive shares as are mine. As my task was primarily to assess the latter, I had, for the sake of consistency, to use the same source of data which I utilised for calculating the variable capital. Consequently, I was not in the position to assess the value of 'other producing branches' as Wilkens did. On the other hand, I evaluated the non-material cost (banking, insurance and other services) of material branches rather generously. As both variable capital and surplus value are realised in the 'other producing branches', whereas in non-material costs only the surplus value is taken into account, it can be assumed that in Wilkens' series the surplus ratio would be somewhat smaller than in mine. It should also be mentioned that the differences between Wilkens' and my national income produced have a tendency to decrease (from 3.3 in 1965 to 1.7 in 1970 and 0.7 per cent in 1972) whereas the share of 'other producing branches' in Wilkens' national income is more constant (between 2.0 and 2.8 per cent of the latter aggregate). From this we may infer that in Wilkens' series the surplus ratio in the FRG is more likely to decline than remain more or less stable as is the case in my calculation.

Table A.2 Surplus Product in the German Democratic Republic

	1960	1965	1967	1970	1971	1972	1973
1. National income produced in million marks 1967 prices (*SJB*, 1974, p. 40)[1]	71,045	84,175	93,043	108,720	113,562	120,090	126,670
2. Number of employed in material production in 1000 (*SJB*, 1974, p. 19)	6,495	6,411	6,426	6,414	6,407	6,401	6,402
3. Average monthly income of full-time workers and employees in the socialist sector in marks (*SJB*, 1974, p. 19)	555	633	662	755	785	814	835
4. Gross yearly labour income in million marks (line 2 x line 3 x 12)	43,257	46,698	51,048	58,111	60,354	62,525	64,148
5. Tax in per cent of average gross labour income (*SJB DDR*, 1974, p. 342)	5.8	6.4	6.9	7.5	7.6	7.7	7.8
6. Tax in million marks (line 4 x line 5 : 100)	2,509	2,988	3,522	4,358	4,587	4,814	5,004
7. Labour income net of taxes (line 4 – line 6)	40,748	43,710	47,526	53,753	55,767	57,711	59,144
8. Budget expenditure on social insurance and pensions in million marks (*SJB*, 1973, p. 312, 1974, p. 310)	9,600	11,802	12,460	14,976	16,220	17,725	19,838
9. Working in material production in per cent of all employed (calculated from *SJB*, 1974, p. 19)	84.5	83.5	83.3	82.6	82.2	81.9	81.6
10. Budget expenditure on social insurance and pensions on behalf of those working in material production (line 8 x line 9 : 100)	8,112	9,854	10,379	12,370	13,362	14,517	16,188

continued

Table A.2 *continued*

	1960	1965	1967	1970	1971	1972	1973
11. Total labour income net of taxes (line 7 + line 10)	48,860	53,564	57,905	66,123	69,129	72,228	75,332
12. Surplus product line(1 − line 11)	22,185	30,611	35,138	42,597	44,434	47,862	51,338
13. Surplus ratio (line 12 : line 11)	0.45	0.57	0.61	0.64	0.64	0.66	0.68

1. Current values were published only with respect to years before 1967. As they are only slightly lower than constant values (70,520 million M in 1960 and 82,802 million M in 1965), and as they do not reflect changes in consumer prices (which were reported as fairly stable) but only in wholesale prices which in their turn were largely offset by subsidies, they can hardly be considered as a more adequate quantification of value relationships than the 1967 prices. On the basis of the national income in current prices the surplus ratio would be 0.44 in 1960; 0.54 in 1965; consequently the increase of the surplus ratio would appear steeper than in the above calculations. Individual price indices, as far as they are available, are reproduced in Table A.8 of the Appendix.

Table A.3 Total Consumers' Share in GNP

(A) FRG in current DM	1965	1966	1967	1968	1969	1970
1. Private consumption	258,670	277,850	285,310	301,770	333,090	369,010
2. Goods and services from social insurance[1]	19,147	21,782	23,913	25,992	28,629	33,062
3. Government expenditure on education, culture and health	22,212	24,162	25,525	27,249	31,545	38,549
4. New dwellings	29,290	30,860	28,890	30,030	31,410	37,140
5. Total consumers' share	329,319	354,654	363,638	385,041	425,584	477,761
6. GNP	460,400	490,700	495,500	540,000	605,200	685,600
(B) GDR in 1967 Marks						
1. Private consumption	62,600	65,300	66,300	70,300	74,000	77,200
2. Goods and services from social insurance[1]	4,407	4,428	4,692	4,922	5,178	5,406
3. Government expenditure on education, culture and health	10,030	10,417	10,982	11,290	11,883	12,771
4. New dwellings	2,340	2,510	2,510	2,750	2,840	3,050
5. Total consumers' share	79,377	82,655	84,484	89,262	93,901	98,427
6. GNP	111,500	117,100	123,500	130,600	137,800	144,000

1. including operation cost.
Sources: FRG: lines 1 and 6, *SJB BRD*, 1972, p. 523, 1974, p. 518; line 2, *Bericht*, 1971, p. 396; *SJB BRD*, 1972, p. 392, 1974, p. 378; line 3, *SJB BRD*, 1972, p. 398 and 1973, p. 410; line 4, *SJB BRD*, 1972, p. 524, 1974, p. 519.
GDR: lines 1 and 6, *Bestandsaufnahme*, 1971, p. 277; line 2, *SJB DDR*, 1971, pp. 317 and 320, *Bericht*, 1971, p. 396; line 3, *SJB DDR*, 1971, p. 316 and 1974, p. 310; line 4, *Bestandsaufnahme*, 1971, p. 292, and *Bestandsaufnahme*, 1974, p. 372.

continued

Table A.3 *continued*

(C) FRG in per cent of GNP	1965	1966	1967	1968	1969	1970
1. Private consumption	56.2	56.6	57.6	55.9	55.0	53.8
2. Goods and services from social insurance	4.2	4.4	4.8	4.8	4.7	4.9
3. Government expenditure on education, culture and health	4.8	4.9	5.2	5.0	5.2	5.6
4. New dwellings	6.4	6.3	5.8	5.6	5.2	5.4
5. Total	71.6	72.2	73.4	71.3	70.1	69.7
(D) GDR in per cent of GNP						
1. Private consumption	56.1	55.8	53.7	53.8	53.7	53.6
2. Goods and services from social insurance	4.0	3.8	3.8	3.8	3.8	3.8
3. Government expenditure on education, culture and health	9.0	8.9	8.9	8.6	8.6	8.8
4. New dwellings	2.1	2.1	2.0	2.1	2.1	2.1
5. Total	71.2	70.6	68.4	68.3	68.2	68.3

Table A.4 Real Income from Employment (wages and salaries) in the FRG

	1960	1965	1967	1970	1971	1972	1973	1974
1. Nominal average net income (in DM per month)	432	643	703	888	975	1063	1149	1265
2. Index of nominal average net income	100.0	148.8	162.7	205.6	225.7	246.1	266.0	292.8
3. Cost of living index of a mid-income worker's family	100.0	114.8	120.6	128.5	135.1	142.2	151.9	162.3
4. Index of real net income (line 2 : line 3 x 100)	100.0	129.6	134.9	160.0	167.1	173.1	175.1	180.4

Sources: line 1: *SJB BRD*, 1972, p. 520 and 1975, p. 515.
line 3: *SJB BRD*, 1974, p. 455 and 1975, p. 448.

Table A.5 Non-consumers' Share in GNP – Federal Republic of Germany

in million DM	1960	1965	1966	1967	1968	1969	1970
1. Government consumption for civil purposes	31,480	52,290	58,710	62,600	67,560	76,330	89,200
2. Goods and services for social insurance	–	19,147	21,782	23,913	25,992	28,629	33,062
3. Government expenditure on education, culture, health	–	22,212	24,162	25,525	27,249	31,545	38,549
4. Line 1 – 2 – 3	–	10,931	12,766	13,162	14,319	16,266	17,589
5. Construction	40,120	70,240	73,690	66,410	71,910	79,300	98,180
6. New dwellings	–	29,290	30,860	28,890	30,030	31,410	37,140
7. Line 5 – line 6	–	40,950	42,830	37,520	41,880	47,890	61,040
8. Defence	9,640	17,740	17,780	18,540	16,780	18,670	19,840
9. Machinery and equipment	32,540	52,000	52,620	48,020	52,870	66,900	82,900
10. Additions to stocks	+8,700	+10,000	+3,600	–1,300	+11,500	+16,000	+15,300
11. Net foreign investment	+7,390	–540	+6,450	+15,920	+17,610	+14,790	+11,170
12. GNP	302,300	460,400	490,700	495,500	540,000	605,200	685,600
in per cent of GNP							
13. Government consumption other than defence and consumer services (line 4)	–	2.4	2.6	2.7	2.6	2.7	2.6
14. Construction other than new dwellings (line 7)	–	8.9	8.8	7.6	7.8	7.9	8.9
15. Defence (line 8)	3.2	3.7	3.6	3.7	3.1	3.1	2.9
16. Machinery and equipment (line 9)	10.8	11.3	10.7	9.7	9.8	11.1	12.1
17. Additions to stocks (line 10)	2.9	2.2	0.8	–0.3	2.1	2.6	2.2

continued

Table A.5 *continued*

in per cent of GNP	1960	1965	1966	1967	1968	1969	1970
18. Net foreign investment	2.4	−0.1	1.3	3.2	3.3	2.5	1.6
19. (line 4 + 7 + 8 + 9 + 11 total non-consumers' share)	—	28.4	27.8	26.6	28.7	29.9	30.3
20. Consumers' share	—	71.6	72.2	73.4	71.3	70.1	69.7
21. (line 19 + line 20) = 100	—	100.0	100.0	100.0	100.0	100.0	100.0

Sources: lines 1, 5, 8, 9, 10, 11 and 12, *SJB BRD*, 1972, p. 523 and 1974, p. 530; lines 2, 3 and 6 from Table A.3 (lines 2, 3 and 4); line 20 from Table A.3, line C.5.

Table A.6 Non-consumers' Share in GNP — GDR

in million Marks	1960	1965	1966	1967	1968	1969	1970
1. Gross investment	16,400	21,000	22,600	24,700	27,200	31,300	32,600
2. Machinery and equipment	7,806	10,734	11,897	12,611	13,808	15,927	17,441
3. Line 1 – line 2	8,594	10,266	10,703	12,089	13,392	15,373	15,500
4. New dwellings	–	2,340	2,510	2,510	2,750	2,840	3,050
5. Line 3 – line 4	–	7,926	8,193	9,579	10,642	12,533	12,450
6. Additions to stock	2,300	3,700	4,700	3,800	1,100	1,500	3,000
7. Other use (i.e. government consumption and foreign balance)	18,100	24,200	24,500	28,700	31,900	31,000	31,200
8. Government expenditure on education, culture and health	–	10,030	10,417	10,982	11,290	11,883	12,736
9. Goods and services from social insurance	–	4,407	4,428	4,692	4,922	5,178	5,406
10. Line 7 – lines (8 + 9)	–	9,763	9,655	13,026	15,688	13,939	13,058
11. Defence expenditure	–	–	–	–	5,831	–	6,752
12. GNP	92,800	111,500	117,100	123,500	130,600	137,800	144,000
in per cent of GNP							
13. Machinery and equipment	8.41	9.6	10.2	10.2	10.6	11.6	11.9
14. Construction other than new dwellings	–	7.1	7.0	7.8	8.1	9.1	8.6
15. Additions to stock	2.48	3.3	4.0	3.1	0.8	1.1	2.1
16. Government consumption other than for consumer services and net investment abroad	–	8.8	8.2	10.5	12.0	10.1	9.1
17. Defence	–	–	–	–	4.5	(4.6)[1]	4.7

continued

Table A.6 *continued*

in per cent of GNP	1960	1965	1966	1967	1968	1969	1970
18. Government consumption other than defence and consumer services and net investment abroad	—	—	—	—	7.5	(5.5)	4.4
19. Total non-consumers' share (lines 13 + 14 + 15 + 16)	—	28.8	29.4	31.6	31.7	31.9	31.7
20. Consumers' share	—	71.2	70.6	68.4	68.3	68.1	68.3
21. (Line 19 + line 20) = 100	—	100.0	100.0	100.0	100.0	100.0	100.0

1. Interpolated.
Sources: Lines 1, 6, 7 and 12, *Bericht*, 1971, p. 368 and *Bestandsaufnahme*, 1971, p. 277.
Line 2, *SJB DDR*, 1971, p. 44; lines 4, 8 and 9, from Table A.3; lines 11, 10 and 9 respectively.
Line 11, *Bestandsaufnahme*, 1971, p. 321; line 20 from Table A.3, line 14.

Table A.7 Purchasing Power of the 'Mark' in the GDR Old-age Pensioner's Household of Two Persons as a Percentage of the Purchasing Power of the 'DM' in the FRG

	Product Mix (consumption basket) as in the GDR		
	1966	1969	1972/73
On total expenditure, out of which	97	111	125
on food	92	94	100
on drink and tobacco	65	63	53
on clothing and footwear	56	62	75
on other industrial products	91	98	116
on services and repair of products	161	227	278
on rent	208	333	400

	Product mix (consumption basket) as in the FRG		
	1966	1969	1972/73
On total expenditure, out of which	88	99	105
on food	89	92	98
on drink and tobacco	44	44	42
on dwelling space (owned or rented)	208	333	416
on fuel and electricity	159	204	238
on household goods	57	61	71
on clothing and footwear	58	61	74
on cleansing products and cosmetics	104	106	118
on leisure activities	139	152	152
on transportation	135	154	143

Source: 'Die Kosten der Lebenshaltung in der DDR im Vergleich zur Bundesrepublik an der Jahreswende 1972–73', in *Wochenbericht,* Deutsches Institut für Wirtschaftsforschung, Berlin-West, No. 21, 1973, p. 192.

Table A.8 Price Indices and the Weight of Subsidies

FRG, 1962 = 100	1960	1964	1965	1966	1967	1968	1969	1970	1971	1972	1973
1. Cost of living[1]	—	—	108.7	112.7	114.6	116.4	119.5	124.0	130.6	137.8	147.3
2. Construction cost	85.8	110.0	114.6	118.5	115.9	120.8	127.2	147.4	162.7	174.3	187.1
3. Agricultural products[2]	—	—	—	109.3	101.9	107.8	113.0	106.0	115.1	128.2	—
4. Industrial products	—	—	104.0	105.8	104.9	99.3	101.5	107.5	112.5	116.1	122.7
5. GNP price index	92.1	—	109.7	113.7	115.0	116.8	120.9	129.5	139.7	148.1	157.0
6. Subsidies in per cent of GNP	0.8	1.0	1.3	1.2	1.1	1.4	1.3	1.4	1.3	1.3	1.5

GDR, 1963 = 100	1960	1964	1965	1966	1967	1968	1969	1970	1971	1972	1973
7. Cost of living	—	100.1	99.8	99.8	99.7	99.9	99.7	99.6	99.9	99.6	99.2
8. Construction cost	—	100.2	100.4	100.9	126.8	125.7	125.7	125.7	125.7	125.7	125.7
9. Transport cost	—	107.5	111.7	111.6	127.6	126.9	126.9	126.9	126.9	126.9	126.9
10. Agricultural products	—	106.9	108.0	110.9	112.9	115.2	123.9	123.0	131.5	130.5	131.6
11. Industrial goods	—	121.1	149.7	149.7	151.2	151.2	145.7	144.6	144.9	146.1	146.9
12. Implicit national income price index[3]	—	99.95	98.37	98.73	99.10	—	—	—	—	—	—
13. Subsidies in per cent of national income produced	2.8	3.8	4.2	4.3	4.5	4.7	4.1	3.9	4.0	4.0	3.6

1. All households.
2. 1961–62 to 1962–63 = 100 (seasonal years).
3. National income in current prices in per cent of national income in 1967 prices.

continued

Table A.8 *continued*

Sources: FRG: line 1, *SJB BRD*, 1972, p. 457 and 1974, p. 452
    "   2, "   "   "   "   p. 450 "   "   p. 441
    "   3, "   "   "   "   p. 437 "   "   p. 433
    "   4, "   "   "   "   p. 443 "   "   p. 439
    "   5, "   "   "   "   p. 523 "   "   p. 518
    "   6, "   "   "   "   p. 514 "   "   p. 508 (calculated from data in DM)

    GDR: line 7, *SJB DDR*, 1971, p. 342 and 1974, p. 328
    "   8, "   "   "   "   p. 328 "   "   p. 321
    "   9, "   "   "   "   p. 330 "   "   p. 320
    "   10, "   "   "   "   p. 332 "   "   p. 324 (unit index of agricultural prices)

lines 7—9 recalculated to 1963 basis with respect to line 11.

line 11, arithmetic average of 32 price indices of industrial commodities in inter-industrial deliveries, *SJB DDR*, 1971,
    p. 327 and 1974, p. 319.

line 12, calculated as differences in per cent between national income produced in current prices (*SJB DDR*, 1968, p. 42)
    and in 1967 prices (*SJB DDR*, 1971, p. 19). Percentage for 1963 was 100.07.

line 13, calculated from data in the *SJB DDR*, 1971, p. 40 and 1974, p. 40.

Table A.9 Purchasing Power of Wages (mid-1971) in hours and
minutes (Hrs/Mins)

Commodity	Unit	FRG Hrs/Mins	GDR Hrs/Mins
Provisions and luxury items			
Rye bread usual variety	1 kg	0/12	0/07
Wheaten flour Type W405	1 kg	0/09	0/19
Egg noodles, packaged	1 kg	0/29	0/40
Sugar, refined	1 kg	0/10	0/23
Butter, brand name	1 kg	1/05	2/23
Margarine, cheapest variety	1 kg	0/29	0/29
Eggs, Grade B	10	0/16	0/49
Full cream milk, 3% butterfat[1]	1 litre	0/07	0/10
Cheese, Gouda[2]	1 kg	0/58	1/43
Beef, stewing	1 kg	1/24	2/21
Pork, cutlets	1 kg	1/07	1/54
Jagdwurst (cold sausage)	1 kg	1/10	1/12
Pickled herrings, landed at domestic ports	1 kg	0/28	0/24
Potatoes, in bags	5 kg	0/32	0/16
White cabbage	1 kg	0/07	0/06
Oranges	1 kg	0/13	1/11
Lemons	1 kg	0/15	1/11
Cocoa powder, maximum amount of oil removed	1 kg	1/13	7/37
Coffee, medium quality	1 kg	2/19	16/40
Brandy (blended 38%)	0.7 litre	1/06	3/56
Chocolate 35% cocoa	100 gr.	0/06	0/55
Tobacco, fine cut	50 gr.	0/12	0/43
Cigarettes, medium price	10 gr.	0/09	0/23
Clothing, fabrics, shoes			
Man's lounge suit, 50% wool	1	25/58	44/46
Woman's dress, three-quarter sleeve 50% wool	1	12/04	18/29
Man's shirt, man-made fibre	1	2/15	11/30
Pinafore dress, cotton	1	2/31	6/06
Man's tie, man-made fibre	1	0/32	2/59
Woman's stockings, Perlon	1 pr.	0/21	1/31
Bed linen, damask	1	5/23	10/07
Knitting wool, baby yarn, 2-ply	100 gr.	0/31	2/03
Man's outdoor shoes, leather soles	1 pr.	5/38	11/29
Woman's sports shoes, crepe soles	1 pr.	5/30	9/34
Other industrial goods			
Folding bicycle, 20 inch frame, aluminium rims, without lights	1	18/45	57/37
Portable typewriter with tabulator	1	31/40	100/43
Man's wrist watch, 17 jewels, stainless steel, shockproof and waterproof	1	11/32	37/16

everything a ton more

continued

Table A.9 *continued*

Commodity	Unit	FRG Hrs/Mins	GDR Hrs/Mins
Vacuum cleaner (cylinder) with standard attachments	1	24/27	46/26
Electric cooker, 3 rings, oven with automatic time-control	1	41/07	152/51
Refrigerator, 130–140 litre, compressor with deep-freeze compartment	1	41/15	261/54
Washing machine with spin dryer, 4–5 kg. dry wash load[3]	1	112/55	285/43
Portable television (black and white) 61 or 62 cm screen	1	78/53	419/03
Car, saloon 45–50 hp.[4]	1	878/28	4226/11
Tariffs, Services, Household requisites			
Railway weekly season ticket, 2nd class 15 km journey normal passenger train	1	1/15	0/36
Electricity, household rate[5]	10 kwh	0/08	0/11
Gas, household rate[5]	10 cbm	0/16	0/23
Radio and TV licences (per set for which one pays)[6]	monthly	1/11	2/23
Haircut for men, basic cut	1	0/32	0/13
Cold permanent wave for women, total	1	2/59	2/17
Shoe mending, men's shoes, leather soles glued	1	1/19	1/22
Brown coal brickettes, delivered	50 kg	1/00	0/50
Dry cleaning, including pressing two-piece man's suit	1	1/09	1/22
Detergent for special fabrics	150 gr	0/08	0/18
Toilet soap, scented, 80% fat content, wrapped	100 gr	0/09	0/10

1. Full cream milk in 0.5 litre bottles, FRG 3% and GDR 2.5% butterfat.
2. FRG 40% butterfat; GDR 30% butterfat.
3. FRG fully automatic; GDR semi-automatic
4. FRG Opel Kadett, 1100 cc. normal model; GDR Wartburg Pkw, 1000 cc. standard model.
5. FRG and GDR without basic rate, which varies according to type and size of dwelling and household and according to region.
6. FRG 3 programmes; GDR 2 programmes.

Source: *Zahlenspiegel,* 1973, pp. 40–1.

Table A.10 National Income by Distributive Shares — Federal Republic of Germany (in million current DM)

	1960	1965	1966	1967	1968	1969	1970	1971	1972[1]	1973[1]	1974[1]
1. Total gross income from employment	142,830	229,990	247,560	247,900	266,310	300,140	353,190	400,220	439,150	498,650	547,330
2. Net wages and salaries	104,900	168,530	178,480	177,630	187,270	206,620	237,150	262,190	286,050	311,190	335,620
3. Income from social insurance and government pensions	37,610	59,130	64,420	70,930	74,370	80,380	86,900	97,100	110,210	123,150	142,250
4. Excess of gross income from employment over net income and transfer payments (line 1 – lines (2 + 3))	320	2,330	4,660	–660	4,670	13,140	29,140	40,930	42,890	64,310	69,460
5. Total gross income from enterprise and property	92,870	125,260	129,530	128,090	150,550	160,510	176,000	185,460	200,740	218,530	217,030
6. Tax and other obligatory payments	20,890	29,190	30,210	29,860	32,390	36,090	34,960	37,120	39,620	49,730	51,070
7. Distributed profits acruing to private households	46,700	71,420	75,180	77,520	86,370	100,060	111,460	124,920	142,310	153,920	162,820
8. Distributed profits accruing to the state	2,840	3,810	3,710	3,100	3,620	4,060	4,160	4,750	3,250	4,200	2,430
9. Non-distributed profits	22,440	20,840	20,430	17,610	28,170	20,300	25,420	18,670	15,560	10,680	710
10. National income at factor cost	235,700	355,250	377,090	375,990	416,860	460,650	529,190	585,680	639,890	717,180	764,360

continued

Table A.10 *continued*

	1960	1965	1966	1967	1968	1969	1970	1971	1972[1]	1973[1]	1974[1]
11. Indirect taxes net of subsidies	40,870	58,940	62,930	65,710	65,740	80,500	81,630	91,110	101,160	109,910	114,640

1. Preliminary figures.
Source: *SJB BRD*, 1972, pp. 514, 520 and 521; *SJB*, 1973, pp. 527 and 528; *SJB*, 1974, pp. 508, 514 and 515; *SJB*, 1975, pp. 508, 515, 516.

Table A.11 Gross and Net Capital Formation — Federal Republic of Germany (in million DM)

	1960	1965	1966	1967	1968	1969	1970
1. Depreciation allowances of the business sector	24,590	44,110	48,280	51,330	54,660	60,430	70,500
2. Depreciation allowances of the state sector	1,140	2,100	2,400	2,470	2,740	3,030	3,670
3. Non-distributed profits of unincorporated enterprises	14,210	13,270	12,680	10,350	16,870	9,900	15,520
4. Corporate non-distributed profits	8,230	7,570	7,750	7,260	11,300	10,400	9,900
5. Government saving	21,760	23,060	24,500	16,430	20,290	36,870	39,800
6. Household saving	30,320	49,030	47,720	45,660	57,960	57,640	73,370
7. Total	100,250	139,140	143,330	133,500	163,820	178,270	212,760
8. of which net capital formation (line 7 – lines (1 + 2))	74,520	92,930	92,650	79,700	106,420	114,810	138,590

Sources: *SJB BRD*, 1972, pp. 507, 511 and 513, and 1974, pp. 498, 501, 502, 505, 506 and *SJB BRD*, 1974, pp. 498–506. Data for further years are not comparable because of the revised method of accounting by the Federal Bank.

Table A.12 Approximate Distributive Shares in the GDR (absolute figures)

	1960	1965	1970	1972	1973
1. National income produced in million Marks of 1967	71,045	84,175	108,720	120,090	126,670
2. Number of workers, employees and members of co-operatives in 1000	7,262	7,336	7,501	7,576	7,623
3. Average income from employment per year in 1000 Marks	6,660	7,596	9,060	9,768	10,020
4. Income from employment in million Marks (line 2 x line 3)	48,365	55,724	67,959	74,002	77,754
5. Wage tax and employees' and co-operative producers' contribution to social insurance in million Marks	6,674	7,746	9,786	11,026	11,663
6. Net income from employment and co-operative production in million Marks (line 4 – line 5)	41,691	47,978	58,173	62,976	66,091
7. Total social insurance expenditure in million Marks	9,600	11,802	14,976	17,725	19,838
8. Residual item : line 1 – lines (6 + 7)	19,754	24,395	35,571	39,389	40,741

Sources: SJB DDR, 1974, line 1, p. 40; lines 2 and 3, p. 19; line 5 calculated according to per household data in SJB DDR, 1974, p. 342 (the percentages in the respective years are 13.8; 13.9; 14.4; 14.9; 15.0); line 7, SJB DDR, 1971, p. 316 and 1974, p. 310.

Table A.13 The Class Structure in the GDR, 30 September 1960

Social class according to the economic sector	Economically Active	Per cent	Resident population
Working class	6,169,600	76.2	13,117,000
Class of co-operative farmers	952,800	11.8	2,031,300
Co-operative craftsmen	146,100	1.8	309,900
Intelligentsia	376,800	4.6	791,800
Employees	347,500	–	–
Members of Solicitors' Boards	500	–	–
Professionals	11,300	–	–
Members of farmers' co-operatives	17,500	–	–
Middle class	372,500	4.6	791,800
Craftsmen	251,200	3.1	533,600
Retail traders	85,050	1.1	189,300
(other) self-employed persons	36,250	0.4	68,900
Capitalists	44,900	0.6	103,300
Industry[1]	13,100	–	–
Construction[2]	2,400	–	–
Transport	1,700	–	–
Wholesale Trade[3]	7,400	–	–
Retail Trade	13,850	–	–
Non-material services	1,750	–	–
Self-employed farmers	34,300	0.4	68,900
Altogether	8,097,000	100.0	17,214,000

Notes:
1. 4,623 Persons in enterprises with state participation.
2. 809 Persons in enterprises with state participation.
3. 39 Persons in enterprises with state participation.

Source: Kurt Lungwitz, *Über die Klassenstruktur in der Deutschen Demokratischen Republic.* Verlag "Die Wirtschaft", Berlin (Ost), 1962, p. 162.

Table A.14 Scale of Preference in Career Choice in the GDR (Opinions of one hundred twenty-year-old boys and girls in the district of Gera in 1964)

Job Content:	Boys	Girls	Total
1. Help, care, education (e.g. nurse, teacher, nursery-school teacher, tutor)	3	25	28
2. Technical professions (e.g. tractor driver, radio technician, crane driver, car repair worker)	16	2	18
3. Office, laboratory or draughtsman's work	7	6	13
4. Not supervised activities (e.g. agronomist, engineer, independent craftsman, music director)	7	5	12
5. Prestige professions (e.g. professor, doctor, scientist, writer)	7	4	11
6. Light work with opportunity to meet people (e.g. hairdresser, taxi driver, hostess or fashion model)	7	3	10
7. Heavy physical work (e.g. co-operative farmer, miner, locomotive stoker, bricklayer)	5	0	5
8. Managerial positions in industry, agriculture and administration	2	1	3
9. Politico-administrative functions (e.g. city mayor, police member, Permanent party secretary, full-time youth organiser)	1	0	1

Source: Peter C. Ludz: *Studien und Materialien zur Soziologie der DDR,* Westdeutscher Verlag, Köln and Opladen, 1964, p. 83.

Table A.15 Specimen of a Personal Form for Screening Purposes [1]

STRICTLY CONFIDENTIAL!

PERSONAL RECORD SHEET

All questions are to be answered conscientiously and in a legible fashion.

Answers in the form of a dash are inadmissible.

If the sections provided here are not sufficient for an exact answer supplementary pages are to be attached.

An uninterrupted *curriculum vitae* is to be attached.

Photo

For applicants for posts:
If you are not appointed industrial concerns and authorities are obliged to return your personal record sheet.

— —

Name (for women, also the maiden name)

Forenames (underline the name by which you are usually known)

Date of birth   Place of birth (district, province etc.)

Citizenship   Nationality (ethnic)

Number and date of issue of identity pass

Addresses of all the places you have lived since 1939 (with exact dates)

From — to

Marital status (single / married / common-law spouse / divorced / widowed / separated).

Education (with the exception of specialist schools attended, in the case of higher education give details of place, dates, area of specialisation, final examinations).

In which foreign languages are you proficient?   Degree of proficiency?

Qualifications for skilled work   Qualifications for semi-skilled work

Areas of specialist knowledge

Examinations connected with your occupation (type, place and date)

Which specialist schools have you attended? (place, date, examinations)

Are you an external student or do you follow a correspondence course? How long have you been doing so? (institute, date, area of study)

In the case of disability, indicate the category of disability (according to established scale) and the number and date of issue of pass.

Employment to date (full uninterrupted list of chronological order)

commencement and termination of employment (month, year)	place of work, locality	employed as	gross monthly income

continued

Table A.15 *continued*

Which state distinctions have you been awarded since 8.5.1945?

Of which parties, trade unions and other social organisations and associations have you been a member? Which do you belong to now? (chronological order)

name of organisation	member from	to	Official functions
a) parties			
b) trade unions			
c) organisations and associations			

Since 8.5.1945 have you been a member of people's representative bodies? (describe the functions for which you were elected)

Were you active as an elected official or did you carry out any other state functions before 1945? (give details)

Which schools and training courses run by parties, unions or other social organisations have you attended? (when, for how long?)

Did you take an active part in the struggle against fascism? (when, where, how)

Are you recognised as having been persecuted by the Nazi regime?

Details about the members of your family and close relatives (for children supply date of birth)

Relationship	Name and forenames	Place of abode	Employment	Place of work, locality

Details about your former military status (also police service and other military units)

Date from	to	Unit or place of service	Highest service rank

continued

Table A.15 *continued*

Which distinctions, medals or party decorations were you awarded before 8.5.1945, when and for what reason?

After 1.9.1939 were you a prisoner of war or an internee? (where and for how long?)

Did you take part in training courses? (when, where and duration)

What was your employment while a prisoner of war?

Have you been convicted of any offence? (details of the offence, penalty and the date of sentence)

Do you or any of your relatives own property and/or land (real estate), or an agricultural or business (trade or commercial) enterprise?

I declare that the above information is correct.

_____ 19 _____

place signature

Attached: *curriculum vitae*

Supplementary questions for holders of, and applicants for, higher positions.

5. Religion (exact details of religious affiliation or sect)

7. All places of abode since 1932 (exact dates): from —   to —

8a. Do you live in your own house or in lodgings?

8b. Do you have lodgers?

9. Name and age of your dependants:

12. Have you been, or are you now, a writer?
    Have you made inventions? (give details)

19. State of health (give details)
    In the case of disability give the level of disability (according to the established scale) and the number and date of pass.

20. Full details of all employment until now (uninterrupted account of ,
    including information about long intervals of schooling, prolonged sickness, unemployment, military and police service, stay in institutions etc., in chronological order);

continued

Table A.15 *continued*

Commencement and termination of employment (month and year)

Name of place and work

Establishment, length of service, school, institution etc. (with details of locality)

employed as

gross monthly income

reason for leaving or change of work

22. Of which parties, trade unions and other social organisations and associations have you been a member?

Which do you still belong to? (in chronological order):

Name of the organisations   Member from —   to —

Reason for leaving: official functions, description of same from —   to —

a) political parties
b) trade unions
c) organisations and associations

26. Were you persecuted and arrested by (representatives of) bourgeois class justice or the police on account of your political engagement? (give details)

27. Information about your close relatives (spouse, common-law spouse, children, father, mother, brothers and sisters, parents-in-law) relationship, name, forename, year of birth and place of birth, party membership,

earlier . . . .   now . . . .
Main employment until 1945.

, Present abode, present employment, name and address of place of work or school.

30. After 1.9.1939 were you a prisoner of war or an internee?

a) When, where and by which military power were you taken prisoner?

b) In which countries and camps were you billetted?

c) Did you take part in training courses? (if so, when, where and length of course)

d) What was your employment as a prisoner of war?

e) When, where and by which military power were you discharged?

31. Have you been abroad? (where, length of stay, date, purpose of stay, including holiday and official trips):

32. Did you have or do you still have, relatives who live abroad: (where, relationship)

Do you maintain connections with them or with other persons living abroad?

continued

Table A.15 *continued*

33. Which of the relatives named under heading 27 had, or still have, functions in political parties?

34. Have you been convicted of any offence? (details of the offence, penalty, and date of sentence)

34a. Do you have similar information about your relatives? (give details)

35. Have you, your spouse (common-law spouse) your parents or parents-in-law owned, or do any of you still own, property or land, or any agricultural, industrial or business (trade or commercial) enterprise or are you involved in such an enterprise? (who, type, size, number of employees, when, where?)

36. Which additional information can you provide besides your answers to the above questions? (about yourself, your spouse, your relatives and your spouse's relatives):

37. Give names, with exact addresses, of people who can supply information about you:

I declare that the above information is correct. I am aware that incorrect information may lead to legal action being taken against me. I further undertake to advise immediately the 'cadre branch' (screening department) at my place of work about changes which affect the content of this personal record sheet.

_____ 19   _____
        (place)   signature

Attached: *curriculum vitae*

1. Translated from the reprint in *Deutschland Archiv,* 1972, No. 2, pp. 179–83.

Table A.16 Banks' Participation in Industrial Enterprises in the FRG

Bank	Enterprise	Percentage of participation
Deutsche	Bayerische Elektrizitätswerke AG	25
Bank AG	Bergmann Elektrizitätswerke AG	25
	Butzke-Werke AG	25
	Daimler Benz AG	25
	Didier-Werke AG	25
	Eichbaum Werger Brauereien AG	25
	Enzinger Union Werke AG	25
	Hapag	50
	Philipp Holzmann AG	25
	Itzehoer Netzfabrik AG	50
	Karstadt AG	25
	Maschinenfabrik Moenus AG	25
	Neue Augsburger Kattunfabrik	25
	Pittler Maschinenfabrik AG	25
	Porzellanfabrik Kahla	25
	Schuhfabrik Manz AG	25
	Gebr. Stollwerck AG	25
	Süddeutsche Zucker AG	25
	Vereinigte Trikotfabriken Vollmoeller AG	25
	Württembergische Baumwollspinnerei und	
	Weberei	50
Dresdner Bank	Bayerische Wolldeckenfabrik Bruckmühl	
AG	AG	25
	Julius Berger AG	25
	Chemie-Verwaltungs-AG	25
	Dortmunder Ritterbrauerei AG	50
	Elbschloss-Brauerei	50
	Engelhardt Brauerei AG	25
	Gelsenkirchener Bergwerks AG	25
	Glückauf Brauerei AG	25
	Goldpfeil Ludwig Krumm AG	25
	Grün & Bilfinger AG	25
	Hildesheimer Aktienbrauerei	25
	Hotelbetriebs AG	30
	Kaufhof AG	30
	Lübecker Flender Werke AG	30
	Metallgesellschaft AG	25
	Norddeutscher Lloyd	25
	Norddeutsche Wolkämmerei und	
	Kammgarnspinnerei AG	50
	Pittler Maschinenfabrik AG	25
	Vereinigte Schmirgel-und	
	Maschinenfabriken AG	25
Commerzbank	A.H.I.-Bau	25
AG	Beton und Monierbau AG	25

continued

Table A.16 *continued*

Bank	Enterprise	Percentage of participation
Commerzbank AG (cont.)	Dampfschiffgesellschaft Neptun	25
	Deutscher Reederei-Verein in Hamburg	30
	Fürstenberg Ehemalige Herzoglich Braunschweigische Porzellanmanufaktur	25
	Heinrich Bergbau AG	25
	Hotelbetriebs AG	30
	Kaiser Brauerei AG	25
	Karstadt AG	25
	Kaufhof AG	25
	Lübecker Flender Werke AG	65
	H. Maihak AG	25

Source: H. Marcus, *Die Macht der Mächtigen,* Düsseldorf, 1970, pp. 88 and 89.

BIBLIOGRAPHY

Abendroth, Wolfgang: *Antagonistische Gesellschaft und politische Demokratie.* Neuwied und Berlin: Luchterhand, 1972.

A bis Z. Ein Taschen- und Nachschlagebuch über den anderen Teil Deutschlands. Bonn: Deutscher Bundesverlag, 1969.

Almond, G.A., and Verba, S.: *The Civic Culture: Political Attitudes and Democracy in Five Nations.* Princeton Univ. Press, 1963.

Angestelltenversicherung, 2 and 3, 1974.

Arndt, H., Doerrer, H., and Ebert, M.: 'Die DDR stellt sich vor'. Dresden: Zeit in Bild, 1971.

Axen, Hermann: 'Zur nationalen Frage'. Reprint in *Deutschland Archiv VII,* 1974, pp. 192–212.

Bachrach, Peter: *The Theory of Democratic Elitism.* London: Univ. of London Press, 1970.

Ball, A.R.: *Modern Politics and Government.* London: Macmillan, 1971.

Bendix, Reinhard, ed.: *State and Society – A Reader in Comparative Political Sociology.* Boston: Little, Brown and Co., 1968.

Beyme, Klaus von: *Die politische Elite in der Bundesrepublik Deutschland.* München: Piper, 1971.

Blank, Karl: *Beiträge zum innerdeutschen Gewerkschaftsdialog,* Band I and Band II. Bonn-Bad Godesberg: Friedrich-Ebert-Stiftung, 1971 & 1972.

Bolte, K.M.: *Deutsche Gesellschaft im Wandel,* 1 & 2: Opladen: Leske, 1967 & 1970.

Bolte, K.M.: *Sozialer Aufstieg und Abstieg.* Stuttgart: Ferdinand Enke, 1959.

Bracher, Karl Dietrich: *Die Auflösung der Weimarer Republik.* Schwarzwald: Ring, 1971.

Bracher, Karl Dietrich: *Deutschland zwischen Demokratie und Diktatur.* Bern und München: Scherz, 1964.

Bress, Ludwig, and Hensel, Karl Paul: *Wirtschaftssysteme des Sozialismus im Experiment – Plan oder Markt?* Frankfurt am Main: Fischer, 1972.

Brinkmann, Gerhard: *Berufsausbildung und Arbeitseinkommen.* Berlin: Duncker and Humblot, 1967.

Brinton, Crane: *Anatomy of Revolution.* London: Cape, 1939.

Bröll, Werner: 'Gegenwartsfragen der Ost-Wirtschaft', Band 6. *Die Wirtschaft der DDR – Lage unde Aussichten.* München-Wien:

Günter Olzog, 1970.

Bundesbank: *Monatsbericht*. November, 1974.

Bundesinstitut für Ostwissenschaftliche und Internationale Studien: *Berichte,* 1971–1973. Köln.

Bundesminister für Arbeit und Sozialordnung: *Reform der Betriebsverfassung.* Bonn: Referat Öffentlichkeitsarbeit, 1971.

Bundesminister für Arbeit und Sozialordnung: *Übersicht über die soziale Sicherung.* 1970.

Bundesminister für innerdeutsche Beziehungen: *Bericht der Bundesregierung und Materialien zur Lage der Nation,* 1971, 1972 and 1974. Kassel: 1971, 1972 and 1974.

Bundesminister für innerdeutsche Beziehungen: *Texte zur Deutschlandpolitik,* Band 8 and Band 11. Bonn: Deutscher Bundesverlag, 1971 and 1973.

Bundesminister für innerdeutsche Beziehungen: *Zahlenspiegel.* Bonn: 1973 and 1974.

Bundessekretariat der Jungsozialisten, Bonn: *Programme der deutschen Sozialdemokratie.* Hannover: Dietz, 1963.

Busch, D.W.: *Berufliche Wertorientierung und berufliche Mobilität.* Stuttgart: Ferdinand Enke, 1973.

Childs, David: *East Germany.* London: Ernest Benn, 1969.

Carter, G.W., and Herz, J.H.: *Government and Politics in the Twentieth Century.* London: Thames and Hudson, 1973.

Claessens, D., Klönne, A. and Tschoepe, A.: *Sozialkunde der Bundesrepublik Deutschland.* Köln: Eugen Diederichs Verlag, 1965.

Dahrendorf, R.: *Gesellschaft und Demokratie in Deutschland.* München: Piper, 1965. (Trans.: *Society and Democracy in Germany.* London: Weidenfeld & Nicolson, 1968.)

Dahrendorf, R.: *Conflict and Contract – Industrial Relations and the Political Community in Times of Crisis.* Liverpool University Press, 1975.

Deutsch, Karl W.: *Nationalism and its Alternatives.* New York: Alfred Knopf, 1969.

Deutsch, K.W., Edinger, L.J., Macridis, R.C. and Merritt, R.L.: *France, Germany and the Western Alliance.* New York: Charles Scribner, 1967.

Deutsches Institut für Wirtschaftsforschung: *DDR Wirtschaft – eine Bestandsaufnahme.* Frankfurt am Main and Hamburg: Fischer, 1971 & 1974.

Doerdelmann, Bernhard, ed.: *Minderheiten in der Bundesrepublik.*

Delp-Druck, Bad Windsheim: Delpsche Verlagsbuchhandlung, 1969.

Dreitzel, Hans Peter: *Sozialer Wandel*. Neuwied & Berlin: Luchterhand, 1967 & 1972.

Dyson, K.H.F.: 'Anti-Communism in the Federal Republic of Germany: The Case of the "Berufsverbot" '. *Parliamentary Affairs*, Hansard Soc., Vol. XXVIII, no. 1, Winter 1974—5.

Edinger, L.J.: *Politics in Germany — Attitudes and Processes*. Boston: Little, Brown & Co., 1968.

Edinger, L.J.: 'Post-Totalitarian Leadership: Elites in The German Federal Republic'. *American Political Science Review*, Vol. LIV, 1960, pp. 58—82.

Edwards, Lyford: *Natural History of Revolution*. New York (re-edited): 1965.

Eisenstadt, S.N.: *Tradition, Change and Modernity*. Toronto: John Wiley and Sons, 1973.

Embassy of the Federal Republic of Germany in London: 'Latest from Germany', 1974, 1975.

Eschenburg, Theodor: *Herrschaft der Verbände?* Stuttgart: Deutsche Verlagsanstalt, 1955.

Engliš, Karel: *Soustava národního hospodářství*. Prague: 1936.

Esters, Guenther: *Workers Co-determination in Germany*. Bonn-Bad Godesberg: Friedrich-Ebert-Stiftung, 1972.

Flenchley, Ralph: *Modern German History*. 4th edition. London: Dent, 1968.

Forster, Thomas M.: *The East German Army*. London: Allen and Unwin, 1967.

Fortsch, Eckhart: *Die SED Die Partei und ihre Mitglieder*. Stuttgart: Kohlhammer, 1969.

Friedburg, L., Horlemann, J., Hubner, P., Kadritzke, U., Ritsert, J. and Schumm, W.: *Freie Universität und politisches Potential der Studenten*. Neuwied & Berlin: Luchterhand, 1968.

Friedrich-Ebert-Stiftung, eds.: *Das Gesetzbuch der Arbeit der DDR. Arbeitsrecht und Gewerkschaftsrechte in beiden deutschen Staaten*. Bonn — Bad Godesberg: 1971.

Friedrich-Ebert-Stiftung, eds.: *Löhne, Preise, Gewerkschaftsrechte. Vergleiche zwischen beiden deutschen Staaten*. Bonn — Bad Godesberg: Verlag Neue Gesellschaft, 1971.

Friedrich-Ebert-Stiftung, eds.: *Parteien in beiden deutschen Staaten*. Bonn — Bad Godesberg: Verlag Neue Gesellschaft, 1972.

Fürstenburg, F.: *Die Sozialstruktur der Bundesrepublik Deutschland*. Opladen: Westdeutscher UTB Verlag, 1967 & 1972.

Galbraith, J.K.: *The New Industrial State.* London: André Deutsch, 1967.

Geiger, Theodor: *Die soziale Schichtung des deutschen Volkes.* Stuttgart: F. Enke (reprint), 1967.

Gesamtdeutsches Institut: *Bestimmungen der DDR zu Eigentumsfragen und Enteignungen.* Bonn: Deutscher Bundesverlag, 1971.

Gesamtdeutsches Institut: *Der Parteiapparat der Deutschen Demokratischen Republik.* Bonn: Bundesanstalt für gesamtdeutsche Aufgaben, 1971.

Gesamtdeutsches Institut: 'Staats- und Parteiapparat der DDR. Personelle Besetzung'. Bonn: (mimeographed), 1974.

Gesamtdeutsches Institut: *Der Staatsapparat der Deutschen Demokratischen Republik.* Bonn: Bundesanstalt für gesamtdeutsche Aufgaben, 1971.

Gesetzbuch der Arbeit und andere ausgewählte rechtliche Bestimmungen. Staatsverlag der DDR, 1969.

Glum, Friedrich: *Philosophen im Spiegel und Zerrspiegel.* München: Isar Verlag, 1954.

Gniffke, Erich W.: *Jahre mit Ulbricht.* Köln: Verlag Wissenschaft und Politik, 1966.

Gratz, Frank: 'Extras für die Bosse in der DDR'. *Die Zeit,* 3 September 1971.

Gripp, R.C.: *The Political System of Communism.* London: Nelson, 1973.

Grossner, K. *et al.: Das 198. Jahrzehnt. Eine Team-Prognose für 1970–1980.* München: Deutscher Taschenbuch Verlag, 1972.

Habermas, Jürgen: 'Strukturwandel der Öffentlichkeit — Untersuchungen zu einer Kategorie der bürgerlichen Gesellschaft.' In *Moderne deutsche Sozialgeschichte,* ed. Hans-Ulrich Wehler. Köln: Kiepenheuer & Witsch, 1973.

Habermas, J. *et al.: Student und Politik.* Neuwied & Berlin: Luchterhand, 1969.

Hallett, Graham: *The Social Economy of West Germany.* London: Macmillan, 1973.

Hamilton, Richard: 'Einkommen und Klassenstruktur. Der Fall der Bundesrepublik Deutschland.' *Kölner Zeitschrift für Soziologie und Sozialpsychologie,* XX, 1968, pp. 250–87.

Havemann, Robert: *Rückantworten an die Hauptverwaltung 'Ewige Wahrheiten'.* München: Piper, 1971.

Hegel, G.W.F.: *Grundlinien der Philosophie des Rechts.* Leipzig: Felix Meiner, 1930.

Herbst, Fritz: 'Kündigung und Kündigungsschutz'. *Sozialpolitik in Deutschland*, No. 13. Stuttgart: Kohlhammer, 1965.

Hermes, Peter: 'Die Christlich-Demokratische Union und die Bodenreform in der sowjetischen Besatzungszone Deutschlands im Jahre 1945.' Verlag der Saarbrücker Zeitung, 1963.

Hofer, Walther, ed.: *Europa und die Einheit Deutschlands*. Köln: Verlag Wissenschaft und Politik, 1970.

Immler, Hans: *Agrarpolitik in der DDR*. Köln: Verlag Wissenschaft und Politik, 1971.

Institut für Demoskopie Allensbach, eds.: *Jahrbuch der öffentlichen Meinung*, 1968 bis 1973. Allensbach: 1974.

Institut für Marxistische Studien und Forschungen: *Klassen- und Sozialstruktur der BRD 1950–1970*. Teil I: *Klassenstruktur und Klassenthoerie*. Frankfurt am Main: Marxistische Blätter, 1973.

Ionescu, Ghita: *The Politics of the European Communist States*. London: Weidenfeld and Nicolson, 1967.

Jacobsen, H.A., and Dollinger, H.: *Die deutschen Studenten – Der Kampf um die Hochschulreform. Eine Bestandsaufnahme*. München: Deutscher Taschenbuch Verlag, 1968.

Jaeggi, U.: *Macht und Herrschaft in der Bundesrepublik*. Frankfurt am Main: Fischer, 1969.

Janowitz, Morris: 'Social Stratification and Mobility in West Germany.' *American Journal of Sociology*, 1958.

Jaspers, Karl: *Aspekte der Bundesrepublik*. München: Piper, 1972.

Jaspers, Karl: *The Future of Germany*. Chicago: Univ. of Chicago Press, 1967.

Jungmann, B.: *Sebehodnoceni a sebeidentifikace in Československá spolecnost*. Ed. by P. Machonin. Bratislava: Epocha, 1969.

Kalweit, W.: 'Ökonomische Stimulierung in der sozialistischen Planwirtschaft.' In *Die Ökonomische Stimulierung der sozialistischen Produktion*, p. 37 & ff. Berlin: Verlag die Wirtschaft.

Karbusicky, Vladimir: *Ideologie im Lied, Lied in der Ideologie*. Köln: Musikverlag Hans Gerig, 1973.

Kehrer, Günter: 'Germany — Federal Republic.' In *Western Religion*. Paris: Mouton, 1972.

Kersten, Heinz: *Aufstand der Intellektuellen*. Stuttgart: Seewald, 1957.

Kosta, Jiří: *Sozialistische Planwirtschaft – Theorie und Praxis*. Opladen: Westdeutscher Verlag, 1974.

König, René: 'West Germany.' In *Contemporary Europe, Class, Status and Power*, eds. Scotford Archer and S. Giner, pp. 279–96. London: Weidenfeld & Nicolson, 1971.

Krejci, Jaroslav: *Social Change and Stratification in Postwar Czechoslovakia.* London: Macmillan, 1972.

Krelle, W., Schunk, J., and Siebke, J.: *Überbetriebliche Ertragsbeteiligung der Arbeitnehmer,* Vol. II. Tübingen, 1968.

Krieg, Harald: *LDP und NDP in der DDR, 1949–1958.* Köln: & Opladen: Westdeutscher Verlag, 1965.

Kunz, Frithjof: *Sozialistische Arbeitsdisziplin.* Berlin: Staatsverlag der DDR, 1966.

Lades, H., and Burrichter, C., eds.: *Produktivkraft Wissenschaft (Sozialwissenschaft in der DDR).* Hamburg: Drei Mohren Verlag, 1970.

Lange, R., Meissner, B., and Pleyer, K., eds.: *Probleme des DDR-Rechts.* Köln: Wissenschaft und Politik, 1973.

Lambrecht, Horst: 'Aussenhandel der DDR 1974'. In *Deutschland Archiv,* 8, 1975, pp. 852–6.

Leenen, Wolf-Rainer: 'Sozialpolitik in der DDR (II)'. In *Deutschland Archiv,* 5, 1975, pp. 512 ff.

Lipold, G. *et al.: Das Zeitbudget der Bevölkerung.* Berlin: 1971.

Lipset, S.M.: *Political Man.* London: Heinemann, 1973.

Löwenthal, Richard, and Schwarz, Hans-Peter, eds.: *Die Zweite Republik. 25 Jahre Bundesrepublik Deutschland – eine Bilanz.* Stuttgart: Seewald, 1974.

Ludz, Peter C.: *The Changing Party Elite in East Germany.* Cambridge, Mass., & London, England: MIT Press, 1972.

Ludz, Peter C.: *Deutschlands doppelte Zukunft.* München: Hanser, 1974.

Ludz, Peter C.: 'Die Entwicklung der DDR'. In *Das 198. Jahrzehnt, eine Team-Prognose für 1970–1980,* ed. K. Grossner *et al.* München: Deutscher Taschenbuch Verlag, 1972.

Ludz, Peter C.: 'Experts and critical intellectuals in East Germany.' In *Upheaval and Continuity (A Century of German History),* ed. E. Feuchtwanger. London: Wolff, 1973, and Univ. of Pittsburgh Press, 1974.

Ludz, Peter C.: *Studien und Materialen zur Soziologie der DDR.* Köln & Opladen: Westdeutscher Verlag, 1964.

Ludz, Peter C.: *Two Germanys in One World.* Paris: Saxon House for the Atlantic Institute for International Affairs, 3/1973.

Lungwitz, Kurt: 'Über die Klassenstruktur in der Deutschen Demokratischen Republik.' Berlin: Verlag *Die Wirtschaft,* 1962.

Mager, F. & Spinnarke, U.: *Was wollen die Studenten?* Frankfurt am Main: Fischer, 1967.

Mampel, Siegfried: *Arbeitsverfassung und Arbeitsrecht in Mittel-deutschland.* Köln: Kohlhammer, 1966.

Mandel, Ernest: *Marxistische Wirtschaftstheorie.* Frankfurt am Main: Suhrkamp, 1968.

Marcus, Hermann: *Die Macht der Mächtigen (Deutschland und seine Wirtschaftsriesen).* Düsseldorf: Droste, 1970.

Marshall, T.H.: *Citizenship and Social Class.* Cambridge Univ. Press, 1950.

Marx, Karl: *Capital,* Vol. III. Ed. by F. Engels. Chicago: 1909.

Marx, Karl: *Critique of the Gotha Programme.* Letchworth: 1933.

Marx, K., and Engels, F.: *The Communist Manifesto.* London: Allen & Unwin, 1967.

Marx, K., and Engels, F.: *The German Ideology.* London: Lawrence & Wishart, 1970.

Mende, Klaus-Dieter: *Schulreform und Gesellschaft in der Deutschen Demokratischen Republik 1945–1965.* Stuttgart: Ernst Klett, 1969.

Mészáros, István: *Marx's Theory of Alienation,* London: Merlin, 1970.

Mitzscherling, Peter: 'Soziale Sicherung in der DDR (Ziele Methoden und Erfolge mitteldeutscher Sozialpolitik).' In *Sonderhefte* 81, 1968. Berlin: Duncker & Humblot, 1968.

Müller, Alex: *Kommentar zum Gesetz zur Förderung der Stabilität und des Wachstums der Wirtschaft.* Hannover: 1969.

Müller, K. Valentin: *Die Manager in der Sowjetzone.* Köln & Opladen: Westdeutscher Verlag, 1962.

Müller-Römer, Dietrich (Kommentar): *Die neue Verfassung der DDR.* Köln: Wissenschaft und Politik, 1974.

Münke, Stephanie: *Die mobile Gesellschaft (Einführung in die Sozialstruktur der BRD).* Stuttgart, Berlin, Köln, Mainz: Kohlhammer, 1967.

Neumann, E.P.: *Die Deutschen und die NATO.* Allensbach: Verlag fur Demoskopie, 1969.

Newmann, Karl J.: *Wer treibt die Bundesrepublik wohin?* Köln: Wissenschaft und Politik, 1968.

Ohligs, Pritz: *Outlines of the History of the German Labour Movement.* Bonn – Bad Godesberg: Friedrich-Ebert-Stiftung, 1972.

Oldenburg, Fred: 'Blick zurück nach vorn.' In *Deutschland Archiv* VIII, 1/1975, pp. 1–7.

Oldenburg, Fred: 'Konflikt und Konfliktregelung in der Parteiführung der SED 1945/46 – 1972.' In *Berichte des Bundesinstitut für Ostwissenschaftliche und Internationale Studien,* 48. Köln: 1972.

Ossowski, Stanislav: *Class Structure in the Social Consciousness.*

London: Routledge & Kegan Paul, 1963.

Österreichisches Institut für Wirtschaftsforschung: 'Die Wirtschaft Osteuropas und der USSR,. 1971 bis 1973 — Ausblick bis 1975.' In *Monatsbericht*, 3/1974.

Pareto, Vilfredo: *The Mind and Society, A Treatise on General Sociology*. New York: Dover, 1963.

Parsons, Talcot: *Evolutionary and Comparative Perspectives*. New Jersey: Prentice-Hall, 1966.

Payne, J.P., ed.: *Germany Today*. London: Methuen, 1971.

Pinson, Koppel S.: *Modern Germany* (2nd edition). London: Macmillan, 1966.

Pleyer, K., & Lieser, J.: *Das Zivil- und Wirtschaftsrecht der DDR im Ausklang eines Reformjahrzehnts (Beitrage aus den Jahren 1969–1972)*. Stuttgart: Fischer, 1973.

Press and Information Office of the Government of the FRG: *Facts about Germany — The Federal Republic of Germany*. Bonn: 1972.

Presse- und Informationsamt der Bundesregierung: *Bonner Almanach*. 1974.

Redlow, G.: 'Die Marxistisch-Leninistische Auffassung von der Freiheit.' In *Freiheit und Gesellschaft*, ed. G. Stiehler *et al.*, Frankfurt am Main: Marxistische Blätter, 1973.

Reigrotzki, Erich: *Soziale Verflechtungen in der Bundesrepublik — Elemente der sozialen Teilnahme in Kirche, Politik, Organisationen und Freizeit*. Tübingen: Mohr, 1956.

Ridder, W., & Scholmer, J.: *Die DKP, Programm und Politik*. Bonn: 1970.

Ritter, Gerhard: *Europa und die deutsche Frage*. München: Münchner Verlag, 1948.

Roberts, G.K.: *West German Politics*. London: Macmillan, 1972.

Roghmann, Klaus: 'The Impact of Military Service on Authoritarian Attitudes: Evidence from West Germany.' *American Journal of Sociology*, 78, no. 2, 1972.

Rostow, W.W.: *Politics and the Stages of Growth*. London: Cambridge University Press, 1971.

Rudiger, Thomas: *Modell DDR — Die Kalkulierte Emanzipation*. München: Carl Hauser, 1972.

Säuberlich, W.: 'Freiheit als bewusste und planmässige Gestaltung der gesellschaftlichen Lebensbedingungen.' In *Freiheit und Gesellschaft*, ed. G. Stiehler *et al.* Frankfurt am Main: Marxistische Blätter, 1973.

Sauer, Wolfgang: 'Das Problem des deutschen Nationalstaates.' In *Moderne deutsche Sozialgeschichte*, ed. Hans-Ulrich Wehler, Köln:

Kiepenheuer & Witsch, 1973.

Schelsky, Helmut: *Auf der Suche nach Wirklichkeit.* Köln: Eugen Diederichs, 1965.

Schelsky, Helmut: *Die skeptische Generation.* Düsseldorf/Köln: Eugen Diederichs, 1957.

Scheuch, Erwin K.: 'Sozialprestige und soziale Schichtung.' *Kölner Zeitschrift für Soziologie und Sozialpsychologie,* XIII, p. 76, 1961.

Schewe, Dieter, and Nordhorn, Karlhugo: *Übersicht über die Soziale Sicherung.* Bonn: Bundesminister für Arbeit und Sozialordnung, 1970.

Schmickl, Emil: *Soziologie und Sozialismustheorie in der DDR.* Köln: Wissenschaft und Politik, 1973.

Schnitzer, Martin: *East and West Germany − A Comparative Economic Analysis.* New York: Praeger, 1972.

Schnitzer, Martin: *Income Distribution − A Comparative Study of the United States, Sweden, West Germany, East Germany, the United Kingdom and Japan.* New York: Praeger, 1974.

Schoenbaum, David: *Hitler's Social Revolution − Class and Status in Nazi Germany 1933−1939.* London: Weidenfeld and Nicolson, 1967.

Shaffer, H.G., ed.: *The Soviet Economy.* London: Methuen, 1964.

Shapiro, Leonard: *Totalitarianism.* London: Macmillan, 1972.

Siebke, J.: *Die Vermögensbildung der privaten Haushalte in der BRD.* Forschungsbericht für das Bundesministerium für Arbeit und Sozialordnung, Bonn: 1971.

Siegel, Ulrike: 'Die Berufstätigkeit der Ehefrau im Meinungsbild Jugendlicher.' In *Arbeit und Arbeitsrecht,* XXIV, No. 11. Berlin: 1969.

Sinanian, S., Deak, I., and Ludz, P.C.: *Eastern Europe in the 1970s.* New York: Praeger, 1972.

Sontheimer, Kurt: 'Grundzüge des politischen Systems der Bundesrepublik Deutschland.' In *Piper Sozialwissenschaft,* Band 2. München: Piper, 1971.

Sontheimer, Kurt: *West Germany.* London: Hutchinson, 1972.

Sontheimer, Kurt, and Bleek, Wilhelm: *Die DDR Politik, Gesellschaft, Wirtschaft.* Hamburg: Hoffman & Campe, 1972.

Staatliche Zentralverwaltung für Statistik: *Statistisches Jahrbuch der Deutschen Demokratischen Republik 1961, 1968, 1971, 1973, 1974.* Berlin: Staatsverlag der DDR.

State Central Administration for Statistics: *Statistical Pocket Book of the GDR 1973 and 1975.* Berlin: Staatsverlag der DDR, 1973 and 1975.

Statistisches Bundesamt: *Statistisches Jahrbuch für die Bundes-republik Deutschland 1972, 1974, 1975.* Stuttgart & Mainz: Kohlhammer, 1972, 1974, 1975.

Steinberg, H.J.: *Sozialismus und deutsche Sozialdemokratie.* Hannover: 1969.

Steininger, H.: 'Die Grundlagen der Freiheit der sozialistischen Gesellschaft.' In *Freiheit und Gesellschaft,* ed. Stiehler G. *et al.,* Frankfurt am Main: 1973.

Sterbeck, Dieter: *Soziale Struktur in Mitteldeutschland.* Berlin: Duncker & Humblot, 1964.

Stiehler, G.: 'Die Dialektik von gesellschaftlicher und persönlicher Freiheit.' In *Freiheit und Gesellschaft,* ed. G. Stiehler *et al.* Frankfurt am Main: 1973.

Thur, Herbert, ed.: *Was willst Du werden?* Berlin: Verlag Neues Leben, 1967.

Tjaden, K.H.: *Soziale Systeme.* Neuwied und Berlin: Luchterhand, 1968.

Tummler, E., Merkel, K., and Blohm, G.: *Die Agrarpolitik in Mitteldeutschland und ihre Auswirkung auf Produktion und Verbrauch landwirtschaftlicher Erzeugnisse.* Berlin: Duncker & Humblot, 1969.

United Nations Organisation: *Statistical Yearbook, 1960–1974.*

United Nations Organisation: *Yearbook of Labour Statistics, 1968–74.*

United Nations Organisation: *Yearbook of National Account Statistics, 1960–74.*

Vaughan, Michalina: 'A multi-dimensional approach to contemporary Polish stratification.' *Survey* 1/1974, pp. 62–74.

Verba, Sidney: 'Germany – The Remaking of Political Culture.' In *Political Culture and Political Development,* eds. L.W. Pye and S. Verba. Princeton: 1965.

Voigt, Dieter: 'Kaderarbeit in der DDR'. *Deutschland Archiv* 2, 1972. Koln: Wissenschaft und Politik.

Voigt, Dieter: 'Sozialstrukturforschung in der DDR.' *Deutschland Archiv* 5, 1975, pp. 476 ff.

Vortmann, Heinz: 'Einkommensverteilung in der DDR.' *Deutschland Archiv* 3, 1974, pp. 275 ff.

Vorwerg, G.: *Führungsfunktion in Sozialpsychologischer Sicht.* Berlin: VES Deutscher Verlag der Wissenschaft, 1971.

Waller, Michael: 'Socialism in the Market Place.' *Government and Opposition* 4/1975, pp. 515–22.

Weber, H., and Oldenburg, F.: *25 Jahre SED, Chronik einer Partei.*

Köln: Wissenschaft und Politik, 1971.

Weber, Max: *Economy and Society — An Outline of Interpretative Sociology*. Eds. Guenther Roth and Claus Wittich, New York: Bedminster, 1968.

Wesolowski, W., Klasy, *Warstwy i Wladza*, Warszawa, 1966.

Wilhelm, Bernard: *Germany — Democratic Republic*. Paris: Mouton, 1972.

Wilkens, Herbert, 'Sozialproduktrechnung in Ost und West', *Vierteljahrshefte zur Wirtschaftsforschung*, 4/1973, pp. 269—80.

Wilkens, Herbert: 'Das Sozialprodukt der DDR.' *Deutschland Archiv*, 6/1975, pp. 601—8.

Wissenschaftlicher Rat für soziologische Forschung in der DDR: *Zur Sozialstruktur der sozialistischen Gesellschaft*. Berlin: Dietz, 1974.

Zapf, W.: *Wandlungen der deutschen Elite*. München: Piper, 1965.

Zapf, W., ed.: *Beiträge zur Analyse der deutschen Oberschicht*. München: Piper, 1965.

Zöllner, Detlev, and André, Achim: *Labour and Social Security*. Bonn — Bad Godesberg: Asgard, 1973.

INDEX